FIGHT, FLIGHT, or FREEZE:

A LOVE STORY

Jim Enderle

RED ENGINE PRESS
PRINTED IN USA

Library of Congress Control Number: 2021941029

Paperback ISBN: 978-1-943267-80-4

Front cover art by Patricia Moya

Printed in the United States

Red Engine Press

FIGHT,
FLIGHT,
or FREEZE:

A LOVE STORY

Jim Enderle

Dedication

To my family, who taught me every sense of love and meaning and joy, and to beautiful Cindy, who created room for them all.

FOREWORD

By Mauricio Velásquez, MBA

President of The Diversity Training Group and long-time admirer of Jim Enderle

I MET JIM WHEN I PRESENTED a workshop at Groton, CT Naval Clinic back in 2010. Admiral Robinson, Surgeon General of the US Navy had me going all over the world—to every base but Diego Garcia. Jim has kept in touch ever since.

We only met once. He asked about writing a book—telling his story. I encouraged him and here we are. I am a Diversity and Inclusion trainer and I said to him eleven years ago, "I am fascinated by the differences among people and the judgments people can automatically attribute to people who are different."

Well Jim's story is about that and so much more.

I have to admit I am not a big reader. I mean, Kelly, my wife and Maya, my daughter are reading all the time. Maya will devour a book in a day or two.

This story grabbed me. So often we look away. We turn off the TV or radio. We put down the newspaper. We don't want to hear about the pain, the sorrow, the tragedy, the conflict. Well, the problem with "checking out" or "looking the other way" or "avoiding pain and sorrow" is that this does not mean the issues go away or are resolved. Too often I see "Eyes Wide Shut"—people just looking away. Well, if you're not a part of the solution you're a part of the problem.

By checking out we never learn—we never grow. If you only "stay in your comfort zone" I will suggest you're limiting your potential to grow, learn, and develop. Time to invest in yourself a little and I think this book can really help. For me, something about a true story makes it all the more powerful.

When Jim asked me to read his book I jumped at the chance. What adventure lay ahead? Well, even I was pleasantly surprised. Jim's story is gripping in many ways. I felt a run of emotions—I was disturbed. I was sad. I felt excited at times, and everything in between—when reading Jim's story. A journey of preconceived notions, reconciliation, resilience, of understanding pain, sorrow, and renewal.

This story made me look at my relationship with my deceased father (Air Force Vet) and my mom. My relationship with my wife and kids—where do I stand? The fact that my father served but I did not—I have thought about that many times. Like I said before, I worked with the US Navy in the past and I always felt I appreciated their commitment, their sacrifice. The sacrifice of all in uniform is under-appreciated once you read this story.

I invite you to be open, to look inward, reflect on Jim and his trials and tribulations and ask, "What does this have to do with me?" I think you will be pleasantly surprised. I suggest to you it is only when we are truly uncomfortable—"outside our comfort zone" that true learning, true personal growth can occur.

Be comfortable being uncomfortable and enjoy the journey. This is a great story and I hope it inspires you like it did me.

Been an honor and a pleasure to do this for you Jim. You did it!

Contents

PART ONE

Chapter One

Death from Above

SOMETHING ELUSIVE FELL FROM THE moonless sky in southern Iraq, its graceful trajectory as alluring as a falling meteor. The sky shifted around it like jagged shards of a kaleidoscope with every shade of darkness. Five months in Iraq in 2007 was long enough that the allure became counter-intuitive—attaching itself to an injurious, even lethal, complacency. I felt a sense of irony that so much in Iraq had turned inside out and upside down, where chaos was more comfortable than safety.

Images appeared in a blur. First, as a toddler, my father lovingly stroked my eyebrow as I drifted to sleep. Then my mother's final look at the airport before my deployment, as if she might never see me again; her question of why her son had to be deployed at all. My thirteen-year-old son, Alfonso defying his autism diagnosis—a predicted inability to love—with a pencil which said "Happy Birthday" for his brother. My eleven-year-old Lorenzo learning how to cook to take care of the family in

1

my stead. Cindy, my wife, asking that I not feel guilty in my final moment if the worst happened.

In that placid moment, one thing troubled me the most: Death didn't bring guilt, but relief.

An ever-present, acrid burn-pit smoke burned into my dirt-lined nostrils. The level path I stood upon was raised about two feet above a blackened pit of football-sized submerged diesel fuel tanks to my left.

The object glided downward in beautiful silence, and I ached for wondrous stillness and serenity. I yearned for the peace only found in an immobile and imminent death. I would not begrudge anyone if that were their final thought.

Fleeing haphazardly would've been pointless. Military marksmen are taught: *Slow is smooth, smooth is fast.* That possible final moment of my life was an exploding consciousness, large enough to move within freely, its trillions of points all visible from every angle, simultaneously and without distortion.

Life had been the blur of the roadside white picket fences back home I'd driven by too fast. I wish I'd delighted in every shade of color and counted and named them. I would've appreciated the sun through leaves over my windshield, the sunlight dancing just for me.

Could the object in the night's sky, teasing my gaze, disappearing when I look toward it, be the end? Maybe I could take the two-dimensional darkness, punching through it like paper or shattering like glass, causing a cacophony of hues into that claustrophobic world.

But the mind's choice of *fighting* was as insane as *flight*. Those efforts would require conviction to be spared. There was no thought of punching my way through the darkness, even if it were as thin as cellophane.

The contradictory nature of war had reared its ugly head. There was a satisfying comfort in death, more so than the curse of a continued life.

I'd lost my way in Iraq. Our mission was exposed against the weaknesses of overwhelming firepower. Bigger and better guns don't win hearts and minds. I had naively believed I could impact positive change while at war. I believed Iraq could be free of its myriad of bad characters and replaced with leaders who represented the best hopes of its people. I believed they could live happily ever after. It was the American way.

And so, I *froze*.

Fyodor Dostoevsky wrote that beauty is both mysterious and terrible, that God and the devil fight at the intersection. Beauty was found everywhere, as it created its own brilliance—a monument to God's victory. To be indifferent allowed the opposite result, giving evil the opportunity it sought. Yet it was the site of all of life's many miracles, most apparent if I'd ever stopped to read life's white picket fence slats.

With a loud metal-on-metal sound, the rocket drilled its way through the hardened dirt. It crashed into the underground tank almost devoid of fuel, which ironically left space for more fumes to facilitate a series of explosions large enough to be seen from the moon.

Underneath my feet, the muffled metallic sound reverberated and trembled through the earth. In that same moment, a wave of dirt landed like a rolling wave, pelting me from head to toe.

But the rocket did not pierce the tank. And although the insurgents did everything right, there was no explosion at Camp Bucca that night.

I paused before picking myself off the ground and walked away as if nothing had happened.

I was alive.

I needed to sleep.

Chapter Two

Meeting Cindy

IN OCTOBER 1987, I'D ONLY been a volunteer at Chicago's National Runaway switchboard for a couple of weeks. Although the toll-free service was nationwide, I found myself talking late one night to a member of the dominant street gang in our North Side neighborhood.

"Sick of the life," was the expression he used, unaware the switchboard was blocks from his home. Much less that I'd been on the receiving end of their, maybe even *his,* wrath. One time a gang member sucker-punched me onto the dusty infield dirt before they closed in to kick me.

At the beginning of the call about two hours earlier, he seemed certain the way through regret was suicide. He seemed to remember every iota of suffering he'd ever inflicted.

For those two hours, I barely said a word as he performed his own version of an emotional exorcism— crying, cursing, answering his own questions.

Finally, he paused, and I instinctively said I was there, still listening.

"You know, you're like a miracle, dude. Maybe I could be one of those guys who goes to high school kids and talks about gang life. Maybe then I would be useful."

I was no kind of therapist, but our switchboard training included being non-judgmental and compassionate. I understood his yearning for catharsis. Going through a divorce I didn't want the year prior, I'd only volunteered because my brother Norm had suggested I apply all my negative energy toward some spiritual development. Since I'd sworn off women until the sun eventually exploded, between the switchboard and delivering the *New York Times* seven days a week, I seemed to have executed the perfect plan.

After hanging up with the former gang member, I received a call from the Fort Lauderdale area from a runaway whose first language was Spanish. Before computers, that required a three-way telephone call to south Florida for available advice and resources.

A young woman from the Switchboard of Miami, named Cindy, answered with a voice that smiled somehow. It reminded me that small talk with random women wasn't my strong point. I'd only dated and then married my high school sweetheart.

"Miami, huh? What's the forecast there?" I asked, silently slapping myself on the forehead.

"Well, continued darkness for the next three hours," Cindy said, hesitating as if she'd actually looked out a window. We both laughed.

She thinks I'm a dunce. What's the matter with me?

Flummoxed, I felt my face blush. It was just after two o'clock in the morning. I recovered, explaining the purpose of the three-way call before we brought the runaway into the conversation.

To accommodate the runaway, Cindy spoke in Spanish.

I'd long been fascinated with bilingual people. Did they dream in one language or the other? I believed each language—with its idioms and expressions—changed the angle of the world we view. Cindy knowing *two* languages provided one more view than I had.

Without understanding more than a few words, I sensed the unexplainable comfort of empathy's universal language. Cindy couldn't pull it off if her compassion weren't tacitly transferred through the phone lines. The runaway wept, maybe at the relief that her trust in someone she'd never met had been rewarded.

I found myself praying that a Floridian in distress would call on my midnight shift, followed by more prayer that Cindy was also working. If she expressed any future plans, I'd state that I just had to know how it turned out. That way, we could look forward to the next phone call. I was dying to ask if she was dating anyone. Probably.

After a few calls over a month, an inner conflict ensued. How could I feel that I'd developed a crush on a stranger's voice over the phone? It was a ridiculous idea that she might also feel that way about me.

I asked, after practicing throughout my workday, if Cindy would correspond with me. So much stress over an innocuous request. Interstate telephone calls in the 1980s were prohibitively expensive. Besides, what were the chances we would ever even meet? We lived 1200 miles apart and moving vans clogged the highways from Chicago to Miami, not the other way. Shockingly, she said yes.

Over the course of sporadic telephone calls and hand-written letters, we learned more about each other. I was correct that her soft-spoken voice and extensive vocabulary were the result of a person who devoured books. In Cindy's conservative and traditional family, a day of fun meant a day alone at the library with stocked shelves of books. From the smell of paper and bindings, a window to the world had opened for her.

Within months, because long-distance telephone charges were at higher rates to a different area code, especially to another state, I received my first phone bill of over $800—but I wasn't deterred. Love has that effect sometimes.

In one phone call, Cindy described a great love for her father. On a family vacation to the Gulf side of Florida when she was about six, they had walked hand-in-hand along the beach on top of water-flattened sand. Cindy had taken a breath of fresh air and looked ahead to a beach that extended to the horizon. She looked down and saw a quarter. She released her Dad's hand to excitedly pick it up, before holding his hand again—her walk then changing to a half-skip.

Further along, she looked down, to find another quarter. Then another.

"Papi, I'm going to be rich!" Cindy exclaimed. "This is the best vacation ever!"

But having three older siblings guaranteed her eternal optimism would have its drawbacks. Once she'd been told that a dress she saw and really loved had been ordered for her and would arrive in the mail in the coming days. Beside herself, she hovered by the front door until she heard the mailman, only to find it hadn't arrived. Days turned into weeks and she continued to meet the mailman at the door. Each of her siblings looked to someone else to deliver the news—a simple practical joke became an unintended, mean-spirited punchline.

Cindy remained steadfast. But weeks blended into months, and she felt something had gone wrong. It must have been lost or delivered elsewhere? Maybe the mailman took a sharp turn and the package fell out? Cindy thought of any possibility except that she had been betrayed. Eventually, after almost six months, she cried and only looked for the mailman with one eye before forgetting about the mail entirely. After those months, she retreated to her room and cried. Alone.

"If there's one thing I know, I would never take advantage of your trust. Never. If I don't know anything else in the world, I know that," I said.

Love had found me. But I felt a sense of impending doom, the kind where only one person is wildly attracted but the other person is interested in a friends-only relationship.

I had an ulterior motive when I asked Cindy what her "type" was, but without knowing what I looked like yet, her response was the tall, dark, self-confident, and handsome Latin Lover. I grabbed a hand mirror as we spoke, and confirmed I was only one series of miracles from looking like Lorenzo Lamas.

Cindy took great joy in teasing me. We started talking on the phone originally just eight days after the Black Monday stock market crash of 1987. She'd read a story of a family whose lives had taken a number of spiraling downturns since, before asking how I felt about it.

"I think that's a real tragedy."

"You're funny. I asked how you feel, and you tell me what you think. I want to know how you *feel,* silly." It turned out that Cindy spoke *three* languages, English, Spanish, and Feelings.

"Uh, well, I *feel* like it's a tragedy?" I responded earnestly.

"We've got work to do, Grasshopper." Cindy laughed.

I'd only confronted that level of insecurity when in love or requiring humility. She dated architects, I dug ditches. I doubted Cindy would be impressed by a Chicago Marathon finish of 2418th place out of 4836 runners, exactly at fifty percent of finishers. In fact, I was spectacularly average. Girls like Cindy had better options than remarkably tongue-tied and the stunningly ordinary.

Even my grammar school achievements weren't noteworthy—I'd miraculously survived eight years at St. Alphonsus without my worst nightmare occurring.

"James," my teacher might have asked, "What is the capital of Illinois?"

"Uh," I would stammer, sweat beads on my forehead, "Ana Arjona (one of the girls I had a crush on)?" The laughs of the class would awaken me from reverie.

Cindy eventually sent a picture and I stared at it the same way I would stare at the annual class pictures of girls in my grammar school I'd been afraid to approach. Those pictures, unaware of my stare, continued to smile.

Cindy sent a portrait from the shoulders up as if she had walked into the room and something to the left had caught her eye. I gazed at the smooth olive skin of her shoulders, her left hand delicately adjusting a black necklace. I imagined her dark, dignified eyes were fixed on me.

Yes, it was I who caught her eye.

If only it were so.

I stared at the graceful, frilly, feminine writing in her letters and traced it with my fingers, wondering what in her mind was responsible for creating such artwork.

I shared with Cindy about my own life. In the revolutionary 60s, I chanced across an equality march of Blacks near my house. That was not unusual for the summer of 1966.

In our area of Chicago's North Side, the marches were peaceful. Everything seemed serene, almost silent for the hundreds of marchers. Demonstrators carrying signs interacted with those watching from the sidewalks. Volunteers from St. Mark's Lutheran Church handed out water to overheated demonstrators. Some even shared a laugh.

A rock in mid-flight suddenly caught my eye. I followed its flight to the left temple of one Black demonstrator who carried a toddler on his shoulder. Immediately before impact was a moment of total stillness, where no sound was heard. And just as suddenly, complete pandemonium.

"I was there, I saw the whole thing," I told Cindy.

The looks on the faces of the Black demonstrators, they weren't scary or dangerous people. They were terrified, bumping into each other unintentionally, some taking refuge in the church. Some cried and the man who was struck bled profusely.

I never did see that boy on his shoulders again.

A long history of discrimination preceded that day, but I didn't realize racial tensions existed before then. The struggle of one group of human beings fighting for equal treatment became real. It was our fault, I thought. I could understand why Black people seemed so angry.

Because Cindy was so moved by that story, I sought to replicate it with other tales she might find endearing.

Passing through Kentucky once, I'd stopped in a restaurant and ordered breakfast where grits were served. Because I'd never tried grits, I asked the dumbfounded waitress if I could try a single grit first to see if I liked it.

The patrons all laughed so hard that one trucker bought my breakfast, while I considered a future in comedy.

With time, Cindy sensed my love of the Spanish language, which had expressions like 'death on a bicycle' and *diente frio*.

"Diente frio? For buck teeth? Why?" I asked.

"Just picture it, because the teeth are..."

"Cold teeth?" We burst into laughter at the silliness of it.

I doubt she'd ever thought of the translation either. If I could make her laugh, wasn't anything possible?

As it was, over the next four years we gave well-meaning relationship advice, laughed, cried, and fell asleep with our phones at our ears, still projecting the other's breathing.

Cindy shared my fascination with travel, and we compared our lists of desired exotic destinations we could visit, like the Pacific or Caribbean islands.

And yet, fears cropped up often over those years. Each time it might seem like a good time to meet, my anxiety would surface. I said at least once that I was afraid of ruining the most valuable friendship I had. I felt once I crossed that line, the entire realities of the relationship would change, and we could never go back. Would it be worth possibly losing a friend as awesome as Cindy?

It was easy for people to say they could be both friends and lovers. But that wasn't guaranteed and in naïveté, I placed demands on love, which were not only impossible but also unfair.

Yet, one time when I was laid off from my electrician's job, we decided to throw caution to the wind and meet. In a whirlwind four days, I'd managed to survive a thirty-two-hour Greyhound bus ride, learned the names of Caribbean fruits and vegetables I'd never heard of before, and asked Cindy's father for her hand in marriage. I thought that would be an appropriate and sincere gesture.

Given her close Puerto Rican family and a nice job and apartment, her stance was she wasn't going to give everything up to move to Chicago as a live-in girlfriend. One option remained: To immediately propose.

Following a lightning-quick negotiation, we departed for a drive to Chicago in Cindy's red 1982 Chevrolet Cavalier with the air conditioner set to frostbite. If she feared the depths of love, on top of turning her entire life upside down to move to Chicago, I admired she didn't seem to suffer the same fears I had.

We took the long way home.

At one scenic stop along the highway, I took Cindy to a bench overlooking the Atlantic Ocean. With the incoming tide flooding the low-lying shrubbery, the sun glistened like tiny mirrors rippling through various shades of greens and browns.

I could've stayed there and not moved until Cindy tired of the view. With my arm around her, I kissed her forehead and said so.

I made a plan and told it to her: In the toughest times we would face, I would think of how I felt then.

Chapter Three

The Envelope

May 2007—Camp Bucca, Iraq

M Y UNIT, ONE HUNDRED AND twenty-one Naval Provisional Detainee Battalion Three members sat on the Kuwaiti runway as three UH-60 Blackhawk helicopters approached. Maybe none of them had thought of it, but I planned on maintaining my personal tradition of having a window seat on each flight.

Not that that mattered as it turned out. The last of eleven fully loaded troops to board, we were immediately buried under an avalanche of sea bags and gear piled almost to the top of the cabin.

The Blackhawks flew three astride, thirty-three men per trip for four round trips over the course of an afternoon in April of 2007. Our mission was to reinforce the overstretched Army units as individual augmentees (or the equivalent of baseball free agents).

The majority of our Army indoctrination training at Fort Bliss, Texas, was centered on guarding detainees at Camp Bucca, the largest detention facility in Iraq with a population of approximately 14,000. The unit as a whole was trained to guard sixteen compounds, each divided into quadrants according to religious sect or affiliation.

Corpsmen like me were exceptions. According to the Geneva Conventions, guarding detainees would conflict with the Hospital Corps Hippocratic Oath, which states, in part, "I will not knowingly permit harm to come to any patient." *Patient* being the operative word. To us, the world was divided into two categories: patients and prospective patients.

Wedging my arm between two sea bags leaning against a small window allowed enough space to see outside. I scanned the southern Iraq terrain for landmarks. I remembered that 997 men died in Vietnam on their first day in the country. I scanned as much as I could.

Empty.

There didn't appear to be a single person before I saw the Camp on the horizon. The flat landscape showed a single shade of brown. The first shadows I saw revealed Camp Bucca. At the top of that darkness, high dirt boundaries with multiple sparkling glints of concertina wire announced the realities of life in Iraq.

As my first foot set in Iraq, all I'd read and heard of Iraq became secondhand. Landing on the helicopter pad, my apprehension amplified. I almost expected to be shot instantly. There was little time to think. Sure enough, we were welcomed later that day with a barrage of mortars.

The helicopter continued to run like a getaway car, ready to collect the next group in Kuwait. We hurriedly formed a human supply chain and quickly unloaded the dozens of sea bags, clearing the way for liftoff.

Iraq became *my* experience.

* * *

The first weeks in Camp Bucca passed innocuously enough, and much of our time was spent moving from one twenty-man tent to the next, in hopscotch movements until units behind us had less seniority. Once that elevated status had been achieved, Jose Rios, one of the unit's many wise crackers shouted, "Sky blue!"—an expression in hopscotch meaning he had won.

It was Jose who beat me to the last lower bunk at Fort Bliss, and between that and our numerous debates over the supremacy of New York or Chicago-style pizzas, we were immediately at friendly odds.

We quickly learned free time for the next year would be spent in one of a small number of places: At Headquarters, which had six computers and a shelf stocked with donated books, or the computer center of the same plywood construction as HQ but with more computers. The largest place was what we collectively called, "Beautiful downtown Camp Bucca with its breathtaking skyline."

The "skyline" consisted of a rectangular arrangement of trailers manned by third-party nationals, contractors from countries like Nepal to Algeria and anywhere in between. In the middle of the rectangle stood a concrete slab with an ever-present eighth of an inch of silty dirt, with basketball rims hanging at each end.

By far, the most popular place in Downtown was the Green Bean Coffee, famous for its frozen drinks. If we walked outside in mid-day, we had approximately two minutes before slush transformed to slurry to cold watery substance, to throwaway tepid.

There was an Army PX, (drawing eye rolls from Army soldiers when Navy personnel called it the Exchange), a Pizza Hut, Burger King, barber and uniform shops, and even a store that sold hookahs.

I had already befriended the Iraqi salesmen there and asked them to write the names of my sons' classmates in Arabic. They obliged and patiently echoed my repetition of the names, where Arabic letters would replicate non-Arabic words phonetically.

Otherwise, it was a small world bound by twenty-foot berms on all sides, a claustrophobia-inducing frying pan. The berms encompassed the base with fortress-like walls with no windows or visible doors to the outside world. Usually, only guards in perfectly spaced towers looked outward to what we imagined was nothingness past the horizon in any direction but southeast.

The presence of al-Qaeda in southern Iraq (AQI) was limited, but there remained a number of Shi'a paramilitary organizations. The powerful Mahdi Army of Maqtada al-Sadr and remnants of the Badr Brigade (a group closely aligned with Iran) operated in the area and launched rockets and mortars from mobile units near the base. Because many high-value militants were detained there, the command hierarchy was on constant alert for a coordinated operation from outside while detainees used the distraction to attempt an escape. With about 15,000 detainees, if enough were somehow set free, the numbers were greatly on their side.

* * *

Two moments defined our early deployment.

As we settled in, while complaining about almost constant moves from one twenty-man tent to another, word spread that one of the members of the unit we replaced had committed suicide. Few discussed the circumstances—his unit had been told they may be extended in Iraq.

One evening I met two friends, Bonifaz and Mariscal, in downtown Camp Bucca. Army Sergeant Elvin Johnson joined us.

"I just wondered what he knew that we don't know. I mean I got here a few weeks ago when you did. It doesn't seem that bad." Bonifaz said. We sat in an area where troops congregated for an Internet signal. The night was pleasant just after sunset.

"Ever watch *Psycho*? You pull up in front of the Bates Motel and it seems like a perfectly nice place at first," Bonifaz continued. Elvin Johnson shuddered at his ominous tone.

I offered that I'd read about "Barbed Wire Syndrome." It was a WWI study of prisoners of war and the effects of long-term detention and increasing pattern of learned helplessness over extended periods of time and was discussed in Viktor Frankl's *Man's Search for Meaning*. The sailor from the previous unit hadn't been in combat, or out of the wire, for that matter. What had transpired that suicide became his best option?

My nicknames for Bonifaz and Mariscal were the "Marshmallow Test Twins", and their steadfast approach was similar. Like the social science experiment in the 1960s, they forfeited a smaller reward for a greater one later. Both deferred everything to the day they were reunited with their families.

Bonifaz's daily objective was to call his wife as she began her lunch break, 7:00 PM daily Iraq time. Mariscal counted backward the days left until we were projected to go home. Normalcy was embedded in routine.

* * *

Our interaction with Iraqi civilians was minimal, often from a distance. The exception was at the camp gate, where visitors entered and were screened under a tent before seeing their detained relatives. Although southern Iraq was predominantly Shi'ite, a majority of the detainees were Sunnis from central or northern Iraq, who had been in power under Saddam.

The Sunni insurgency, as such, was particularly violent and large. The collective term 'detainees' was used and a majority of men at Camp Bucca had not been formally charged with a crime. Their open-ended detention without charges was a consistent source of complaint in the court of international opinion.

Stepping into the shade of the massive tent didn't provide much comfort from heat, which regularly reached over a hundred and ten degrees by the time visitor hours began. Occasionally, I would be assigned as the medical person at the tent, tending to family members who were often overheated and dehydrated.

One day, two young women in flowing black abayas stood patiently in the queue. Niqabs covered their faces from just above the eyebrows to the bridge of their noses and extended sideways to their temples on either side.

The young women avoided eye contact with anyone but the two children beside them. A little girl of about eight wore a mostly yellow dress with an irregular pattern of off-white splotches. Her brother of about six stood silently, holding a dusty, semi-inflated soccer ball against his button-down white shirt. One of the young women, most likely his mother, reprimanded him and pulled the ball away, brushing dust off his shirt.

In the little girl's hands were what appeared to be a set of about twenty popsicle sticks that covered the entire color spectrum. She was not the least bit intimidated by armed American soldiers towering over her. She plopped down in the dirt and arranged the sticks in color-coordinated combinations until she found satisfaction with the arrangement and her hands moved away, palms up like a magician. She smiled at our applause before getting back to work on the next arrangement. The only distraction was when she'd impatiently push back her dark hair as if it interrupted her creative process.

Eventually, I followed the family to their detained family member—the young women's dignified strides apparent even through flowing robes. When they reached out to hold the children's hands, their sleeves rode up to show gold bracelets.

The little girl impressed him with her sticks. The boy competed for attention by doing soccer drills, all the more impressive with a half-inflated ball. The father smiled. They were all relatively subdued, maybe aware they were being watched. The father messed up the boy's hair and one of the women rested her head on his shoulder as they spoke quietly. The little girl remained animated throughout—a real ball of fire, that one.

Who were the prisoners, I wondered? I wished for Cindy's head on my shoulder on our long rides through the Connecticut countryside. I wanted to make paper airplanes and mess up my two sons' hair, aged eleven and thirteen. I pictured Lorenzo, with his handwritten notebook of family favorite recipes, and Alfonso, who likely asked Cindy daily how long one year was. Cindy and I found the concept of time was as difficult to explain as it was for Alfonso to grasp. I imagined changing places, just for thirty minutes.

Soon, the visiting family was ready to depart for their long trip to Iskandariya—one of the cities of Iraq's notorious Triangle of Death—from what our interpreter Hussein said as he looked through the family's visitor application. They drove a 1998 white Toyota Tercel with worn tires and no air conditioning.

While speaking with a few gate guards, we stood by the car as if we were seeing off relatives after Thanksgiving. The women interacted with nods and spoke only with the interpreters, but the children looked at us with smiles curling mischievously, before waving. I maintained their gaze, as the Toyota pulled off seemingly in slow motion and the kids knelt on the seat looking out the back windshield.

Two days later, word passed that their car had been struck with a roadside bomb. They had been apparently targeted as the family of Sunni extremists, exemplifying the omnipresent eyes of the desert. Someone had the dirty job of telling the detained man. No parent deserved news their entire family had been murdered. I wished I could've warned them.

Until then, it had been only a curiosity to look outward from the base. But during the day I found myself climbing the eastern berm of Camp Bucca, all the way to the concertina razor wire.

* * *

When I sought solace as a kid in Chicago, I climbed to the roof of our apartment building and look outward, wondering what I didn't know about the world around me. The high-rise buildings of the Cabrini Green Housing Projects, then considered the most crime-ridden neighborhood in the world, were a mere two miles away, yet at least a solar system from where I stood.

* * *

The Iraq landscape just south of the Hammar section of the Mesopotamian Marshes was dirt, baked into concrete hardness by months of heat without moisture, with a top layer of silty sand. Could that have been the biblical wetlands, the birthplace of Samson, before an angered Saddam Hussein, frustrated with the resistance based in the Marshes, had them almost entirely drained to remove the insurgent sanctuary?

On that berm, looking outward, I grieved. I would never look at dirt and sand without seeing gold trinkets, colored sticks, and an old, dusty, half-inflated soccer ball.

I stared across the barren expanse—just dirt, rocks, and sand as far as I could see in any direction. About any of the 5000 military personnel would see what I saw: nothingness, with barely a plant or living thing—a piece of land the world had abandoned.

I needed perspective. How could anyone love such a place? I needed Sayyed.

* * *

When a frame of reference was needed, many in the unit approached Sayyed, one of the unit's most seasoned interpreters. Sayyed was usually the right man to ask, as he cherished the opportunity to represent his country and was a natural storyteller. I found I could ask what time it was and Sayyed would respond how Iraqis invented the watch. Any answer to the presented question seemed to begin centuries ago.

In a short time, I had taken a liking to Sayyed. Unusually spry for a man in his mid-sixties, I hadn't even noticed him until one of the medics told me he was teaching anyone interested in learning Arabic.

I approached him and asked when he was teaching, and he answered, "Any time I see you."

I felt an immediate bond.

Sayyed believed learning languages, eating local food, and traveling was a basis for peace, or at least understanding among people. Any time we met after that seemingly had something to do with sharing a meal.

A former professor of Middle Eastern History, he proved capable of convincing me anything in the world had either originated, or had been invented in Iraq, and I'd glimpsed magnificence and sensed Iraq's history through Sayyed's expressions.

Had Cindy fallen in love with small details of me in the same way?

Staring at the bleak horizon, I missed Cindy so. If she were there, she would not have seen the unending state of mourning and catharsis. She would have seen the nation waiting to burst, dancing with unbridled joy two generations of Iraq had never known. I was sure of it.

As I looked eastward, on the very plains where two of the bloodiest battles of the Iran-Iraq War occurred in Khorramshahr and Operation Beit ol-Moqaddas.

Sayyed described a similar empty distance where his eyes met with those of his future wife as she traveled on her father's vegetable cart on the way to the town market.

Maybe my affection for phone lines and meeting Cindy would be lost on future generations. Sayyed's association with an empty expanse, or my connection with phone lines, was small or insignificant to others. We felt gratitude for them, nonetheless.

* * *

Within a week, a detainee in one compound tested positive for tuberculosis. A group of medical personnel was tasked with testing the entire compound to avoid the possibility of a very contagious disease quickly spreading. A reality of the compound politics, the Medical Department approached the compound's hierarchical leadership and arrange the testing, with the understanding that they could deny access. In that compound, classified as one with an extremist ideology, many of the men had little interest in interacting with Americans. Even eye contact was avoided for the most part.

If the leader of the compound (the *zaeim*) ruled the test was necessary, not one of the men would disobey.

I was impressed that not a single man was late, and soon they silently stood in orderly lines. Medical personnel and interpreters stood at the front of the poorly lit tent and the detainees normally approached with heads down, their arms exposed below the elbow and extended. Several politely murmured *shukraan* [thank you] and filed back into the compound. The single-level and rectangular structure allowed for dormitory-like conditions.

What the zaeim said, went. In one case, he demanded a ping pong table, and it was promptly delivered. Still, the command was wary of each item the zaeim ordered.

The items were inventoried carefully as detainees had demonstrated resourcefulness in captivity that would make our Code of the U.S. Fighting Force [military parlance which defines behavior while held captive] proud. They creatively turned the simplest items into digging tools or makeshift weapons.

For the most part, detainees didn't have strong grudges with medical personnel. We were visible to them through the Hospital [a series of connected trailers] at the compounds' center and were responsive to various medical needs. We didn't carry weapons, as directed by Geneva Conventions. To their benefit, many of them were able to order glasses or have dental work done.

One man, about eight back in the line, seemed to be trying to get my attention. As he leaned forward, straining to see my name over my right pocket, I ignored him before he laughed. A few of the men directly in front of him stifled their own laughter. Looking up after administering a test, I saw the man's eyes widen. With my eyes on him, he reached into his yellow jumpsuit and revealed an envelope.

We had portable lighting directly around the front of the line which produced a glare, so I leaned forward past the light and squinted into the more dimly lit part of the tent.

On the envelope was an address sticker in the upper right corner, like the ones the American Legion sends. My parents used them.

The writing on the envelope had cursive writing that reminded me of my mother's handwriting when she would send me to the corner store as a kid. It also had other stickers of hearts...like those my mother attached to letters she sent to Camp Bucca.

The detainee smiled and nodded with a mocking wave of the envelope.

I stood there, breathless. He had my parents' envelope, which meant he wasn't alone—it probably would've been passed to others, too. And many of these detainees were eventually released or further radicalized while detained.

I imagined a group of militants approaching our Connecticut house with only my wife and boys while I was stuck overseas. I thought they might kill them. It would be effective psychological warfare against every man and woman who had to leave their families to fight in Iraq. *You did this to yourself.*

The numbness didn't prevent me from moving down the line in his direction to physically confront him. However, Sayyed and two medics intercepted me before I took a full step, taking me off the testing line. The man and I continued to stare. He taunted me. Other interpreters grabbed the envelope and removed him from the line without being administered a test. We still did not break eye contact.

"Doc, we have the envelope. He's trying to get a reaction. Just ignore him. Look at me," Sayyed said, holding me by my shoulders.

I'd been in fights in my life. I'd been disliked, but I couldn't stop asking myself what I'd done to him. It was a hate I'd never confronted before. It was so personal, and I felt so utterly powerless.

"There's only one way this ends, Sayyed. He just made the biggest mistake of his life," I said as the man disappeared into the compound.

With his last wide-eyed smile, my vantage point reversed. I now saw my apartment building from Cabrini Green as if I'd never lived anywhere else.

Chapter Four

Enlistment

Chicago 1992

FOUR MONTHS FROM MY THIRTY-FIFTH birthday, I was in a quandary. The end of October marked my transition from electrician's apprentice to journeyman. Rather than celebrate that high mark, a lay-off sent me dejectedly toward our union hall.

With a shrug and accompanying chuckle, I learned another job in Chicago for seven to ten months was unlikely from my bench seat at the bottom of the union's seniority list.

After reviewing my skill set, I found no want ads for DITCH-DIGGER. MUST DIG STRAIGHT AS A RAIL, THREE-FEET-DEEP, FOUR-FEET-WIDE, WITH SQUARE CORNERS. 100 FEET/DAY UNLESS WORKING IN A DRIVING MONSOON, THEN SEVENTY-FIVE FEET/DAY MINIMUM.

After working as a journeyman electrician seven twelve-hour days a week brought more money than I'd ever seen, I took a job delivering pizzas for a weekly sum that just a week earlier was earned in a single twelve-hour shift.

Cursing my luck, I reported to my first day. I was immediately reprimanded for walking through the restaurant and told to enter from the alley entrance, just past the rusty dumpsters' blended smells of tomato sauce, rat poison, and smelly socks.

Introducing myself to my new co-workers, I re-marked that until that moment I thought tomato sauce went well with everything else. Crestfallen at the idea of hustling for tips, I took my seat with the other drivers, oblivious to the clangs, metal-on-metal scrapes, and slamming of pizza oven doors.

As orders came through, I quickly slid down the bench until I was in front of the delivery dis-patcher. He looked as happy to be there as me, his muscle-tee sweat-soaked and stained, a toothpick hanging from his lips at an impossible angle.

At one time he may have been a weightlifter, but he was overweight and the faded, naked lady on his upper left arm didn't dance as much as she used to when he flexed his muscles.

When the dispatcher called my number, another driver cut ahead of me. Grabbing two pizzas he whirled toward the rickety screen door as if I wasn't there.

"Where do you think you're going?" I asked, moving between him and the back door. "Those are my pizzas. I waited my turn."

"Can't you read?" the man asked, blindly pointing over his shoulder.

A sign explained the driver with the most seniority could jump the line if it were one of their repeat delivery destinations. He moved again toward the door before I blocked his path. I couldn't stand another minute.

"I don't care what the sign says, that's my three dollars." I stared at him as menacingly as I could and realized how absurd it was fighting over two pizzas.

"Perhaps we could settle this out back." The man looked at the three other pizza delivery guys, apparently digging in.

"Perhaps we could," I answered, purposefully moving to just outside the screen door.

My adversary was maybe twenty years older and heavyset. I hoped to call his bluff. There seemed to be no way out.

Putting the pizzas down, he moved with less conviction toward the door. I thought of the irony of another driver taking the pizzas while we fought for our lives in the oily, smelly alleyway.

His eyes bulged and watered as he stepped into the alley. Maybe ten seconds later, he wretched. I stood there, wondering if I was going to fight or resuscitate him. He put his hand up as if he needed to lean on the wall before rethinking.

"Smells awful out here," he said, wiping his eyes and trying to spit the taste of the alley onto the pavement. "You take this one. You look like you need the money more than I do."

My relief was a hollow victory, overpowered by a sense of arrested development. I was thirty-four and a flurry of punches short of being face down in a smelly alley over a three-dollar delivery. I was just scrappy enough to posture my way out of a fistfight.

When I got home, Cindy suggested keeping an open mind, apparently underestimating the possibilities. She was the person who pointed out a want ad for firefighters at 1-800-FIREFIGHTERS. Amazingly, that number was for a Navy recruitment office.

Life was kind of funny that way. I had an annual exercise of trying to imagine the year ahead of me against reality. In the past four, years, I wouldn't have imagined life playing out the way it had.

* * *

The ensuing months brought change at a dizzying pace. I had gone from a union electrician on one side of the fence of the Great Lakes Naval Base to a recruit doing jumping jacks while being screamed at on the other side.

Life had prepared me well for the rigors of boot camp. Outside of being in supreme physical condition, I carried a work ethic with my thirty-four years. In all, I had learned from sports involvement to music lessons. I exemplified the lessons of my family, where finding a way to contribute wherever I fit was ultimately what lead me to success. I was perfectly content doing the work few relished because it was my key to being welcomed into a group.

* * *

Boot camp passed quickly, as did Hospital Corps School at Great Lakes, before being assigned to the Portsmouth Naval Shipyard (New Hampshire).

Near when I arrived, the base Master Chief organized a volunteer opportunity in Boston. One of the city's representatives set up a full day for homeless veterans to come to a centrally located park where a small temporary city, buzzing with military personnel and manned tents, provided services and resources.

At no charge, the homeless veterans received immunizations, selections of clothes, bicycles, job resources, mental health referrals, VA doctors for quick physical exams, and more. Most amazingly, the Navy Seabees set up a tent where showers and haircuts were offered.

It was a mystery to me where the hot running water came from. The only water source visible was a single concrete water fountain on one side of the park. Small wonder the Seabee motto is: THE DIFFICULT WE DO NOW, THE IMPOSSIBLE TAKES A LITTLE LONGER.

Our bus full of Hospital Corpsmen departed New Hampshire at 4:15 AM. By the time we arrived, a throng of maybe a hundred people waited. They stood in an orderly line, some of them smoked cigarettes and talked quietly. As the clinic's bus pulled up at 5:15 AM, they broke into a raucous cheer.

As the screeching of the brakes ended, we piled off the bus. The sun was just bringing the park out of darkness.

Volunteers wearing dungarees and polished Boon-dockers found it impossible to get off the bus. Senior personnel asked the gathered veterans to step back.

As I stepped onto the curb, one of the men waved as if he recognized me.

"Doc!" I looked away thinking he must have been talking to someone else, but he persisted as he worked his way toward the front of the group.

"Doc, hallelujah man. I knew it, I knew you'd get here. You sure took your sweet-ass time, though," he said with a big grin.

Perplexed, I wondered how early he might have wanted us to arrive. Our precious first cup of coffee was going to have to wait. I'd imagined sitting in the park with the others until later in the clear autumn morning.

"Lance Corporal Coleman, USMC," he said, the grin dropped from his face, subtle in the low light at the crack of dawn. "I knew you'd come back for us. You know why? You *know* why," LCpl Coleman nodded, answering his own question.

"Uh, why?"

"Because you crazy SOBs always...we know you'll always come back for us."

I couldn't clearly see LCpl Coleman in the early morning light—the man's shadowy outlines swallowed hard, his shoulders raised, the posture square and plumb. He'd initiated me to the pride of serving as a Corpsman.

I'd only been in the Navy for ten months.

People joked that my single award, the National Defense Ribbon awarded upon boot camp graduation, was upside down and I would still check if that were true, forgetting that single symmetrical ribbons were Seaman Recruit-proof in orientation.

I was the beneficiary of reflected and historical glory. Hospital Corpsmen killed in action, Medals of Honor awardees, tales of bravery and valor could be quantified, but only then could I distinguish between enumeration and magnitude.

I smiled at LCpl Coleman. So far, I'd merely shared hallways with those men and women.

* * *

Blessings and curses came early in my Navy life. During Corps School at Great Lakes, Cindy and I learned we were expecting our first child. Because we moved from Illinois to Connecticut to Portsmouth, New Hampshire (I didn't know New Hampshire had a coast) over her first two trimesters, we were ready to move again by the time we were introduced to her doctors. Cindy often joked that we would someday laugh about our trials and tribulations, and I would have to wait almost the entire pregnancy for her to lose her temper.

As with many first-born children, Alfonso decided to go past the full term. In early December, with snow over three-feet-high, while waiting for me to pick her up for a doctor's appointment, Cindy took out the trash and lost her balance in the icy parking lot, suffering the indignity of a headlong dive into a snowbank. Testing the "we'll laugh at this someday" theory,

I could describe the Miami girl, nine-months pregnant and bundled like the Michelin Man with only her feet cartoonishly kicking from a snowbank.

Then, just over one year after digging ditches as an electrician, far from any home we'd ever known, I witnessed the miracle of childbirth.

When Alfonso was nineteen months old, a doctor identified definitive signs of autism. Because my only introduction to autism was the movie *Rain Man*, we silently sat in the parking lot with two-year-old Alfonso between us. When a mosquito landed on his left thigh, I promptly swatted it.

Between the sudden movement and sting of perceived betrayal, Alfonso cried, and Cindy reflexively scooped him from the car seat and rocked him. I hoped it would be the last time he was hurt by my protection. Cindy mentioned later that a mosquito had landed on me almost simultaneously and I instinctively swatted the mosquito on Alfonso's leg first. She saw that as reflexive unselfishness—a glimpse of who I was. There were two ways to see it—I was moved Cindy chose to think of me favorably.

After a few minutes, we drove toward home until Cindy asked me to stop at an upcoming church, the first spoken words since the doctor's office.

We walked into the rear of the empty and darkened church. The marble altar and sacristy were illuminated as if the area gave off its own warm light.

Cindy quietly turned into the room and I followed, putting Alfonso's car seat on the pew before we knelt in unison, sniffled, and burst into a cleansing cry. I didn't know enough to even ask a good question about what we would do next.

Soon enough answers revealed themselves. Cindy planned to visit the sanctuary of a library. She would leave no stone unturned while I denied the doctor's diagnosis. *The doctor saw him for minutes. What did that doctor know? Alfonso's our son. All he needs is a loving home.*

I wasn't going to follow the half-baked diagnosis from someone who had seen him for a matter of minutes. In fact, I declared, "She's probably forgotten about him already. Responsibility for a loving and supportive home will fall on us."

The sliver became a wedge, which soon widened into a chasm. Our language changed. Cindy resented my lack of support as I insisted we were creating our own troubles. Cindy buried herself under volumes of books on autism while I focused on work and enrolling in school. We encountered our first moments of sitting at opposite sides of the room, wondering aloud what came next.

Finally, one night I found Cindy sitting on the couch with her stacks of books reading Temple Grandin's newly released *Thinking in Pictures*. I repeated my assertion she should find balance.

"Get some sleep," I suggested, "and go back to being undeterred tomorrow."

I ran a hot bath, adorned the counter with candles, and handed her a glass of wine. Then she could turn in for the night. Climbing momentarily from our trenches, we shared a tender moment.

"You have a switch, Jim. You can turn off. I feel like our life is on fire. If you don't love me enough...Alfonso is your son, too. Couldn't you at least talk about this for his sake?"

"I do love you enough, Cindy."

I didn't offer more of an explanation and Cindy didn't reply. I had thought of using the same logic for Cindy to agree with me. "If you love us," I could have said, "let's avoid early intervention programs for autistic toddlers."

Waking up for work in the morning, I found the bathwater cold. The untouched wine was warm and the candles had burned themselves out. Cindy dozed fitfully with two lights illuminated, erasing any chance for shadows. Books jabbed into her ribs—*how tired does one have to be to sleep like that?*

I stood there for a moment on the verge of tears, unable to move and unsure what to say before I helped her into bed and left for work.

As I locked the door behind me, I knew my life changed but words were inadequate. I could only imagine breaking a concept like love into digestible pieces. It seemed impossible to explain to a person, my son, the emotional elements of love. I felt a skittish, half-conviction I could love a person who could not love me.

Chapter Five

Tunnel to Everywhere

May 2007

S AYYED WINCED. EITHER HIS TEA was too weak or too strong. He shrugged, apparently accepting his fate.

"Here's one thing I don't get, Sayyed. I mean al-Qaeda is what, about two-point-five percent of the country? Why don't people just rise up if they don't want them here?"

Sayyed nodded, his salt-and-pepper hair close-cropped and thick. His hair and a choice of light-colored shirts contrasted with dark skin that had survived too many tans. When he wore his black, thick-rimmed glasses, he often heard that he looked like Tariq Aziz, the international voice of Saddam's regime.

Originally from eastern Iraq's Maysan Province, much of his youth was spent in the al-Amarah River on the northern edge of expansive marshes made famous by T.E. Lawrence, also known as *Lawrence of Arabia*.

To Sayyed, his home of Amarah was the best place to take the pulse of his nation. Throughout history, when life was difficult there, its struggles invariably rippled to the remainder of Iraq.

Less than twenty miles from Iran, during the Iran-Iraq War of the 1980s, the city was almost overrun by each of three human-wave attacks by the Iranians trying to cut the main artery between Baghdad from the southern metropolis of Basra.

He only spoke haltingly if it did come up, his eyes moistening and turned toward the floor.

"When Iranians ran out of men, they sent...teenagers, children, and we had to do it. I kept hoping our shells would miss them and they would turn back."

Saddam Hussein, having survived America's Gulf War and frustrated of the Marshes acting as a natural sanctuary for Shi'ite-led insurgency, ordered them drained, disrupting a way of life that went back to the Sumerian Empire.

The area, rich with wildlife one wouldn't normally associate with Iraq, had been Sayyed's childhood playground.

With his father, Sayyed hunted sand foxes, Indian mongoose, and European hare. Water buffalo were relatively common, and before they were drained, deeper in the Marshes, Sayyed swore there were otters.

Often, the difference between having a main course of meat or not depended on Sayyed's accuracy with his slingshot.

Sayyed said mud was the most elemental fabric of the *Ma'dan* [Marsh Arabs]. It was used as mortar, glue, and ammunition.

At seven, his job was to mold and dry mud balls, before eventually becoming amazingly adept at hunting birds and small animals. His aim, Sayyed said humbly, was a direct result of being hungry.

Sayyed, always a survivalist, despite reservations, had begun to work with the Americans when tens of thousands of uprooted people from Ma'dan came to Amarah with few skills or prospects for work.

"You said you're from Chicago, Jim?"

"Yeah, but you're avoiding my question, Sayyed."

"Not at all, my friend. I'll answer your question with one of my own." A former professor of Middle Eastern History at the University of Baghdad, Sayyed held an academic's propensity for the Socratic method. "In Chicago, how many people there rose up against Al Capone and the mob? They had guns, organization, and they were ruthless. Your grandparents, maybe? There's a big difference between complicity and being horrified into submission."

I looked out the window and saw Sgt. Johnson quickly running across the basketball court. Dust jumped up before heavily settling back on the concrete. Johnson had a panicked wave as he burst through the screen door of the café.

"Doc, do you have wheels? Sayyed, you, too. The Hospital—now." Johnson bolted from the café and into a vehicle waiting barely in sight between the trailers of downtown Camp Bucca. Moments later, a cloud of dust rose just behind the café.

"The tea is not good today, anyway. Remember, straight to the hospital," Sayyed said, repeating his almost daily mantra to stay away from Compound Eight where the man with my envelope resided. He was certain the detainee's goal was goading me into an international incident to advance his cause.

When the Abu Ghraib torture scandal came to light in the Spring of 2004, it exceeded any recruitment goals of al-Qaeda in Iraq and support the United States had garnered in tribal areas was frayed. The worst-case scenario was to provide indications that we were the evil occupier portrayed by al-Qaeda.

Just outside the café was one of the base's five desert tan ambulances. If the tan color offered any camouflage, that was nullified by a huge medical symbol—a white circle filled in with a thick red cross. The entire inside of the ambulance was dark green metal.

The trusty old vehicle immediately started but I had to pause for a moment to put on gloves—everything inside was blistering. I often wondered how many Corpsmen and medics had been in that old ambulance and how much death and human suffering played out within its shell.

A dusty distance of about a half mile spaced the detention compounds from living areas and downtown Camp Bucca. As the concertina wire of the compounds drew closer and the rough ride prompted Sayyed to wonder if the shock absorbers were as old as the vehicle. Another time, he congratulated me for "not missing a single bump in the dirt road."

* * *

I was not the same since the envelope incident. In a world of every hue of brown, I only saw black and white. There were only predators and victims. My enemy had obliterated moral neutrality.

I was no victim. Victims demand discourse and memory and validation, while I had taken on a predator's natural silence and secrecy. I told not one soul, but Sayyed deftly noted my change of language.

"You've been a bit preoccupied since that night in Compound Eight," Sayyed had said. "Maybe you're famous now with them. Eyes are on you. And ears, too."

The change was subtle, and only in the last two weeks had I used words like "neutralize", "eliminate", "clear". From language comes mentality. Actions follow words if they're left there long enough.

"You're overthinking it, Sayyed," I said. Words failed me.

But Sayyed *was* right. I had used language that would take responsibility for that foe's death deniable. My expressions had become sterilized and clinical. Rationale and emotions weren't interchangeable. I remained calm because the situation required it. I would resist the urge to shout

from the top of the magnificent Camp Bucca skyline after I killed him. No person alive would
ever know.

"What's that ahead?" I asked.

In the middle of a road of leveled dirt was what
appeared to be a construction crew. A backhoe sat
with its arm up, while the machine pivoted under
the direction of two soldiers. Everyone was looking at the ground.

"Looks like they're building something."

As we pulled up, the guards at the gate waved our
ambulance through. Within a dusty few minutes,
we'd arrived at the hospital.

A group of soldiers gathered around a long trench.
A troop transport truck had its back two tires in the
ditch. A backhoe dug away, piquing the curiosity
of detainees in neighboring compounds.

If the main road through the compounds was a
mile long, every inch of the double-height chain
link fences was lined with amused detainees, en-
joying the sight.

"Why did Johnson have us respond? It doesn't
look like anyone was hurt."

There had been rumors of an escape tunnel for a
few weeks, detainees were up to something. Ironically, the better detainees behaved, the greater
the chances of some grand scheme unfolding just
out of view.

Sayyed shouted what sounded like an Arabic expletive. Jumping from the ambulance, he looked at detainees along the fences.

"Move the ambulance, Jim. You're right in line."

"Move it where?" I looked at the truck near the hospital and the backhoe, then at my ambulance, then onto the nearest compound where a group of soldiers furiously dug alongside the backhoe.

A surveyor couldn't have placed our ambulance more centered between the two points. On either side of the roadway dividing the two sets of compounds were detainees packed near the fence. Army guards waved them back.

"Doc, over here." I heard Sayyed, who'd already jumped into the trench.

It became apparent there was a collapsed tunnel. A troop transport, much heavier than my ambulance had been waiting for the shift change and, because of that extended time in place, its idling diesel engine had loosened the tunnel walls. The weight of the huge truck, engine vibration, and gravity took over.

Sayyed ran his hands through his graying hair. "It's the work of *muqanni*," Sayyed said, a term I'd not heard before.

What remained of the tunnel was an architectural wonder. About five feet in diameter with a flat floor, the tunnel was ramrod straight. The rounded sides were as smooth as hardened concrete—not like sand at all.

Whoever was responsible for that was a meticulous artisan. The tunnel had a cold, calculating personality—straight, direct, and determined.

Tunnel warfare may have originated in the Middle East. The Assyrians in the 9th Century BC used tunnels to weaken fortification walls during a siege. Walls were only as strong as their foundation. But it wasn't walls the miners were looking for.

"Who the hell is Muqanni?" I said, mistakenly thinking muqanni was a proper name.

"Remember the qanat? They are the tunnel diggers."

Just days before, Sayyed argued that in that area of the world, man had discovered a way to make ice. A qanat was a method of digging a cavernous upside-down beehive-like structure with vents positioned exactly in a way to take advantage of every relatively cool breeze. Yes, indeed, almost back to prehistoric times, the ever-resourceful Persians and Arabs had found a way to chill water into ice right there where the temperatures soared into the one hundred and tens.

"Muqanni are held in high esteem because they make and repair the water sources and design the tunnels that feed the qanat. The survival of a town depends on them." Sayyed shook his head sadly. "They aren't warriors. Their work vanishes and they wind up here, where they do the bidding of the zaeem."

I tapped a part of the rounded tunnel with my fist. Not a grain of sand came loose.

Eight-to-ten feet below the ground, the tunnel revealed inaccurate perceptions. One might see a compound and be thankful that almost two hundred possibly dangerous men per compound were kept under wraps, removed from the battlefield. The tunnel was exquisite.

"That's great but they're going the wrong way." I felt bad the sentence indicated a sense of superiority over detainees. "This is going toward the middle of the base." I continued. While feeling bad over my bias, I felt giddy at their ineptitude. "If they wanted to escape, this is the long way."

"Escape was never their intention, Jim." Sayyed responded. "You have to think like them or you're going to get killed. Say twenty of their best fighters faked illness and were brought to the hospital at the same time. If it were coordinated during a rocket or mortar attack, every .50 caliber facing outward, they couldn't dig a tunnel far enough to be out of range. So, they chose the alternative. No, not the wrong way at all. You're underestimating them."

Within each compound were up to a couple hundred detainees. When the zaeem ordered anything from the command, it would be reviewed. They could request innocuous things like pillowcases, a soccer ball, or an extra table tennis racket.

Soccer balls could be halved and used as shovels; the pillowcases reduced to a spool of thread. Detainees showed an incredible capacity to make requests that over time provided all the components of a weapon.

Those two hundred men of shared purpose—escape—had nothing but time on their hands. The worst of them ate, slept, and drank with the singular purpose of disrupting the American mission. If names were removed or replaced, we would hail them as heroes and exemplary of our Code of Conduct for prisoners of war.

It became clear the insurgents dug into the hospital compound, where weapons were checked into the armory, as none were allowed around detainees per our security protocols. Once inside, the stage would be set. The best fighters with weapons would use the tunnel and come up to the surface unnoticed as they would be under the Hospital—which was situated in a series of trailers.

With so many detainees having been in the trailer, they were intimately familiar with the layout of every section. Coming up under the armory, they would have enough arms and ammunition to take hostages or kill the unarmed medical personnel. Subsequently, they could fight their way outward from there.

It was in all probability a suicide mission for them but would likely inflict a great cost for American soldiers and a huge morale boost for the detainees. All that time, we were the equivalent of the hapless victim in a scary movie, panic-stricken and running through their house to lock all the doors and windows, only to find the monster had been in the home all along.

The 15,000 detainees had been held for anything from petty theft to the killing of American soldiers.

Outside the base, it was well-known that extremists with blood on their hands were being held. These dangerous Sunnis, the religious sect associated with al-Qaeda and the most turbulent areas of Iraq, were likely the true targets of the rockets and mortars launched toward the base.

Sunnis detained in southern Iraq were guilty by association. The area was dominated by the opposing Shi'ite sect and presented an opportunity for vengeance.

Al-Qaeda's stated mission was to initiate an Iraqi civil war, which would almost guarantee the involvement of the entire Middle East. The most extreme view among al-Qaeda affiliate was the belief that the end of time had begun and the war was a formality.

As for American forces at the camp, the high number of detainees also outnumbered coalition personnel by almost four to one.

"Which of them knew what was going down? The ones who were laughing?" My mood shifted from glee to dread. "Or was it those with no expression on their face? They're the scary ones," I said to Sayyed, scanning the fences lined with yellow jumpsuits.

My head wasn't in the game. I was digging tunnels of my own, planning every detail for that one opportunity I needed, picturing each step, rehearsing, and conditioning for what had to be done. Only God and I would know, and I'd deal with the consequences then.

What muqannis had taken centuries to learn about tunnels I found terrifyingly intuitive.

"I thought we had a great relationship with the detainees."

"True, that's why they'd quickly kill you. It's the others they'd want to see suffer."

Those guys knew what they were doing.

I had haunting images of what could have been if not for the randomly parked troop transport truck.

Even then, the hundreds of detainees were reading the body language of Americans as we discovered their intentions. We were surrounded by a determined and ingenious foe and they weren't close to defeat.

It was going to be a long war.

Chapter Six

The Last Night

THE NIGHT BEFORE MY DEPLOYMENT with the *USS Wasp* (LHD-1) to the Mediterranean Sea in February of 2000, Cindy had flown back from Miami. As if grieving the sudden loss of her best childhood friend wasn't too much, I would deploy for six months a few hours after she got home from the funeral.

Her eyes still swollen and red, she fell into a sleep out of sheer exhaustion. Alfonso drifted off to sleep after checking to see if his mom was home. He'd never been separated from Cindy in his six years for more than a few hours at a time.

The timing for deployment couldn't have been worse. Cindy finagled Alfonso into an autism early intervention program, and he responded with a seemingly endless cycle of setbacks followed by resilient optimism. Alfonso awakened each day and seemed to think "this is my day."

At Lorenzo's fifth birthday the previous December, Alfonso had defied autism's expected "lack of awareness of others" symptoms by presenting with no prompting, a pencil which read "Happy Birthday," among countless instances where he defied projections. *Exceptional parents*—in the autism community, meaning the parents of children on the spectrum—can take these increments and build a monument around them.

Fair-skinned with reddish-brown hair, Alfonso could go from laughing and sociable to maddeningly frustrated, dropping heavily to his knees and banging his head on the floor. As with most children with autism, routine was critical. Alfonso's anxiety dramatically increased when my explanation of how long I'd be gone further confused him. He would wake up to a house with neither his father nor an adequate explanation.

Lorenzo (our second son) though, was wide awake. He had just turned four and I was trying to explain how long six months was.

"Dad, can I come with you? I'll be good, Dad, I promise," Lorenzo pleaded.

I momentarily stared at the ceiling, pained, and wondered when the damn taxicab I called would arrive.

"Lorenzo, it doesn't work that way. Sailors have a lot to learn. A person could get hurt if they don't know what to do."

"But I'll stay in the x-ray room and eat sandwiches. I won't even leave the room, not even once." Lorenzo was undeterred. His eyes brightened. To him, it was the perfect solution.

"I wish I could bring you, Lorenzo, but this job is only for adults. But six months will go by fast. I'll be back in the summer, and then we'll have fun. I promise."

Lorenzo slumped and his bottom lip quivered.

When will that Goddamn cab get here?

I gave his tiny body a tight hug, wondering why I'd ever enlisted. With negotiations over, Lorenzo handed me his favorite Power Ranger to look over me. A honk of the horn told me the cab had arrived.

Why did it get here so quickly?

I had to physically move Lorenzo from the doorway in order to walk out the door—the hardest thirty pounds I'd ever moved.

As the cab pulled away, Lorenzo's silhouette with my much-too-big *USS Wasp* hat askew, his right hand waving meekly, seared into my memory.

How selfish was I? As the cab moved, I thought of Lorenzo running with that joyous skip only children have. Even in haste, there was time to half-skip. *Will he be too old to run that way or hold my hand when I get back? What small details will be mere memories by the time I get home?*

Military families have entirely different definitions of incremental landmarks in family dynamics. The changes aren't so dramatic from day-to-day, but I was gone six months at a time. We returned to homes where our children's voices were changed and unfamiliar, and our spouses had assumed our roles. Even the furniture was arranged differently. They couldn't help having to adjust to my absence.

* * *

Almost seven years later, I learned I was deploying to Iraq and I told Cindy I would tell the boys. So, I offered Lorenzo a ride for ice cream. Within a block of the driveway, he looked away from me outside his passenger window towards the submarine base in New London, Connecticut across the Thames River.

At eleven years old, Lorenzo was quiet and thoughtful, with an impish and mischievous sense of humor. When he first learned to tie his shoes, if we pointed out they were on the wrong feet, he would cross his feet with a big smile before fixing them. Maybe our favorite game of all was the *Why* Game.

"We have to go grocery shopping. Let's go!"

"Why?" Lorenzo responded in a sing-song manner.

"Because we need food."

"Why?"

"Because we ate the last week's groceries."

"Why?"

"Because we were hungry."

"Why?" Each question brought a bigger smile from both of us.

"Because we need to eat to have energy to do stuff."

"Why?"

"Because the house would get messy because we'd be tired all the time without food."

"Why?"

"Because we don't want the house to be messy."

"Why?"

"Because then the house would have so much stuff it would collapse."

"Why?"

"Because God said so."

Lorenzo stared at the submarine base across the river, maybe hating that the Navy was ready to take me away again. As much as we loved the *Why* Game, it was an unusual time humor couldn't find its way. One of his classmate's fathers was leaving for the Middle East, setting his fears in motion.

"You're going to Iraq, aren't you?" he asked flatly.

Because of the military family dynamic, Lorenzo was already overly responsible and seemed to defer his eleven-year-old problems for the good of the family. Like medical triage in emergencies, there were always other more critical crises.

"Well, Lorenzo..." I stammered, surprised how much a child his age could learn from passing television news flashes.

Saddam Hussein had been unceremoniously hung on December 30th, 2006, after American authorities turned him over to Iraqi authorities. The symbolism of Hussein going to the gallows on the first day of *Eid al-Adha* [Feast of the Sacrifice], a day when many Islamic countries pardon criminals and few are put to death, was interpreted as differently as one could imagine by Shi'ites and hard-line Sunnis.

The Sunnis immediately declared the hasty decision was directed by Americans, making the Shi'ite-led government a puppet of the occupiers. The country teetered on the verge of a devastating civil war.

In whatever way Lorenzo had processed the news, he struck the exact fear I'd tried to suppress.

"You're going to die there, aren't you, Dad?"

"Lorenzo, I'm going there as a Corpsman. I'm going there to help people," I said, knowing the truth was that militants deliberately injured unit members, and then trained their sniper rifles directly over the fallen soldier. They knew the Corpsman would respond to render aid.

My short explanation comforted Lorenzo, if at all, only slightly.

When the boys were toddlers, deployments seemed less complicated. I could say I had to leave because I "had to make sure there were no bad guys out there in the world,"—an explanation that worked until Cindy objected to the implication that *we* were the good guys and *they* were the bad guys.

Lorenzo was wise beyond his years and could sense subtle changes in mood and language.

Resilience and survival instincts of military families have been a recurring theme in talk shows, but Cindy, at times, had the look of a scared roller coaster passenger, strapped in just after the cars had bolted from the boarding area. All that was left was to get through it.

Cindy assumed every fatherly role, Alfonso was forced to adjust to disruptions in his routine, and Lorenzo became an eleven-year-old man of the house. *What have I taught them?*

With a year-long separation before us, I incorrectly believed the week's appointments should've been a simple formality. Monday at 9:00 AM brought an appointment with the Legal Officer and me to sign a power-of-attorney necessary for Cindy to assume full control over our finances.

I didn't pay attention to his horror stories of military members returning from their deployment to an empty house or a spouse finishing a no-fault divorce and remarried. Undeterred, I insisted on an unconditional power of attorney.

I was thankful Cindy wasn't there. Even without a clear picture of what our unit would confront in Iraq, I was adamant to maintain separation between Iraq and my home life.

In the waiting room, I read Victor Hugo's *Last Day of a Condemned Man*, which describes the thoughts of a convicted man hours before his execution.

"A revolution had taken place within me. Until the death sentence was passed, I felt myself breathe, palpitate, live, in the same atmosphere as other

men—now I distinguished a sort of wall built up between the world and myself." (page 57)

At 11:00, I signed my Final Will and Testament in which I expressed my wishes in how my property would be distributed upon my death—a much more sobering task than I had imagined.

How often did it happen a service member saw their mortality in ink and that moment was prophetic? *Will I be one of them?* I walked back to the Submarine Base Clinic with no memory of which path I took.

Everything moved quickly in chaotic order, like the contrast between a gentle undercurrent and the violent riptide. Although it was a matter of days, it seemed to be minutes before we, as a unit, placed belongings we'd continuously carried throughout our lives into crackling manila envelopes.

I wasn't sure if the contents were held for us or sent home. We wouldn't have room for belongings and the memories they bring. For the first time in my life, I understood the plight of Hugo's hapless condemned man.

"Besides, in this anguish, the only means to suffer less from it is to observe it. To paint it will prevent me from feeling it." - (p. 59)

I dropped my car keys into the envelope, a simple task so dramatic. I wished I'd expressed more, said more, or written more.

An overweight and impatient sergeant took my driver's license, my currency and change, my wedding band, wallet, and phone—noting that I had no use for them where I was going. He told me that, apparently unaware of the magnification of words and their meaning to deploying troops.

Finally, all my clothing was placed in a box and mailed home. It was my final act before awaiting definition in an assigned identity. As of that moment, I wore the same clothes and carried the same gear as everyone else.

By the time I had completed training at Fort Bliss, Texas, some questions about our mission crystallized.

In a short stopover between training and deploying, my family in Chicago had a party and my trepidation turned every word into snippets of eulogy. I debated with my sister-in-law about the idea of going to Iraq when she reminded me that the President was my Commander-in-Chief.

Thoughts, feelings, and instincts were meaningless. I was only a soldier. I requested time with a priest for a short blessing.

Soon, I had nothing but the uniform I'd been issued. The only thing verifying my name was the uniform tag on my right breast. If I changed uniforms, and it fit properly, I could have any name or be any person in any unit. I held an itinerary which said our airplane departed at 0400. Everyone was accounted for.

The passenger boarding bridge made a sharp left turn, so it appeared to be a dead end. I had only one door left to traverse. The signal came from our leaders to move forward in prompt and orderly fashion.

Jim Enderle

"It is impossible that I will be pardoned... ah! The wicked wretches!... they are coming up the stairs... four o'clock!'

* * *

Once I found my airplane seat, I thought of the previous night.

It had only been a few hours since Cindy's anxiety was out-screamed by my own. Her only crime was expressing her anxieties, which seemed minuscule next to my own. Cindy verbalized her lists of responsibilities and tasks, on top of maintaining the house and the boys, on top of her concerns for me.

In the meantime, my focus was black and white. As the deployment approached, if it wasn't an imminent threat to me, a problem was a mere annoyance.

We were driving to get some groceries, and after a couple of miles of silence, I sensed disconnection, a way to maybe transition from daily life to the family of a deployed military member.

Later on the night before, as 2:00 in the morning approached, the house had fallen silent. I sensed the boys were sleeping uneasily. Cindy and I sat close and looked at the television as if some mesmerizing movie was on, but the television was off. After a while, Cindy joked at my wanderlust and made me promise not to venture away from my unit to see the Hanging Gardens of Babylon. I'd never hesitated on the ship's deployments to Europe to jump on a Eurorail train and escape anyone who spoke English.

"This is not that kind of a deployment," I chuckled, admitting to myself that I'd join any convoy passing through that part of Iraq if I could.

How intriguing the Hanging Gardens of Babylon or a ziggurat would be to visit among the hundreds of historical places there.

Cindy's tone changed. "Jim, I have one thing to ask because I know how you are."

"Okay," I said. I accepted what came next without any idea what that meant, and it occurred to me that after sixteen years of marriage, I should have known better.

"If something happens to you," she said slowly, "I want that your last thought is that we love you and will always love and honor you—just in case."

Cindy gave a sign of the cross, bowed her head, and kissed her hand as if finalizing her prayer. She was unable to pass a homeless person or car accident or say a prayer without that understated motion. As her head lay on my chest, she extended her arm and gave me a tight hug. When she looked up at me, I nodded while looking at the darkened television.

"If you die, we wouldn't want you to believe you've let us down, not for a second. I would not want that to be your final thought. Please know we'll always love you."

I felt guilty to think I just wanted the moment of departure to arrive. The waiting was excruciating. All we needed to say or were willing to say had been expressed. It was time to go. I'd have walked in the grass barefoot and counted the shades of green from our back deck if I thought of it.

I thought of a conversation on one of my last duties at the clinic. One of the young Corpsmen told me to be careful. I responded, "I am from Chicago, Iraq doesn't scare me" with false bravado. I immediately regretted the words.

Service members I'd known had been killed or injured in Iraq. There were daily reports of Iraq being on the verge of utter civil war.

It was selfish of me to speak that way. The Chicago I spoke of were neighborhoods I'd only seen from the rooftop of our apartment building.

Chapter Seven

Munawwar and Abdul-Hayy

9 June 2007

ROCKETS AND MORTARS RAINED DOWN upon the camp, bringing a problem for the insurgents within indirect fire range of our base: They struck in the area of the base where detainees, their own allies, were housed. Militants launched the attack just after we'd finished our breakfast.

By the time one serves in Iraq for four months, mortar attacks missing their mark and barely marshaling the force to make a pencil roll off our plywood-constructed tables were hardly noticed. I normally felt a complacent annoyance. That time mortars were accompanied by rockets, which shook building foundations bringing the smell of dust, angry at being awakened, to our nostrils.

Within moments of the first explosion, the visceral joy I felt from seeing where the rockets landed was hard to suppress. It was at least close to the compound where my adversary was housed. My obsessive prayers had provided an opportunity.

It had been three weeks since the detainee in an al-Qaeda compound read the name tag over my right pocket and deliriously pulled an envelope from his waistband, letting me know my family's addresses had been compromised.

What were the chances? The al-Qaeda militant couldn't believe his luck, seemingly elated he could personally notify a deployed service member of danger to his family, especially a family he wouldn't see for another seven months. Just the idea broke any pretense of safety on that Army base.

Interpreters tried to keep the envelope away that night, but I recognized the writing. Our eye contact immediately became personal, as if he had just walked into my living room unannounced and taken my family hostage. I hated him. He was everything I came to Iraq to fight.

Maybe the joy I felt wasn't strong enough—it was closer to elation. I saw him in black and white, with no redeeming qualities, no family who loved him. He was evil, it could *only* be that he was evil.

During attacks, the proper procedure was to muster in a predetermined location to account for everyone before being dispatched to where we were needed.

Hospital Corpsmen had their own sets of rules: We ran toward explosions. Mustering with our unit was determined on a case-by-case basis.

The ensuing chaos allowed me to carry my weapon into the compound area, while under normal circumstances all weapons were turned in at the armory.

Even luckier, a personnel transport headed toward the compounds drove by trailing a huge cloud of dust. Although the truck had no room for more passengers, I still dove into the back of the carrier, aided by those seated in the back. They pulled me into a tangled sea of legs and arms. The planets were aligning in my favor.

The *Art of War* states: *"If you know the enemy and know yourself, you need not fear the result of a hundred battles. If you know yourself but not the enemy, for every victory gained you will also suffer a defeat. If you know neither the enemy nor yourself, you will succumb in every battle."* But I had a new one for Sun Tzu—what if I knew my enemy better than myself?

I'd learned enough of my foe and had even heard another detainee refer to him as Manuwwar. He'd been captured in Husaybah, Iraq, a city in western al-Anbar province in April of 2004. He'd been part of a group of insurgents trying to take some pressure off the siege of the city of Fallujah to its east, hoping the Americans would divert man-power to quell the attack in Husaybah, allowing insurgents in Fallujah to break free.

I felt horrific fear my family was in the same danger, or more so than I was. What of the idea of fighting our wars overseas to prevent war from being found in the United States? Too much evidence al-Qaeda militants were cagey, resourceful, and not to be underestimated was discussed at daily briefs.

Guards waved us through the gates, where inside utter confusion reigned. Detainees in yellow jump-suits ran free of their compounds as the fences were destroyed. In a surreal scene, instead of fleeing or fighting, they screamed for help and led medical personnel to aid their fallen comrades, pulling at the American's uniforms.

I grabbed a length of spare rebar and walked toward the compound with a gait that felt as if I were walking uphill or against a strong wind. Walking into Munawwar's compound through a hole blown in the chain-link fence and barbed wire, I came upon an area that had an eerie quiet, with a barely audible, but menacing hiss. There, three bodies were strewn on the sand, two dead and one still clinging to life. The rebar felt blisteringly hot even in my gloved hand.

The lone living man, my adversarial al-Qaeda mil-itant, was grievously wounded. Lying awkwardly on his left side with his left arm extended, pain on his face showed pain too great to writhe. His right arm clung to his side to brace against an open, exposed wound.

Kill him. He would do the same if the situation were reversed.

My pace toward him quickened. It had to be done to make my family safe.

But I knew nothing of killing a human being. There were intangible and indescribable qualities needed for killing. Despite the adrenaline in the moment, I thought of a high dive. You don't walk to the end of the diving board and look down if you're afraid of heights. Just run and block everything else out. Once you're clear of the diving board, it's done.

An investigation would trace bullets back to my pistol, so I grasped the hot rebar. In a moment of premeditated clarity, I decided the rebar would be the necessary mechanism of death. Actions follow words. I'd "neutralize the enemy," as military language says of killing. The expression deliberately sounds so harmless and impersonal. It was the language of war. Yet it was clear to me it was a bridge that once you cross, you never go back, so I prayed.

Oh my God, I am heartily sorry for having offended thee...

The man's clothes were torn in two different places with skin sticking to the fabric from obvious third-degree burns. Two tourniquets were shoved in my left cargo pocket. Rebar in my right hand.

I slowly walked into his line of sight. No sympathy struck, but he was no threat. I'd imagined lunging at him but hesitated, unsure if it was because our eyes met. Rather than that wild-eyed look etched in my mind for the last three weeks, these eyes were pleading. Maybe ten feet from me, I was close enough to hear his labored and irregular gasping and coughing. He looked up and recognized me.

The fire of hatred didn't burn as intensely. It likely occurred to him he was looking at the person who held his last hope. Or perhaps not.

He muttered some words in Arabic I didn't understand, something with a lot of "Ls" and "As." If I'd wished for it, I found when it came true it was a miserable feeling—not as vindicating as I'd ever thought. As all the thoughts flew around and our eyes locked on each other and our facial expressions softening, I kept praying.

And I detest all my sins because of thy just punishment...

His left hand clawed at the dirt as if trying to grab hold of something. My enemy was operating on instinct over rationale, trying to pull himself to somewhere else, anywhere else. His effort was heroic but invariably futile.

The muscles in his left arm strained, revealing a pool of blood that had been absorbed into the thirsty earth. His right arm was not useful as the upper arm had an apparent fracture. Try as they might to somehow get away, his weakening fingers did not even penetrate the dirt—the concrete-like Iraqi parched earth.

The temperatures soared into the one-hundred and teens and sweat steadily dripped from my nose onto my left arm crossed in front of me, my hand grasped the rebar, which didn't feel quite hot enough. I rearranged my sweaty fingers around the ridges of the steel.

As I looked downward, a drip of perspiration fell from my nose about every three seconds. Only the steel tips of my combat boots were dry, as the humid morning had not left a speck of uniform that wasn't soaked through. Tourniquets in the left pocket, a tool of death in the right. The prayer in my head continued:

But mostly because they offend thee, my God, who are all good and deserving of all my love...

There is a Hippocratic Oath that Corpsmen take, almost identical to that sworn by doctors where we swear to do no harm, to care for all casualties. And that part of my brain outlined steps taken quickly to sustain life.

End it, he would do that and more if I were lying there. Kill him.

I was conflicted because their dedication to tribe and family was something I admired and respected. He uttered more "Ls" and "As." *Is that a poem or a prayer?* He likely would have respected my match of his convictions.

The whole "winning the hearts and minds in Iraq" all came down to two enemies staring into each other's eyes and making a choice. Then I discovered it was no choice at all. The joke was on me. So, for what it was worth, I chose.

An enemy with whom there is no path to negotiation has our names and address, and as such, not even our sleepy corner of Quaker Hill Village would be safe.

I stared at his outstretched left hand, as if some force held it in place, turned upward, fingers spread, looking to absorb as much hope as possible. Was he asking for my help—for my forgiveness?

"La illaha illallaahul...." the dying man muttered, barely audible, before stopping abruptly. His face twisted in a grimace, his eyes closed tightly before opening them again. He blinked. Even blinking his eyes was in slow motion. His fate had been sealed before I arrived. My enemy was dead. His blood soaked into the ground and with any breeze, the sand would disguise it—along with trinkets, soccer balls, and colored sticks.

Death had no dignity. A Bible quote read, "It is done. I am the Alpha and the Omega, the Beginning and the End."

He lay on the ground that's like a frying pan in his own blood, with burnt skin and exposed intestines his right arm was still trying hold in, each with an unforgettable smell of their own, death now identified as body odor emanating from my pores. Not my clothes, they can be washed or replaced—tattooed onto my skin. Hundreds of layers of sand and dirt covered his blood on my boots, but it's still there. It's all I see when I look at them.

His hand remained extended hopefully upward until the end of the world, unanswered until the end of time.

I pleaded to the cast of thousands in my mind, my hands extended in front of me. I couldn't synthesize it. The prayers to his God unanswered, his final moments alone with his mortal enemy, and all I imagined I represented to him.

I thought I was ridding myself of him. But from that moment on, all I'd see was his face. I wish

I'd have closed his eyes, then the memory of him would be that he was in a peaceful sleep.

The enemies in Iraq didn't need a well-coordinated, worldwide network of ruthless terrorists to bring the war home. My actions hand-delivered it right into my own living room. They didn't have to do anything. I was sorry I couldn't stop it.

I firmly resolve, with the help of Your grace to sin no more and to avoid the near occasion of sin. Amen.

* * *

With a step backward, I remained unable to look away. Time was impatient and fate was finished with me. The frenzied sounds of bedlam return to my ears, along with the sight of an Iraqi man struggling in the hazy humidity.

The smoke just hung there, dirt and sand still settling. And the smell of the bombs—like grease, sweat, metal, and some kind of propellant or fuel. It was a translucent synesthesia. It didn't seem to block the sun, as I was wishing it would be thick enough to cast a shadow.

I lost track of time. It felt as though I'd barely turned away from Manuwwar when I saw that man needing help. I couldn't help but felt a sense of impending doom. The rocket and mortar attack was likely over, but if not, I'd never know what hit me. It was a common method of insurgent attack to stagger the waves of rockets, hoping to catch medical personnel or others retrieving the dead and injured to maximize casualties.

I ran toward the man but felt disconnected from my legs, as if I stood on a wooden floor and someone heavy was walking, causing the floor to reverberate. I pulled the tourniquet from my pocket as the man helped another badly injured detainee. There was a rush of other medics into the area, the sounds of directions and cries for help.

My focus stayed on the struggling man, heavy-set like a fireplug, bending over with his back to me to carry something or someone too cumbersome for him. Perhaps the tourniquets would have a use after all.

The blazing morning became even more unendurable, some celestial magnifying glass burned that exact patch of earth. The sun shined off the man's perspiring bald head.

The man appeared to be scolding a boy who, as I got closer, I realized was a severely wounded teenager, maybe sixteen—not much older than my own son. Blood soaked into the father's pant legs as he knelt in the dirt, but I couldn't tell if he'd been injured. I guessed he may have been confused as it seemed he wanted to run from where he was through an opening in the fence.

There was no escape from the camp, though it appeared to be open desert. I wondered what the heavy-set man desperately looked for. He looked right, then all the way to the left, before dropping his head.

"*Think,*" he must have thought to himself. He had the rest of his life for regret.

If the man had been injured, adrenaline bypassed his pain. He scolded the boy as if the young man was merely being stubborn.

He yelled in Arabic, maybe saying *"Look at me when I am talking to you! Look at me when I speak to you!"* He held the boy by the shoulders and gently shook.

While my brain pressed me to run, my body settled for a trot. Approaching him, the man's movements were frantic but halting. He was too caught up in his tragedy to notice anything around him. Within seconds, I stood behind the man, close enough to smell the smoky scent of burnt skin.

Over his left shoulder, the boy looked gravely wounded. Already, two tourniquets were in my hand, but the boy's death was imminent by partial impalement of a twisted piece of rocket shrapnel, like a thick metal shaving, protruding from just to the left of his heart. Blood trickled from his mouth and nose. Weakened coughing and desperate gagging did not clear his throat.

Whatever young boys do in Iraq, he should have been doing any of them. But instead, all energy he had was spent in an all-consuming attempt to continue breathing.

As I looked over the man's left shoulder, the boy's eyes met mine. His first reaction was terror. His right hand rested on his father's lower leg before limply dropping.

Then his eyes looked through me, they lost focus.

What was wrong with me that the young man's impulse was dread at the sight of me? Certainly, I was the last person on earth on any list to witness a moment that intensely personal. His father was there.

The young man looked up at me and his eyes lost focus, and he too mercifully died. But even mercy was tragic there.

The father continued to whisper. His body language shouted, *"Look at me! Stop being obstinate!"*

There was no one in front of him or around us. The man never realized I was there. The father spoke to an invisible group in front of them, *"He must be alive! He must be alive! His eyes are still open! See? Look! He is alive! He's just being stubborn! This cannot be true."*

Slowly, it sank in.

After a few moments, he let out a long, involuntary, agonizing cry as if wherever God was, he could hear his tortured grief. The tormented shriek was audible until the father completely ran out of breath and his voice trailed, leaving no residual air in his lungs. He took in a deep inhale as if drawing in all the air in the world and let loose with another cry.

"Laa-aaaahhh! La-aah!" The Arabic word for *no* was broken into syllables that denied and desperately pleaded. His voice cracked.

That scream was beyond human. I prayed I'd never hear it again. But I've heard that scream ever since.

He fell forward over the boy's body with weeping sobs. Kneeling back up again, I saw his bloody hands extended to the heavens. There would be no intervention from God, no miracles. The world never contained them.

I instinctively reached for the grieving man and placed my left hand on his right shoulder. The man, with no idea who was behind him beyond a sympathetic figure, placed his left hand over mine and tightly squeezed.

For that brief moment, two men sworn to the destruction of others were only fathers. Somewhere the boy's mother cried out, perhaps not even knowing why.

* * *

Over the next hour we provided medical care. At one point, I helped to carry one badly wounded man to a helicopter waiting to transport him to the next highest level of hospital care.

Kneeling at the man's feet, it was an older man whose hands were entirely limp, even with the uneven bouncing of the team of four litter bearers. It was the Compound Eight zaeem, hardly recognizable with the left side of his face burnt.

As other medics scrambled to prepare for liftoff, I was momentarily left with him. The zaeem, who hours earlier called every shot for his compound helplessly lay there.

"I'm sorry we can't save you. Rest easy," I said awkwardly. "Where you're going, you'll understand my words."

Jim Enderle

The helicopter was prepared, and I ducked and stepped back, feeling a dizzying sense of urgency. Working my way to a bank of port-a-potties I stepped in and locked the door.

The sun was so brilliant the walls were illuminated. Barely making it to the toilet, oblivious for the moment of the steamy scent, I violently vomited. An involuntary, rumbling sound emanated from me—grief and agony rolled into a single sound.

Suddenly, I realized where I was. My sense of smell returned. *What if someone heard me?*

As much as one can possibly pull themselves together in a cramped and smelly toilet, I collected myself and straightened my soaked uniform.

As I swung the door open, the door of the next portable toilet opened. It was one of the senior enlisted men—he'd been within earshot the entire time. He reminded me of screaming comic Sam Kinison with a flat top—there were no situations that left him speechless or without a plan. Until then.

He looked into my eyes, red and swollen and we looked at each other for a long moment, before we nodded almost reverently and walked away. Our eyes never broke away.

Maybe he recognized my destination had no return route.

Chapter Eight

The Call Home

THE TELEPHONE WASN'T GOING TO dial itself.

I sat alone in the Troop Medical Center (TMC) at almost midnight, my hand on the receiver. I stopped. I stood up and paced around the sick call area with both hands running through my hair. It had been two full nights since I'd slept, and attentiveness was fleeting.

I'll count to five, pick up the phone, and dial. I have to focus.

Earlier that day, I asked Sayyed questions of the two men who had died. Maybe knowing something about them might resolve my thoughts? By the end of the day, Sayyed had gone through personal effects before they were sent home. He said it included letters from their loved ones to both men and the unsent letters they had written.

He'd transcribed and copied all of it for me—my request.

The TMC was dark after hours, but I suspiciously checked every door and office before muttering aloud what I would say. Nobody was there but me.

I'd say I couldn't talk long but that I'd been thinking of Cindy and wanted to hear her voice. She'd surely ask what was wrong and I could say I was just tired from the heat. Maybe Cindy wouldn't remember my best marathon times were in the heat.

Sixty-three hours after the deaths of Manuwwar and Abdul-Hayy and two tormented nights of trying to picture Cindy's face. I couldn't see it anymore without looking at a photo. How could I not recall her image after fifteen years of marriage? *It must be because I forfeited the right to her image.*

In the corner of my eye, I saw someone standing. I fumbled for a light switch before realizing I had a flashlight. Terrifying closet monsters of my childhood returned, represented by Manuwwar. They weren't a figment of my imagination.

Who stood in that corner—a fellow detainee who witnessed Manuwwar's death? *Do they blame me for watching him die?*

Within Islamic law is a compensatory system of dealing with those responsible for a relative's death which decides from among three choices. He can demand *qisas* [equal retaliation as in *an eye for an eye, life for life*] in the name of the family or *diyeh* [financial compensation in the form of assets, traditionally a set at a hundred camels for a free Muslim male, or an equivalent amount of money]. He could also choose forgiveness as an act of religious charity.

But he hadn't escaped from his compound and broke into the TMC and hid in a dark corner to forgive me. He had come to collect.

After almost frantically ripping my cargo pocket off my pants, I pulled the flashlight from my pocket and turned it on with an unsteady hand, only to see a uniform hanging from an IV pole.

I laughed loudly, crazily. If it had been a hostile stranger, he could have killed me five times before I directed the beam into the corner.

I needed sleep but there were more important matters at hand—remembering Cindy's face.

Standing in the dark, I bent slightly at the knees and wrapped my arms around her imaginary frame. My arms remembered exactly how she fit so I squeezed knowing how tight the hug would be. I slow danced, never wanting to let go. Her image came to my mind, but through a camera lens smeared with Vaseline.

I filled in the blanks. Her dark hair was naturally wavy and full of bounce. Only recently had she even considered highlights. Her eyebrows were a work of art. Cindy did meticulous research before a stylist could touch them. I used to joke that applying for a home mortgage was less complicated. I could only see her dark eyes as if they looked just beyond my shoulder.

No, please look at me, Cindy.

I pictured each facial feature, but separately. Unable to put them together in one portrait, I dropped to my knees near the IV pole, and clung to it as if holding myself up. I wept. I couldn't picture her. She wouldn't look at me.

Every facet of my life had changed in the three-and-a-half weeks since I'd last spoken to Cindy. Emotions were seemingly exponentially magnified during deployments. Email messages not immediately returned went unnoticed at home, but within the borders of Iraq, the calculus changed. A day without a message or response brought fears of abandonment and betrayal. *Maybe I am easily forgettable, after all. Perhaps people are only being polite when I'm around and really wish I would just go away.*

The lines the last time we spoke were long and beyond patient, even cheerful. Immense gratitude overwhelmed me until I thought of members of the unit who had joined the Navy after Hurricane Katrina devastated New Orleans. They'd enlisted on the verge of homelessness, having lost family members and almost anything else dear to them. Did those men and women have anyone to call?

I'd called Mom first at about 11:00 AM, Chicago time. With limited time, Mom told me she knew I was in difficult circumstances and that I had always been conscientious and thoughtful, fair-minded, and sensitive. She didn't understand our rush to war in Iraq, but she had no doubt if anyone could bring reconciliation to the Middle East, I was the one.

"Just do your best, I know you will. Just keep trying."

"We're trying, Mom. Happy Mother's Day. I love you." I was thankful for the delay and usually poor reception on satellite phone calls.

A two-second delay meant a maddening overlap of voices, then both sides would stop talking, producing silence, before talking at the same time again. Maybe that time, it worked in my favor and my mother didn't hear my voice break. It would have given me away. I had to be careful. A slip of emotion like that would beg a line of questioning, especially around loved ones.

The next call to wish Cindy a happy Mother's Day caught her by surprise. She and the boys were just leaving, invited by friends to a picnic and a late-night swim.

Other days, Cindy found any free activities that would get them out of the house, since the school year was coming to an end. Still, I had a sneaking suspicion there was a lot of their daily lives she kept to herself.

"We love you, don't forget to duck!" Cindy said cheerfully.

It was our inside joke from when I'd told her I was working in an air-conditioned x-ray room. Within the safety of that belief, we'd found a way to defuse the tension of the deployment.

"Okay, I'll remember," I said, just as cheerfully, "I love you."

But I knew the transition, especially for Alfonso, had to be difficult. About everything we did while I was home was done as a family. I knew transitions and upheavals in Alfonso's mind were stressful. Cindy didn't mention any difficulties. I didn't ask.

In the wheeled desk chair, I rolled toward the desk and placed my hand on the phone as if inertia would carry through picking up the receiver and dialing.

We could make satellite calls from one military base to another without incurring charges. I could call the submarine base in New London and they transferred the call to my home number, bypassing both the dangers of a phone call being overheard and government expense.

The impetus didn't translate.

Think! What did I say last time? That phone call went well. I'll just say what I did last time. Maybe if I hear her voice, I'll be able to picture her face. I'll use the same words. The call will go just as well. What words did I use?

Could I have spoken to Cindy about the hijacked envelope and my reaction?

To speak of militants having our address, I might as well have been trying to explain color to a blind person, in what language a deaf person thinks, or what water tastes like. The thickness of the stolen envelope that separated us had become a chasm as big as all of Chicago.

My hand moved off the phone again. The boy—his name was Abdul Hayy—should never have been there. His father had coerced him into stripping out-of-commission generators for scrap metal to feed the family, I had read that in their rap sheet.

Manuwwar begged for the confrontation, the bastard. It was his fault. And the stupid war. I only behaved that way because of the stupid war. He would've killed me if the situation were reversed. That's it—he would have. For sure. I can't tell anyone that, they weren't there, they'd never understand.

I picked up the phone and dialed the number for the clinic. *That task will become easier in time. I'll focus on the job. Besides, anyone who knows me, who would even believe I could be capable of that?*

I could confess everything, and nobody would believe me. It won't happen again, anyway. This is an anomaly. I'll allow myself to feel guilty and saddened by it, then it's about moving forward.

It must have been progress that I'd avoided the compounds since then, even though I realized the militants would still come after me. I just didn't know when. They were famous for holding grudges for generations before exacting retribution. It was just my imagination with the IV pole, but the next time it might not be.

I must steel my resolve, even once I'm home, to protect my family because they'll come. Or am I bringing the threat home with me?

A sailor answered the phone on the quarterdeck of the clinic back home.

"Hey, Enderle. How's it going over there? We were just talking today about how hot it is there. Is it that bad?"

"But it's a dry heat." The expression never made sense to me but brought a chuckle from the other end of the line.

So far, so good.

"Could you put me through to my home phone, please?" I provided the number and waited, the suspense rising.

"Hello? Jim? I was just thinking about you."

"Hello, Cindy," I said plainly. I hoped she would ask questions and I could just answer. Either that or I could ask questions and listen to the sound of her voice.

They would be safer if I didn't return. That might satisfy the militants enough to leave my family alone.

"How are you and the boys?"

Cindy answered that they'd found an antique auto show that was free. The boys got preferential treatment from the car owners, some of whom let the boys sit behind the steering wheel. Our car almost broke down and a local mechanic, after hearing we were a military family, had Cindy pay only for the parts as a thank you. I barely heard anything, only comforted by her voice.

"See? Some good has come from this deployment. We got a discount! That was so nice of him, he wanted me to say thank you."

If Cindy had met me within the last couple of weeks, she wouldn't fall in love with me. If I weren't my parents' son, they would reject me. That image my mother instinctively etched into her mind would not return, certainly as she remembered. I couldn't bear to be thanked. My plan had gone from failed to failure. I still couldn't picture Cindy's face.

"I wish I had more time, but I have to go. I'll call when I can. I love you."

I had to rest and stay sharp. I must finish our unit's mission. I had never felt so mentally exhausted and confused.

"I love you too. Don't forget to duck!"

Chapter Nine

Blindfolds

August 2007—Baghdad International Airport

Since Navy units were tasked with supplementing Army units, we remained flexible and were used as necessary. Participating in convoys from Camp Bucca was not a part of our Army mission until I approached the first sergeant with a slip relieving his medic from the next mission.

"Consider yourself overruled, Doc."

"He went to Baghdad yesterday, First Sergeant," I argued the man had episodes of diarrhea and worsening dehydration. Surely, someone could switch with him.

"Doc, you're new at this, but I'm going to do something I never do." I felt happy to see his pensive look. "We're sending him to his rack [bed]?"

I nodded approvingly.

"No, knucklehead. I'm going to repeat myself. You're overruled. He's going out." The first sergeant turned to walk to his office.

"You can't send him in that condition, First Sergeant, he can't keep anything down," I said, not anticipating resistance.

"What do you want me to do, Doc? Cancel the movement? Who am I going to send? You?" he sneered. "Because unless I'm sending you, you're overruled."

"Send me, then!" I felt backed into a corner. "The Army won't show me something I've never seen with the Marines."

The first sergeant hadn't known I had never seen combat with a Marine unit.

* * *

By the tenth convoy to Baghdad—I'd become a part of the first sergeant's bullpen—the rhythm of our movements begged complacence. Seven months after our arrival, it was impossible to keep everything as an imminent threat. It could've been. But anything could happen anytime, anywhere, if you thought about it.

Our convoy departed after the sun abandoned the sorrowful country. History says Alexander the Great was so enamored by the sunsets in Iraq that it was his favorite place in his Empire (which was most of the known world at that time).

I thought that maybe the sun was just sad, though. Maybe it would drop below the horizon so it wouldn't have to see the plants and trees it enlivened leaning away, terrified, because the rockets and mortars had blown them back.

Throughout every convoy, I identified every landmark to find on a map of our routes. Each of the team members was alert for any environmental changes—a hole in the ground, a pile of trash, animal carcasses— from one day to the next. Bombs could and did hide in any of those.

After the final remnants were drained from the sky, we left with a mission of transporting fifty suspected militants from southern Iraq to Baghdad for trial. After dropping the detainees off at the Baghdad International Airport, we returned with an equal number of new detainees with enough evidence against them to be held.

The movement was not without risks. The omnipresent watchful eyes in the desert were well aware that many of those transported were the minority people of Iraq, Sunni, and possibly among the extremists trying to sow chaos through assassinations and bombings wherever Shi'ites congregated in large numbers. The ultimate goal desired an all-out sectarian civil war. Eyes in the desert would have loved the chance to kill a large group of suspected militants with one well-paced daisy-chain of roadside bombs. In that instance, the killing of American soldiers would be incidental. It was high-value militants they sought.

Attacks on convoys had been on the rise throughout 2007. A British announcement to leave their base in Basra in early September and a number of successful high-profile roadside bombings (including the killing of one of the chief organizers of the Anbar Salvation Council who had pledged support to Americans over al-Qaeda operatives) raised the militant's confidence.

Additionally, an article I had read detailed a haughty proclamation on the front page. An al-Qaeda senior official declared that his "Lions of the Martyrs' Brigade" would familiarize American troops with fires witnessed only by those sent to Hell.

He stated he was proud to announce the source of his hubris was the recently developed Explosively Formed Projectiles (EFPs) launched a mass of molten lava hot enough to melt its way through a Humvee and anything or anyone inside.

*Would that be **my** death?*

The detainees wore blindfolds, their hands bound to the belt around the detainee's waist in front of him, their feet shackled. Guards yelled instructions simultaneously and the men grew disoriented. We deliberately moved them in ways that kept them slightly off-balance. Sometimes we used opposing commands like "stop" and "move" within seconds.

With little choice but to cooperate, the detainees tried to follow orders but blindly bumped and tripped. Between the vehicle and the C-117 that flew the last leg of their trip to Baghdad, our team set up a checkpoint of three inspectors—an Army Soldier, and interpreter, and me as the medical representative.

The soldier ensured they were properly secured, and I checked prescriptions against medications and documented conditions. (The prisoners sometimes requested drugs they didn't actually need.) Their earthly possessions were relegated into a single baggie, shoved between medications and maybe a picture or two. As the interpreter, Sayyed meticulously looked at letters or photos, as they sometimes contained coded messages.

Once, we found a diagram that showed the layout of the diesel fuel tanks, military tents, chow hall, and anywhere troops in Camp Bucca would congregate for any reason, ingeniously illustrated into a picture of a brick wall. Another time, a photo included information on compound negotiations. And yet another, a diagram and estimated time of completion of an escape tunnel.

As the line of the detainees stumbled toward us—a cross between the Keystone Cops and an accordion-like traffic jam—I said, "And there they are, the Lions of the Martyrs' Brigade."

The sergeant next to me appreciated my mocking tone, but I immediately felt regret, wondering what Sayyed may have thought.

I looked at Sayyed to my right, his eyes squinted as if he was calculating and analyzing. Maybe he hadn't heard me.

A short, heavy-set man tripped and fell in front of me. He struggled to get up. Nobody helped him. He sweated profusely, and the dirt he fell onto already dampened his yellow jumpsuit. It looked like he landed in mud. He'd blinked his blindfold down.

"Pick up and tighten the blindfold. What does he have?" I asked.

The guard abruptly pulled the baggie from the man's grasp. It contained one prescription for a heart condition and matched the small plastic bottle's contents, I noted after going through it.

The guard moved quickly, as the man's body turned without resistance, putting up and tying his blindfold.

The blindfolded man stood before me and I towered over him. He'd been absorbed back into the dejected, demoralized line of detainees. The Lions were at every disadvantage.

One of those men could have been the one who'd come to my Connecticut home to avenge Manuwwar's death. It was *their* law, after all. One of them might have even known my secret. But at that time, I was judge, jury, and executioner. I wanted all those men to lose all hope.

I was one shredded photo away from that man giving up entirely.

"Is that everything?" I imagined asking him like the guard to a Jewish man in Arthur Miller's *Incident at Vichy* who'd provided his degrees and accomplishments, hoping for special consideration.

"Yes," the man might have responded, surely thinking I wouldn't bother with his one single picture.

"Good, now you have nothing." I would say, callously tearing the picture and tossing it over my shoulder as if it were meaningless. Perhaps he would have given up. If enough of them gave up, broken, that stupid war would have been over.

"Everything okay, Doc?" Sayyed words brought me back to reality.

"Prescriptions for a heart condition. What about the picture, Sayyed?"

My flashlight shined on a picture with bends and frayed edges. A young girl, maybe six years old wore a bright yellow dress shadowed by earthen browns. I imagined her cared for, spotless, before the more recent bombing of an apartment building—maybe her home. Her innocence contrasted the bullet holes and destruction.

A broken bed frame rested behind her, a teapot on the rubble to her left. Over her right shoulder, what appeared to be a woman's shredded dress or pajamas lay almost within the child's reach. Someone had lived there when the building was leveled.

With my flashlight on the picture, Sayyed eyed the Arabic writing on the back of the photo for a long moment. Even in the darkness I sensed Sayyed firm his facial expression, but he couldn't disguise a hard gulp.

"My daughter, sir," the detainee said, who by then had blinked his blindfold down again.

"Your daughter? Why is her birthday on here?" Sayyed asked. "You don't know your daughter's birthday?"

The man burst into tears before explaining he was not home when his youngest of five children was born. With a cracked voice, he claimed to be working on an oil field for extended periods of time. He hadn't been there for her birth and had regretted it ever since.

"Please sir, five children. They take everything from me. My youngest daughter, it is all I have." He lowered his head and looked down. "I'll die before I see her again. Please, sir."

"What do you think?" Sayyed asked, seemingly past his hard gulp.

"Let him keep it, and pick up his damn blindfold," I told the guard alongside him.

The man sobbed. "Thank you, sir."

"Get him out of here, we have to hurry."

In the background, the engines of the C-17 transport plane to Baghdad roared. The convoy team leader seemed edgy.

I took one last glance at the detainee, his left hand grasped his baggie—all his earthly belongings—as he stumbled walking up the ramp onto the C-17. The detainee in front of him fell backwards onto him. He did not brace his fall, instead protected the baggie, then accidentally got kicked in the face.

"*Astayqiz* [get up]! *Naql* [move]!"

The man struggled to get up, stood himself up with his fist while white-knuckling the baggie. He carefully kept the picture intact and with no new folds. The line of detainees disappeared into the gaping mouth at the back end of the C-17.

I asked Sayyed what it was about the picture that had almost overcome him. Hopefully, the family had long abandoned the building, even though a pair of pajamas hung on a laundry line and the small teapot were in the photo.

Sayyed said the family may have followed a tradition of leaving some belongings in their home, so maybe, someday, they could return to life as they fondly remembered. Everything would have been there as they'd left it.

I had an admittedly rare look into the Iraqi man's eyes since they were always blindfolded. He was sweaty. The ugly jumpsuit was far from fashionable. Every move he made was contingent on the men in front or in back of him. I had freedom of movement and could have executed plans of the powerful over the men.

Landing in Baghdad, we delivered the men to another convoy team in exchange for another group to be held in Camp Bucca. Almost five hours later, the camp appeared in the distance. The sun continued its uncomfortable relationship with Iraq, reluctantly rising.

"Lately, you've expressed a real dislike for so much in my country." Sayyed didn't say *Iraq,* he said *my country.*

I apologized if I said something that made Sayyed feel defensive of his homeland. He was correct in pointing out my negativity. I stated that even scorpions and camel spiders hated that place. The sun couldn't wait to set.

"Not all of these men are guilty, Sayyed," I also added, trying to come to meet him at his perspective.

Our conversation then returned to what was written on the back of the man's picture. Sayyed had translated not only for its literal meaning but how it could have been used as a transfer of information. He pursed his lips, a look of certainty he'd made the best decision he could.

"What was written on the back besides her birthday?" I asked.

"Some of it wasn't legible, but what I could read included a short poem by Abdul Wahab Al-Bayati in which he describes death as a tragedy, yet within heartbreak life blooms."

From my frustration, tearing up the picture of his daughter seemed like the shortest path to resolution. I felt badly the thought had crossed my mind and even worse than Sayyed noticed my wandering mind, and maybe even my evil intent.

"What was her birthday, Sayyed?"

"September 11th, 2001."

Chapter Ten

New Year's Eve

31 December 2007

I WALKED ALONG A WOODEN BOARDWALK between the tents and pods after sunset, which already had Christmas lights and decorations alit. Groups of soldiers in sweats and flip-flops sat in chairs with lukewarm two-percent beer from the DFAC.

I entered my living space, about one-third the size of a mobile home and situated behind blast barriers. I closed the door behind me.

Inside the linoleum-floored trailer beamed two fluorescent light fixtures, with two beds on opposite ends and a wall of four lockers. Windows allowed pulsating light shows from flashing helicopters to fill the room.

I picked up a card Cindy sent that played Barry White's *My First, My Last, My Everything* when opened, and sat on the edge of my bed. I smiled at her attempts to send happiness from home, knowing she and the boys were visiting her family in Miami for the holidays.

An explosion suddenly rocked the pod, powerful enough to knock the blinds from the window near my bed. They likely targeted the helicopter pad, maybe a quarter mile from my front door.

The sounds of every imaginable curse word simultaneously answered the blast. The pods' metallic walls groaned with the concussive blast. Doors flapped open and I was sure a window broke, too.

The urgent sound of a dozen boots landing and sprinting through pea gravel emanated above every other sound.

More explosions came, lights flickered, and Cindy's card flew from my hand. One of the explosions almost struck pay dirt, before another blast landed between the dining hall and the berm. An indirect flash flickered through an opening I had never noticed in the pod.

The same people who provided terrorists with our addresses likely drafted detailed plans of the base, the locations of our DFAC, living quarters, and underground diesel tanks had certainly given them the locations of our muster points.

Maybe that was a diversion to the real attack. We'd been bombed almost daily for months but never like that. I shivered at the thought of a well-trained team or two coming up from a tunnel under the camp, under the cover of a more prolonged attack. It wouldn't be the first time terrorists figured a way to bypass the lethality of perimeter machine guns.

Earlier that year, insurgents posing as a security team in American uniforms, proper identification, and speaking flawless English infiltrated a U.S. base in Karbala, killing five and wounding three. *Impenetrable* was loosely defined.

I slowly picked up Cindy's card and ensured it was secured in my cargo pocket with ammunition clips, except for one I locked into my M-9 pistol before chambering a round, safety off.

It was difficult to feel where the cross-hatched pattern on the weapon ended and the sweaty palm of my hand began. My breath masked the panicked sounds of attack. I checked my chest pocket as if I had either a lot of time or a moment. A translation of Manuwwar's Nizar Qabbani poem was right next to Cindy's picture in the pocket over my heart, safely secured in a Ziplock baggie.

Then, a third detonation. A sense of touch returned with the concussion coming up through my boots. My five senses seemed to be working separately from conscious reaction to them. I feared the same helplessness and powerlessness I felt at the moments of Manuwwar's and Abdul-Hayy's deaths.

A fraction of a moment after yet another explosion, I sensed a different feeling of pressure. Startled, I whirled behind me and saw a flash low to the ground screaming in the opposite direction.

Looking to the sky, I saw something that appeared to be an airplane blow by before a series of explosions. Artillery on base had returned fire, using advanced technology, within seconds.

Insurgents learned of that capability and countered with a number of strategies to neutralize our technological advantage. At times, they fired from rooftops of those friendly with American forces.

Enemy forces also mobilized small teams in pickup trucks with a mortar tube welded to the bed. That tactic was more of a nuisance as shooting a mortar from a moving truck on a bumpy and uneven desert floor all but guaranteed inaccuracy.

Accuracy may have been at the bottom of the list for terrorists. The attacks were designed to draw fire from the base. When innocents' homes were struck, they exemplified how unintentionally reckless Americans were, in the hopes of turning the population against our occupation. Attrition was their victory.

* * *

Arriving at Headquarters after everyone else, I approached the unit muster point—the members still in sitting in concrete blast compartments shaped like squared-off pup tents—and flipped the safety back on. One of the Senior Chiefs chatted with the others.

"Did you see that counter artillery? It had to be about two hundred feet off the ground."

After the response, the attack ended instantly. No infiltration of the base had occurred.

I walked through the gravel path back to the pod and sat on the edge of my bed.

During the attack, it was clear survival was not due to any skill on my part. There was an equal chance a mortar would fall on my head or miss the base entirely.

Running to Headquarters seemed so futile and, in an instant, I felt so certain of infiltration by militant special forces, I took the darkened areas between tents. That was where the terrorists would be.

I almost wanted to laugh out loud. I placed a clip in my M-9 and chambered a round, safety still on.

As I walked, I felt tension at first, walking as if against a stiff wind. For a second I wanted to drop all gear but my weapon and shed my clothes. I wished to be free of the weight of my gear, the uniformity and constraint of my clothes, and be seen as I was.

I would finally confront those who had been tormenting us, those who'd dug their tunnel toward the base hospital, those who'd stolen my family address.

It was my moment to fight.

Chapter Eleven

So Long, Sayyed

5 January 2008

THREE DAYS LATER, THE UNIT received orders we'd be redeployed from Iraq in three waves, the same way we'd been brought in. Headquarters was crammed with personnel looking to see which of the waves they'd be in. Noticing I was on the first wave, I approached the master chief and requested to depart on the last wave.

"So, you're requesting to leave three days later?" Master Chief Rose said, squinting his eyes at me.

"I should be the last man on the last bird, Master Chief. I just want to know we're all out first."

"You're crazy, Doc, but I'll put you on the manifest for that day. I don't think you'll have to twist arms to be the last man on."

"Thanks, Master Chief."

"Hey, Doc," He waited for me to stop and face him. "Thanks, I appreciate that."

We stood for a moment nodding before I left without a word. He may have perceived my request as a patriotic notion. The truth was I had one task I could not leave Iraq without completing.

Outside Headquarters sat a group from the unit, some of whom I hadn't seen very often during our deployment. They seemed happy to see me.

"What's up, Doc? Hey, these guys think I'm nuts, so you have to settle this," one said before snapping at mumbling from the others. "Screw you, guys, I'm not the only one."

"This I've got to hear, Boats," I said.

"Okay, so I put in for an extension for another year. Think about that for a minute. The money the government saves by not training and sending someone in my place—didn't they say at Fort Bliss that they paid like a bazillion dollars each to train us? I rest my case."

"You want to extend for another year?"

"Yep," Boats said without hesitation. "Tax-free, baby. Ryan, too, right man?"

Maybe each of us had our reasons. I felt a guilty comfort at the idea of calling home and telling Cindy we'd been extended, and the decision was out of my hands. The transition home induced more fear than Iraq. Moments before, the master chief thought I might be the bravest patriot in America, but I'd misled him.

Ryan looked sheepishly at first before steeling his resolve against some inner struggle. "Either that or I'm coming back as a contractor. We're talking big bucks, dude."

A moment about two months before, when our convoy pulled off the highway into a remote fuel point, flashed through my mind. Our convoy, much like apex predators, were most vulnerable when we stopped for a bathroom break or to get fuel.

Every man in every vehicle scanned the horizon in every direction, which was barren. Two Iraqi contract workers were at the service station, in addition to their military supervision. Our interpreter that night, Blackie, approached one of the men in great pain. He was leaning so far toward his left side that I thought he'd fall over—most likely kidney stones. From my vantage point somewhat far away, his grimace almost looked like a smile.

I recognized that same paradoxical look on Boats' and Ryan's face of being happy or in great pain. Or both.

The other gas station attendant, his backgammon opponent as we pulled in, said something and laughed. Even the man in pain laughed until doubling over in pain. I wondered what could possibly be so funny to make a person in such a condition laugh. Nothing in the universe could be that funny.

"Come on, Doc, give me some credit. I'm thinking *in* the box—the *sand box*."

Each of us burst into roaring laughter until we wiped away tears. Nothing I heard was funny. Sometimes, I supposed, people just needed to laugh.

I had a concrete reason for being the last person in the unit to board just as I would have a flawless rationale for requesting an extension for another year in Iraq: Fear.

Three days later, only the last wave from Iraq to Kuwait had remained. I would board the helicopter in four hours, but I had one thing I would not have left Iraq without completing.

Sayyed waited outside his tent and smiled as I approached. I placed my hand over my heart and bowed slightly, the traditional and respectful Arabic greeting, and extended my hand. He embodied everything good I had seen in Iraq.

Sayyed, momentarily surprised, returned the gesture.

"DFAC?"

"No, somewhere else," I replied. "We can finally walk as if there is nowhere to be in a hurry."

We'd just completed a long handshake and as we turned to walk, I held my hand out and Sayyed instinctively held my hand, a common show of respect and friendship in the Middle East.

We walked on an uneven dirt road toward the base perimeter until we reached the berm. After a moment, I climbed the berm and Sayyed followed.

I looked outward from the same spot I'd climbed the first weeks of my deployment. The horrific battle of the Iran-Iraq war, Khorramshahr, was still out there. I saw more, half-inflated soccer balls, colored sticks, and teapots than before. Every shrub and plant seemed to lean away, petrified in time by the horrors inflicted around them—some of them by our presence. Nothing and everything had changed. The world was cast only in browns.

"Is there hope, Sayyed?"

"Jim," Sayyed responded, for the first time using my name. "Don't try to be like this desert. Heraclitus said, 'No man steps into the same stream twice, for it's not the same river and he's not the same man.' You've done what you can."

We stood on the berm, hand-in-hand. Sayyed had deftly avoided my question as we looked at the same expanse over which he'd fallen in love decades ago.

I reached into my left breast pocket and pulled out a piece of paper I'd carried daily for the past seven months, Sayyed's translation of Nizar Qabbani's *In The Summer* found in Manuwwar's pocket after he died. The poem was an unsent letter to his fiancé:

> *In the summer, I sit on the shore and think of you. If I told the sea what I felt for you, it would leave its shores, its shells, its fish, and follow me.*

"I was wondering if you remember this."

"Or course I do. You've carried that around since June? I'm glad you liked it so much."

"Do you think I should give it to Cindy?"

"If you think it's beautiful, yes, you should. Why not?"

"Yeah, you're right. She loves good poetry." I wrestled with the idea of hand-delivering a part of Iraq for which there was no discussion.

The man who had copied the lines of the poem would have killed me without a thought. Something about handing his words to the love of my life grated against my mantra: *What happened in Iraq, stayed in Iraq. It will remain, unchanged like the desert.* Yet, I kept the poem, ragged and sweat-stained, since Manuwwar's death. I knew of no explanation why I'd kept it in my pocket, right next to Cindy. That didn't seem unnatural, but to bring it home did. It was just paper. I felt I should throw it away.

"Have you thought of taking your family from Iraq, Sayyed?" The high mortality rate of interpreters had been shown on at least two occasions just on that base, during that deployment.

"And you ask *me* if there's hope?" Sayyed smiled. The university professor couldn't resist one final teaching moment.

"Pick up your wife and leave. Go to Europe or come to the United States."

"You're very kind, but I'm too old to be the least favored of the already unwanted. And my wife, she's already too tired of swimming upstream to start over."

As if it were deliberate, the late afternoon shadows brought hues of pinks, lilacs, and yellows against a brilliant sky. Iraq was saying goodbye, hoping perhaps I would have some good memory to share with the world—the place must be salvageable if I could finally find beauty in my last moments with it.

We spoke until the last possible minute before Sayyed and I tightly embraced and walked to the helicopter pad.

"God bless you. I'll never forget you, Sayyed."

I grabbed both sea bags and walked toward the line of waiting sailors—and swore I wouldn't look back.

The sound of three approaching Blackhawks built to a crescendo. I checked my pockets for the third or fourth time. Everything had been mailed home, but there were three things I didn't trust to anyone: Cindy's picture and Sayyed's translation of *In The Summer*. Bulging from my right cargo pocket were Sayyed's translations of Manuwwar and Abdul-Hayy's letters from home and their unsent responses. The originals had been mailed to their respective families.

I may have been the first person in the history of warfare who had such intimate accounts of his enemy's personal lives. Inexplicably, I had no real intention of ever reading them. I was afraid of what I might have read. Curiosity compelled my keeping of their accounts, though.

Getting to my unit, I couldn't help but wonder if Sayyed remained there. He was looking from the distance just like my own parents at the airport on the day I deployed. Maybe he waited to see if at least one of us would get out of Iraq alive.

In the last moments, Sayyed removed his glasses for a moment, possibly shedding a tear. It was impossible to know what he thought. I waved. Sayyed only turned and walked back toward his tent, but only after waiting to see me, the last man on the last bird, climb on board.

I would never see Sayyed again.

PART TWO

"If we could read the secret history of our enemies, we should find in each man's life sorrow and suffering enough to disarm all hostility." - Henry Wadsworth Longfellow

Chapter One

Partial Confessions

21 January 2008—Quaker Hill, CT

A BELCHING, AGONIZED SHUDDER CAME FROM an angry Earth. Startled from an uneasy sleep, my body quivered as if an electric shock had passed through, a tremor from the floor to my chest. Something mounted on a wall crashed onto the floor. An orange light pulsated off the wall, sending its reflection to the room's darkest corner like a bolt of lightning. The light may have come from helicopters. I hadn't remembered mortars being that terrorizing. That one must have been close.

Springing up, I immediately collided into some immovable person and crumpled to the floor, landing hard on my right side.

They're here.

The flashing light that had been on the wall behind me suddenly flashed against the opposite end of the room as I looked up. My weapon hung on the post, but I'd fallen away from the head of the bed. Instead, I grabbed a cold metal object.

That's when I felt a bear hug. Startled, I rolled and landed on top.

"Jim, what happened?" The person I'd grappled with put up no resistance. "It's me, baby. It's Cindy!"

Shocked, I finally realized, the sounds I'd heard came from a passing snowplow.

The source of light passed. The vibration from the floorboards slightly faded. I lay on the carpeted floor, the fading, blinking light showing the wood-paneled wall in front of me. My face, tight as a clenched fist, softened and I calmed down. Cindy and I lay on the floor as the snowplow passed in the other direction before vanishing down the hill toward the Thames River.

"Jesus Christ, where did *that* come from?" I forced a laugh.

"My God, what's the matter? Were you having a bad dream?" Cindy sat against the wall, groping for the lamp switch. I moved closer to her.

"I'm sorry, it's been a long trip, I guess. Are you okay?"

I'm screwing up. I'll adjust. I'll know better next time. I hardly noticed snowplows before. Were they always that loud? I know Cindy's going to ask questions now.

"I'm fine. Do you think you can sleep? It's been one day." Cindy said optimistically, perhaps to make me feel better. "After the last *Wasp* cruise,

I think you slept for a week." We both rolled to our knees and stood up.

"It's great to be home in my own bed. I've been dreaming of this for the last year." I held Cindy's hand as we climbed into bed.

I'd been home all of two days, which I filled with sharing some pictures and telling Cindy and the boys of my talks with Sayyed. I showed the boys a video of a sandstorm recorded at Iraq's Ayn al-Asad [the Lion] base. The video showed an imposing wall of sand that resembled a moving brown mountain, the landscape devoid of vegetation.

Telephone calls from both families filled our days. The boys and I laughed at funny outtakes from Army training videos, mostly with soldiers expending nervous energy with various pranks and schemes—like knocking over portable toilets with soldiers inside.

During the deployment, I'd sent email messages to my parents of what I'd learned from Sayyed. Mom said she hoped the deployment had been as fascinating as it sounded. Dad had been reading the newspaper daily to see the temperatures.

I forwarded a picture of a misplaced thermometer with its red needle, topped out at one hundred and forty degrees. Julie said my six-year-old niece Monica really enjoyed the video of me reading the Velveteen Rabbit. One time I read Monica a story at bedtime on a stopover before the deployment.

Everyone was just happy I'd returned.

Yet, I was petrified at the thought of seeing my family again. I needed practice at being the same old good guest I'd been before.

"You're hyperventilating. Are you okay, Jim?"

My attention snapped back to Connecticut's wintry night.

On the way to bed that night, I'd stopped at the top of the stairs and stared out of the window. It held a clear view I'd treasured of both the river and Mamacoke Island, a bird and duck sanctuary for migrating birds heading south and throughout the winter. In the summer, red-tailed hawks circled gracefully high above our deck.

Looking north up the river was blackness with few homes or streets with water views. Even with a long list of home improvements, we were grateful to have such a comfortable place to live.

The snow fell, leaving an outline on each branch of the hundreds of trees between our home and the river. It must have been damp snow with temperatures just above freezing. From that window, far to the right one could see the outline of the Gold Star Memorial Bridge.

I saw a white picket fence halfway down the hill and it appeared a sign was hung but I wasn't able to read it.

Turning toward the bed, illuminated with a soft incandescent light, I'd felt sudden anxiety before bedtime.

The snowplow brought the point across.

In the middle of that serenity, I felt by the next day, it could be teeming with an Iraqi hit squad. I drew in deeply and released a long exhale.

Cindy was more nocturnal than I and had a propensity to think of all unsaid or incomplete thoughts right about bedtime. She also had a mostly endearing affinity for asking a series of questions, eventually arriving at the exact query she wanted to ask all along. I was certain the Socratic Method was taught to the great philosopher by the woman of his life and he stole the credit.

I was fretful. Even before my reaction to the snowplow, I wondered when she would ask about the deployment.

"I promised I would let you sleep. You're still tired, aren't you?" she asked, as I turned the light off and slid under the covers. After deployments, inordinate amounts of sleep were the norm.

"Yeah, jet lag, I think. I'm a little nervous about work, too." A gust of wind blew and the snow hitting the roof sounded like sandblasting. Every couple of minutes a small group of cars passed, the sounds deadened by newly fallen snow. As my eyes got used to the dark, the dim streetlight shone against the far wall, punctuated by moments when cars passed.

There was no escaping the reality of my life since that day with Munawwar and Abdul-Hayy. I discovered a deep, evil facet of humanity which lurks within each and every person. Maybe that was what every veteran hoped to preserve: The privilege of the innocent never knowing what humanity entails.

"Okay, a promise is a promise. Do you think you can sleep?" Cindy asked.

I'd already thought of a couple stories—they were stories like those I told before I left. I hadn't explained thoroughly to Cindy why I was taking sleep and anxiety medications, only that I was getting used to the new time zone and settling into a new routine. My anxiety receded and I drifted to sleep, thinking that new schedule with a consistent bedtime was the answer to my sleeping difficulties.

"I'm okay."

A battle ensued as we climbed back into bed and both of us lay there, facing the ceiling. I felt a need to talk about and process the deployment, yet that idea was overwhelmed by the thought to be protective of my family. *They can't know the enemy might follow me home.* I couldn't have had them live in fear. There was no good reason to explain our family address was in the possession of terrorists.

I felt an inability to catch my breath, not like my automatic reactions in Iraq. I thought maybe the terrorists had obtained the coordinates to our house by then. I'd walked in the house and took an inventory of every item in the house since I'd been home. Alarm clock. Cookie jar Cindy brought from Miami. Pictures Lorenzo had drawn in middle school. Alfonso's artwork made of colored pipe cleaners.

We lay in silence before Cindy grasped my hand, then turned and put her arm around me. Her head lay on my chest. That had never made me apprehensive before.

"It's so good to have you home. I know you have work tomorrow," Cindy said, squeezing my hand. "I wish we had some time off together. Let's go away for a while."

"I have work. I'd like to take time in the summer when the boys aren't in school."

It was an all-or-nothing world, but in Cindy's reaction, I had lost some of my resolve. Maybe talking about it wouldn't have been as bad as I'd feared, but I was convinced I couldn't bear the thought of bringing that level of pain I felt to my family without tarnishing their view of the world. I loved that they believed the world was what we made it. Ten feet away from us hung my uniform with her picture, Manuwwar's love poem, and Sayyed's translations stuffed into my cargo pocket.

"Jim, was it a hard deployment?" Cindy hesitated as if she were afraid to ask.

"Yeah, sometimes. Most of the time, we were sitting on our hands." I answered flatly, still trying to catch my breath. I intentionally tried to sound sort of bored with the idea of talking about Iraq. Maybe if Cindy thought there wasn't much to talk about, she wouldn't pursue it.

Why did I bring that poem home, where someone could find it? What if she does laundry? I have to move it.

"Did you...see anyone die there?"

I noticed a cottonmouth sensation with a cold sweat and a quickened heartbeat. I felt coldness and looked around the room as if a window had been opened. I shivered. Cars passed on the street below, oblivious to the chill I felt in my body. More lights moved across the wall, like sitting on a train as it leaves the station.

"Yes." My voice had the sound of a creaking door. My mouth tightened.

The bedroom fell into utter silence, a dreadful stillness. The snow outside still sandblasted the roof, but I felt both our hearts pounding. I was holding up. I was going to make it. Maybe that was the question Cindy wanted to ask and that was over.

"Women..."

She knows!

"...or children? Did you see women or children—"

"Goddammit..." Cindy didn't get all the way through her question. "It was so horrible." I wept. A cleansing cry burst with surprising pain; an aching agony only described after all the painful weight had been released. Cindy wept before she finished her question, the one she really wanted to ask all along.

Only a short-yet-vivid collection of images appeared as Cindy questioned me. A child's hand, like Lorenzo's, dropping limply and followed by screams of human anguish. Manuwwar's eyes—so unlike those taunting me before the rocket attack.

Teapots, half-inflated soccer balls, and colored Popsicle sticks. They all appeared together.

"I'm so sorry you had to live through that, Jim." Cindy seemed to find a moment in which we could bond again over what had happened. I was drawn to the centripetal force pulling me into the middle in spite of resistance.

"I know your heart. That must have been so difficult to carry alone." Perhaps Cindy had noticed something in the first moment I walked into the airport terminal in Providence.

"It's okay, Jim. You're home now."

* * *

I awoke before the alarm clock, Cindy and I unmoved from before. If it were my goal to keep Iraq over there, I was quickly failing. I was losing the momentum of my promise to keep Iraq as a place on the map, and no more. Feelings could be minimized with rational—or whatever you could convince yourself was rational—thought.

The snow-covered streets were deserted at 5:15 AM. I thought maybe other businesses would be closed, but Submarine Base New London was certainly open. I needed to have been at work. I needed to clear my mind.

There was no possible good in bringing Iraq home. Cindy would just have to understand that I'd spoken of Iraq for the last time. The attraction of going halfway across the world to fight a war was that my family could stay in our town with comfort and freedom, with Cindy tending to their busy lives. It had to stay that way. That was my mission in Iraq and that had not changed. It would be my mission for the remainder of my days.

Historical examples abound of those with the conviction to find something so integral to their character that they could not deny it, even when facing the ultimate price. The earliest of American martyrs, Nathan Hale, stated he only regretted he had "but one life to lose for my country" as he stood at the gallows. That admirable set of beliefs went back to the beginning of recorded history.

Socrates, condemned to death with charges of disrespecting the Gods and corrupting Athenian youth could have been saved, but the Greek philosopher refused the opportunity to escape his unfair death sentence.

I felt the need to steel my resolve, even if no person who knew and loved me would understand. Maybe I would be denied by them if it came to it, but there would be no concession. I was the only person who understood the ramifications of allowing Iraq into my home.

Cindy and the boys would be changed by the terrorist threat. I recalled the resigned looks on Iraqi women's faces, kids moving without joy and innocence, all their withdrawn body language from facing an incessant threat. That was all I'd ever bring home.

Not my family.

I supposed it was the same thing parents of Munawwar and Abdul-Hayy had wished for them.

Chapter Two

The Airport

17 January 2008—Atlanta, GA

DAYS EARLIER, AS THE BOEING 777 landed with a slight bump in Atlanta from Berlin, there were unrestrained whoops and hollers, even some hugging among the four hundred military passengers returning from Iraq. Our unit, assembled only for the purposes of supplementing the Army mission, would catch connecting flights in every conceivable direction to every corner of the United States.

Reservists would melt back into their life's work while active-duty personnel reported to their commands. Eddie Huck would go back to his post office job in Iowa without any winner in the 'Great Dairy Farm Debate' with Jason Mullin from Minnesota, over which cows produced the best milk and why. Steven Chin would no longer have to hold his own as a Green Bay Packer fan against Chicago Bears fan Matthew Lawson. Chuck Lokey would pursue his dream of teaching history and Reggie Williams would report to his police unit patrolling the streets of Miami's Liberty City. Carlos Bonifaz and Robert Mariscal would no longer have the need to count down the days until they returned to their families.

The flight was nine hours and fifty minutes and I'd spent much of that time cycling between avoiding conversation to being unusually talkative before an aching sense of inevitable abandonment. I feared many from the unit would just go back to their busy lives and soon forget our assurances to stay in touch.

Our unit walked across the tarmac and through a long, empty, echo chamber of a corridor. We found ourselves going from the reverberating sounds of hundreds of boots in what may have appeared to be a military invasion—that time of an airport food court. Airport patrons continued to move about, oblivious to our sudden entrance. Of much more interest to them was the overwhelming scent of fresh pastries and bagels.

* * *

One year ago, as the boys and I "spied" on Cindy as she shopped, systematically cutting TJ Maxx into quadrants in order to report her movements to Lorenzo (who acted as Command Control). On that final February night in the United States, the light-hearted entertainment reinforced *patriotism* and *bravery* into simple actions and roles in the minds of my boys.

When I broke the news of the deployment, I promised my family my purpose with the unit was the health and well-being of all men on all sides. That night, war seemed to be an idealistic game.

People all around us lived normal lives that night; I'd been oblivious to noticing that before. I felt somehow then connected to their right to live freely as had been provided for me by men like those at the Homecoming Statue dedication after the bombing of the *USS Cole* in 2000.

* * *

As we landed, I wasn't sure to what grand plan I was attached.

Atlanta's terminal floors at 7:30 AM may have been the most reflective surface in the world, like walking over a second sun. When I heard the airport public address system, a conscious effort was required to not shush the thousands of people in the terminal—I'd gotten used to silence during any intercom or radio communications in Iraq. I walked with my eyes straight ahead mostly, seeing people in my periphery without eye contact. Civilians were foreign. I wore my own creased uniform and looked for others in military garb.

Moving from one long walkway to the connecting flight, I felt I was being watched. An inordinate number of people had noticed me the longer I spent in the airport, their gaze held on longer, even after my eyes met with theirs. A little girl with dark hair and a white dress hugged her mother's leg and shyly peered at me. Other people smiled, children waved, and I had the feeling either my fly was open with fluorescent underwear or that I had a gigantic stain on my shirt.

But if the hero some of them saw could've explained little things like walks through an airport were terrifying, they'd all probably would have looked away. It must have been someone else's hero—the one whose world hadn't been turned inside out.

Maybe marching in a pressed uniform proved I was bullet-proof to civilians. I felt if half of them witnessed what I knew of myself, they wouldn't approvingly look at me. The little girl would hide behind her mother's leg but without the smile. I suspected the other half of people were beyond indifferent. Nobody knew.

An acquaintance of Cindy's was surprised I was coming home from Iraq.

"I thought the war was over," she told Cindy.

I looked around as I strode forward. A young boy of about eight didn't look up from his PlayStation 3 war video game. His fingers couldn't release bullets quickly enough and a musical sequence indicated he needed to find a recharge station or press the reset button. After his temporary setback, he forged ahead with a fresh new life, happily blasting everything in sight.

At the next terminal, I noticed an enticing bar with ESPN visible from every tall wooden stool at the next terminal. The pull of alcohol, even at 8:00 AM called out. I wished to dull the sensory overload of one of the busiest airports in the world. I thought a "topper" might have done some good until I remembered I'd be landing in Providence in three hours and twenty-three minutes.

The bright morning sun obliterated my view of the travelers nearest to the window. But alongside the mirror-like aisle, a group gathered around a DVD player, totally engrossed with a war movie action scene. None of the group of five looked at me, but I felt I recognized them. They could've been the first people to call me a hero.

* * *

In 2002, I attended a speech to a Hospital Corpsmen graduating class. Congressional Medal of Honor awardee, the keynote speaker, Robert R. Ingram was asked about the meaning of bravery and courage. The Medal of Honor was the highest award given for valor beyond any arduous circumstances one can imagine.

"Everybody fails to define courage, and courage is a conscious decision made moment by moment to do the right thing. Courage doesn't make you a hero. I hate that word, 'hero.' I don't understand what it says, what it means."

* * *

My Hospital Corps insignia on my left collar drew a salute from a man with a black and gold Army baseball cap. I nodded, taking in the sounds and senses around me—perfumes, the reverberation of shoes click-clacking on a concrete floor, luggage rollers, multi-colored clothing. If the Soldier was a combat veteran, he certainly saw the blood dulled under layers of dirt on my boots.

After a life of hoping for being exceptional, I felt uncomfortable with my idea of the assumptions people in the airport held. They probably were the same assumptions I'd made before I deployed.

There was no blame in not understanding war, I just wished for better *listening*. Each member of my unit had a story worthy of America's time.

As I walked down the center of the wide aisle, I was aware I'd perfected a stride in Iraq meant to startle, intimidate, and create space. The accompanying look on our faces removed any doubt and citizens in Iraq instinctively moved away—as magnets with a like charge.

Sure enough, on one convoy, Sayyed encountered a man with a horrified expression. The man told Sayyed that shortly before the original Gulf War, Iraqi propaganda blasted that U.S. Marines were cannibals who would kill everyone.

In certain parts of the airport, I saw people in the crowds on cell phones casting glances at me. *Terrorists have my family's address. Maybe they are here already, waiting for me.*

Uncomfortable with attention on me and my double-starched uniform, I distracted myself by wondering about the lives of other people at the airport. One young woman walked along. More than a walk, really. It was buoyant stride of a young girl maybe going on her first vacation alone and independently. Her heels clicked. Her hair had the bounce of a softly coiled spring. She was confident, pulling her wheeled luggage, looking forward and feeling alive. I imagined her flowered skirt with a solid, cream-colored top was her favorite outfit. I surmised the woman relished some life achievement, something gigantic—overcoming agoraphobia, an abusive relationship, something. She was freed.

Another woman walked past me on my right. She moved with a posture that fell inward like she was embarrassed by her height. Maybe that was it. I didn't think she was too tall.

I felt as though I had no name and had a stranger's past. I had to concentrate on the person who deployed and how he would have reacted. My own past seemed obliterated. I didn't understand veterans who said they came home a different person. My problem was that I'd returned the exact same person. I was the pretender who had deployed a year before.

I felt resentment at the idea of being that *new* person, but the die was cast. To be anyone else would invite conversation and analysis, opinion, judgment, and speculation.

I looked around the airport. My unit was gone—dispersed in every direction. It was just me. Nobody knew the secret.

I thought more about Mr. Ingram at the commencement ceremony for Hospital Corpsmen. Having been awarded the Medal of Honor, talking about his award had also described the award as:

"...a burden, a curse. Everywhere I go, this is my identity...yet that twenty minutes is the very thing I wish I could escape. I just can't run fast enough."

As a child, one friend fascinated with magic tricks described what was known as *equivocation*, in which a magician gave someone an apparently free choice but framed the next stage of the trick in such a way that each choice had the same end result.

In order to pull it off effectively, the magician took advantage of the disparity between what the subject thought they knew and what they actually knew. I could only compare that walk through the airport with my family's last day in that shopping center a year prior as a point of reference.

I discovered throughout our cool-down period in Kuwait I felt an odd emptiness at living outside daily life in Iraq. I clung to the very conditions which had changed my life and perspective. Even with an unsettling absence of resolution, it had become comfortable.

I was one flight from landing in Providence, Rhode Island. Cindy said Alfonso and Lorenzo had grown about four inches in the past year—twelve months of their lives I'd never get back. Cindy must've had innumerable crises to solve in that year.

Along the west side of the aisle, away from the bright sun, a crowd watched airplanes landing and taking off. I'd forgotten my fascination of flight, but I continued to walk ahead, suddenly saddened by the thought that Sayyed would probably not live to see his wife or lasting peace.

Looking ahead to a new hopeful mission, I held that somehow Iraq's trials and tribulations were meaningful. Perhaps it would take the passing of a generation to see whether our sacrifice bore fruit. For me to insinuate otherwise spoke against the efforts of all four hundred twenty-one men and women in the unit. If I had any promise to keep, it would be that what they forfeited was worth their exertion. I was terrified to think we spent a year in Iraq and advanced nothing.

At one end of the terminal hung a gigantic red, white, and blue banner that read: LAND OF THE FREE BECAUSE OF THE BRAVE.

Chapter Three

Welcome Home

17 January 2008

SEEING CINDY AND THE BOYS after a year of being away immediately became a moment etched in my mind—like the being present for the birth of both of our sons, or the night Cindy said she would marry me. It was one I'd anticipated, imagined, and practiced for almost a year. I thought of our sons' births. We had no idea of their sex or personalities, only that our lives would never be the same again.

I hoped I hadn't ruined the moment by giving Cindy specific instructions for our meeting. I wanted nobody at the airport, only to get in the car with her and the boys and go home.

It was an impossible chore not even a multi-tasking military wife could manage. When a member of a command was deployed, a receiving committee headed by a senior-enlisted leader, welcomed the member back.

Changing airports was a simple solution, but flight arrangements were made through the command and they received a copy of any itinerary changes.

I shuddered as I stepped from the plane into the loosely sealed terminal chute. They allowed Cindy and the boys to come to the gate. After September 11, 2001, that was only done in special circumstances.

I avoided eye contact, disguised by giving everyone a joyous hug. When anyone asked any questions, I quickly said that it had been a long trip, without further explanation. I was about twenty pounds lighter than when I left. I held a fear that the more I said, the more my family might notice that facet of myself I'd held close since Munawwar's blood-soaked prayer, and Abdul Hayy's quick death.

"Welcome home!" Cindy and the boys said in unison as I walked into the terminal and we made a confused attempt among the four of us to all simultaneously hug.

"I tried, Jim, I really did. I'm sorry." Cindy said as we rode the down escalator and the welcoming party came into view.

After a year of the bizarre normalcy of just staying alive, it seemed the entire day was filled with oddly unnerving change. Many of the unit's days were planned, almost to the minute, over the last year. Even combat felt complacent with time.

Cindy and I held hands and I focused on how I'd forgotten the small joys. There were homemade signs and some applause. Travelers at Providence, Rhode Island's Starbuck's kiosk smiled and joined in, maybe out of curiosity, almost doubling the size of the welcome party.

"That's okay. I'm just glad to be home." We exchanged glances and I smiled for fear Cindy would ask what was wrong. "I just want to get in the car."

The Senior Enlisted Advisor stood at the front of the amassed group of fifteen uniformed members, many of whom I didn't recognize. He had a relaxed demeanor and was quick with a joke. I feared the master chief would try to bring some levity to the situation, as if he felt compelled to compress a year of my life into a single witty remark. I felt a weird allergic reaction to lightheartedness.

In the crowd, I saw the face of our radiologist, Dr. Cardi, with whom I had solved every problem of the sports world before I left. My world seemed smaller by the second. I felt like I was breathing the air I'd just exhaled, over and over, as if I stood in an upright coffin. I focused my attention on Dr. Cardi.

"Welcome home, HM1. It's great to have you back." The master chief wore an infectious smile.

Before deployment, he and I had a number of constructive debates from politics to educational techniques. He'd taken pride in being a well-read, critical thinker. Usually, conversations with the master chief involved a homework assignment or a book recommendation.

Without releasing Cindy's hand, I shook the master chief's hand and nodded without saying anything. I stared over his shoulder at the doctor, anxious to be finished with the formalities.

The Navy personnel from the clinic greeted me, some stationed at the clinic for almost the entire year I was gone, making me a bit of a new check-in. They wouldn't know what to expect from me. There were few secrets among those in my unit, and that closeness seemed to have been all I knew.

"So, you're not planning on killing yourself or anyone else, are you?" Master Chief asked in one of those awkward moments.

The entire airport seemed to be without noise while he spoke. I imagined his voice boomed. A long, uncomfortable moment of silence ensued. The silence even seemed to extract air from the airport.

Outside of Fleet Marine Corpsmen, few Navy personnel saw war from the perspective of ground troops. The master chief had never deployed with Army or Marine units.

A morose sense of humor was also a staple of the Hospital Corps' collective coping mechanism. I restrained creeping resentment. I stared at the man who represented those who sent me to Iraq, apparently with no idea of what they were asking of me.

For a second time, I recognized the rhythms and sounds to identify the words as English without an immediate understanding of their meaning. Usually, that initial part of a conversation called for pleasantries to set the tone for the ensuing banter. A smile and appreciation for the person's effort was considered polite.

I felt a quivering sensation to cry—nobody in my unit would have dared ask that question. The senior leader at the portable toilets in Iraq knew better after Manuwwar and Abdul-Hayy's deaths. He computed that between my vomiting episode and bloodshot, tearful eyes, that maybe a wordless nod or an empathetic acknowledgment was enough.

I missed my unit. They understood.

"Not at the moment, Master Chief," consciously trying not to break Cindy's hand with my grip. Doctor Paul Cardi smiled and waved out of ear-shot. At my response, everyone laughed.

Perhaps the master chief somehow saw the blood on my boots and was trying to distract everyone's attention from the inevitable questions right there in front of Cindy and my sons. With a feeling of urgent dread, I scanned the eyes of the assembled Sailors.

No. None of them were looking at my boots.

I realized I hadn't planned the following few minutes, and improvising felt foreign to me. Some person deep within me screamed for help I didn't realize I'd needed until then. I sensed relief that the question and answer were for public consumption. A watered-down version was easier to digest, reduced to witty exchanges.

"Are you planning on taking any leave before coming in to work?"

"No, Master Chief. I'll be there Monday morning." Cindy's hand squeezed mine in protest without saying a word.

I looked at her. "I'd rather have the time off during the better weather."

"You're coming in on the Martin Luther King holiday? Slow down, hard charger."

"Oh, right. Tuesday it is."

* * *

The windchill factor in Rhode Island, in single digits, belied the clear and sunny day. Either I shook because I was unaccustomed to the cold or I was overwhelmed at the number of strangers on the way to the white Navy transport vans.

I was a person who had been given a stranger's past and I struggled to remember exactly who I had been. To pull that off, I had to be inside his mind in how he responded to questions.

Don't over-think. Just allow the conversation to unfold. Or get them to talk instead, that's even better.

Maybe I'd lost my proclivity for bad puns, and if not, I'd have to relearn I was the only person who thought they were funny.

We pulled onto the highway for the hour-long drive home. Alfonso was fascinated with the idea of my being on the opposite side of the world only a day earlier, before he asked how something so big and heavy could fly. We passed a restaurant at which we'd stopped, right next to an outdoor Christmas tree farm.

Sights and smells returned, and I moved away from the vehicle's heater—even in the frigid temperatures, I'd had enough of oven-like heat. The Mystic Aquarium and the diner just off the highway came into view.

Lorenzo and I talked about my progress on Star Wars Battlefront II. Cindy rested her head on my arm. The sailor at the wheel asked if it was good to be back and what I missed the most.

"Not even close, my family."

After driving to the base to pick up our own car, we drove to our house where our neighbor shoveled his sidewalk. We had a mostly polite, neighborly relationship but he seemed pleased to see us pull into the driveway. He stood alongside the car as I climbed out.

"Welcome back, Jimbo." John nodded with a squinting, knowing smile as if I had only at that moment gained his approval. He extended his gloved hand.

"Yeah, thanks, John." Cindy and the boys went inside to escape the February temperatures. John and I stood in the cold. Once the door closed behind them, John's eyes widened.

"So, did you kill any of them sand niggers?"

"Them what?" I asked, feeling breathlessly ill. All I wanted was to get inside our home, but I stopped in mid-step. I'd never heard the term before, certainly not from any member of my unit.

I felt a compulsion to provide the intimate details of death: The sounds, smells, Manuwwar's pleading look, the limp drop of a teenager's hand. Maybe I could have sickened John and make him think there was a gruesome world beyond anything he'd ever imagined. Unlike a war movie, I wanted to make it three-dimensional. Or I could've made him fear a person with a real experience of death.

I imagined John backing away from me, nervous while turning his back. War's powerful momentum surged inside me like an itch I couldn't scratch. I wanted him to experience sleepless nights and wonder daily why he hadn't committed suicide.

Mostly, I hoped John would never ask that question again. Nothing about it was polite or dignified or glorious.

John and I stood in the frigid cold for a long uncomfortable moment. His words hung like icicles from my gutter before John realized I'd make him wait until the Spring thaw to get his answer.

I had no idea how to answer. I felt pangs of guilt. I wished I could express man's capacity for evil beyond anything John had ever imagined. Enough to sicken or embarrass him, if I had done it right.

I flashed to the group watching a war movie on the DVD player and the young boy playing the video game complete with explosions and bullet ricochets.

I hoped their wars were fun.

Chapter Four

The Workshop

March 2008—Hartford, CT

C INDY BELIEVED IN THE TINY window the night of the snowplow that talking was necessary. She became frustrated since that night, seeing us crying ourselves to sleep as a breakthrough or even a possibility to bond over the experience.

I made the decision to deploy to Iraq and, like all unilateral choices in a marital relationship, there were repercussions. Cindy nibbled around the edges in an incremental fashion, and then chipped away from different angles, hoping to find a way into facing the problems together. I had built sensitivity to that tactic and countered by systematically closing each path. The results were a series of symptomatic arguments where each of us seemed to understand the real issue.

"You really *hate* to use your turn signal, don't you?" Cindy asked, emphasizing the word hate, as we drove to pick up groceries.

"I don't *hate* to use my signal, I just didn't use it that time," I said, answering her impatience with frustration. I emphasized the word hate, exaggerating her dripping sarcasm. My well-read wife didn't often choose her words by accident. "There's a difference."

"The *difference* is you're being a jerk. I'm just pointing it out," Cindy retorted, returning the favor of using my own choice of words. "I can't say anything to you anymore."

Over time I bought a reprieve by suggesting I see a counselor about my deployment. Cindy brightened, not realizing a post-deployment assessment was mandatory, saying she just wanted me to speak with someone. Cindy expressed fear at how low my frustration threshold lay.

"Your anger, it's just under your skin. If you broke into a sweat, it would come out of your pores and I'd smell it."

I didn't respond. It was getting late. I offered to go to a restaurant that never closed and had fresh desserts. It was a family activity and I imagined each of us was escaping any day's problems. We sat and blew the straw sleeves at each other and congratulated the good shots while consuming decadent pistachio pie.

I asked what the boys had learned while I was gone.

"We found out Mom can be fun," Alfonso volunteered, before catching himself.

Cindy was undoubtedly the disciplinarian while I was more like the boys' favorite uncle—the guy who splashed through every puddle in the road, shooting waves from the tires as if we were in a speed boat.

"No really, Mom was a blast." Sure enough, Cindy's creativity for road trips, county fairs, and free activities was the stuff of legends. Cindy smiled.

"I just wanted to stay busy, so we didn't just sit around and think. But we did have a lot of fun, didn't we? And both boys are in the Boy Scouts!"

As we talked, Cindy revealed Lorenzo had something very important he wanted to tell me.

"Dad, we couldn't wait for you to come home all year. You're here and we're happy, but it feels like you never came home."

* * *

I sat in the hallway of the Veterans Affairs (VA) building outside the psychologist's office before standing and pacing. Cindy asked me to sit back down.

After being home for almost two months, the post-deployment nurse referred me to the VA for a neurological assessment. *Volun-told* is the military term, where a task one would otherwise avoid was placed on the personnel tracker and followed by a superior.

"Talk to me. What's wrong?"

"It's nothing. I hate psychologists."

"It's just a formality, Jim. What's the worst that can happen?"

"That they tell me I have something that cannot be fixed."

Since my return seven weeks before, I'd been evaluated and ordered to counseling, mostly because I'd been exposed to blasts. My fears were two-fold, each of them hard to explain. I believed people who questioned me about Iraq would understand through their own trauma. Secondly, my trepidation stemmed from my inability to put my experience in words and the terror of being turned away.

Because wars were fought elsewhere, it was natural civilians felt war happened elsewhere and didn't affect them except as a curiosity. I wished I could just run a marathon or parachute at twelve thousand feet to have my story told. It seemed so daunting.

* * *

Many things around the treatment of returning veterans had changed even since a big group of Corpsmen from our clinic deployed with Marines to both battles of Fallujah in 2004-5. Even for our unit, there were no pre-deployment assessments done, besides a single questionnaire.

In post-deployment questioning, no questions asked if I was so tired that I hoped for an accident or that I would get sick. The body and brain eventually did that as an act of self-preservation. I felt certain the course of my treatment would continue without confronting the most pertinent questions.

At work, falling back into the routine seemed easier than I'd imagined. My reputation had preceded me, and I was given collateral duties outside of my job in charge of the clinic's radiology department. I was approached and tasked with attending a suicide intervention workshop.

Like sending a recovering alcoholic to a bartending class, I felt I had unresolved thoughts about suicide and had little time to process. But to turn down the class might have drawn attention to me. Away from the attention—evaluation perpetual cycle, my issues manifested in other ways.

* * *

"Good morning. How can I help you?" It was our final practical exam of a three-day suicide intervention class—a one-on-one session with another student as suicide intermediation.

I approached one man, Tom, over the three-day course with a single purpose. He was confident, well-spoken, and others in the room seemed to defer to him. He'd offered good suggestions throughout the class of about twenty, and if anyone could help a suicidal veteran, he seemed the most likely to accomplish it.

"I don't think you or anyone else can help me. I'm not sure why I called, I'm going to go now." I fell silent. I felt I actually would have ended the call.

After each of the previous sessions, the class had a critique and a discussion of our methods. On previous days, we went over various studies and approaches, the dos and don'ts of dealing with a suicidal phone caller. Anger welled within me as it seemed each time we intervened; we felt the satisfaction of a magical happy ending. We talked each of the possible subjects off the proverbial window ledge or bridge.

How dare any of them see happy endings! My experiences at the National Runaway Switchboard when Cindy and I met had proven the fairy tale ratio was much lower than one hundred percent. If anything, I saw my own suicidal tendencies oscillate.

"Sir, I'm here. You're free to go, but could you at least tell me what made you call?" Tom had a good grasp on keeping the conversation moving.

Tom sat immediately in front of me, from a better vantage point than a phone counselor. I focused on looking as apparently withdrawn as possible. I looked at Tom and saw he looked away with eyes darting as if he were looking for answers near my shoes.

We'd learned to allow any caller free choice over their words and actions. If the person called, on most occasions, that was a sign of hope. If a person was talking, there was a chance.

"I don't know man. I'm just sick. I'm sick of life."

We sat facing each other in front of the class. To a person, they leaned forward with undivided attention. We were the last pair. Each of the previous suicidal calls had been resolved with provision of resources and counseling. All happy damned endings. And with each resolution, I felt an increasing weight.

"My name is Tom. Can you tell me more? I have all day, okay?"

"Well thanks, Tom, but that's more time than I have."

Maybe Tom would hang up and go back to thinking of a job promotion or a beautiful young woman he had been trying to impress. His life was one of possibilities, all of them excitingly pivotal.

I looked at Tom, who was momentarily thrown off. He stammered before regaining his composure. His headed tilted and his eyes turned upward as if the answers were legible just over my head. I noticed he was unable to return my gaze. Maybe it occurred to him that it was not simply role-play.

"Are you...are you thinking of committing suicide, sir?"

"Uh, yeah." The answer was unemotional and matter-of-fact.

The class emphasized the importance of asking the hard question and shining light on the obvious. Being non-judgmental at that moment shifted the power to the caller and validated their right to choose their options.

"Okay. Have you felt this way for a while? Could you tell me your name?"

"My name is Jim. I've felt this way since Iraq."

Tom had a breakthrough. He'd been given a small opening through which he could start a dialogue. He looked back into my eyes, while mine hadn't looked away from his since the beginning of our "phone call," except to see our classroom full of people in the periphery.

I owed that exercise to my unit. I was training the very people who would answer our call to a veteran's suicide hotline, maybe even my own last gasp at resolution. They must understand if it was for them or not. There was no room for pretenders.

"Jim, is it okay to talk about Iraq? What was your job there?" Tom shifted, seeming to balance himself in his chair, possibly thinking the pieces of the puzzle were falling into place.

It had been just over a year that our convoy traveled to Iraq's Basrah airport on the outskirts of the city. A solitary figure moved in the darkness and from my view just behind the driver. I called out. I heard the legs of the gunner as he whirled his .50 caliber toward the suspicious figure, apparently seeing movement before I did.

"My family, they're gone. Even those around me are only being polite. If they had a choice, they would rather I just die. I have nothing."

"Jim, did this all happen after Iraq? The way you feel?" Tom tried to focus on whatever incident seemed at the root of my present troubles.

When I didn't answer his question, he shifted again to a side, placing his left hand on his left knee, his elbow outward. His brow lowered in thought. My posture didn't change, but I felt tightness in my neck.

"Let me ask you a question, Tom. And I want you to tell me what you'd do. Let's see if this was like the movies." I described a tactic used by insurgents to rain holy hell on convoys. Timing was critical, especially when coordinating various movements among teams in different areas of the country. Our convoy arrived in Iraq and dropped off one group at Baghdad's International Airport, and a convoy from Baghdad's Green Zone brought those deemed dangerous enough to be held for our team to take back to Camp Bucca.

The airport's terminals, still pock-marked from the American attack just after the 2003 ground invasion of Iraq, had become a hub for communication. Still, under cover of night, rocket and mortar attacks were launched. Few things were more vulnerable than a convoy sitting still for very long. Our movements had to be seamless and precise. Amazingly, our timing had been excellent on each convoy. One convoy had a twist.

"You're in a convoy moving along and a young woman is trying to run in front of the convoy. She's screaming, pleading for us to help her."

Terrorists knew we were schedule-driven. Insurgents would have a herd of animals or people just happen to cross the street, anything to slow or stop a convoy, making a successful attack exponentially greater. They had various methods at their disposal, like pre-staged daisy-chain Improvised Explosive Devices (IED), and Explosive-Form Penetrators (EFP), which turned a steel plate into a self-forged, semi-molten projectile capable of blasting through both sides of a Humvee and anything in between, passengers included.

I looked at Tom. He seemed sincere. He looked up at me and studied my face. I didn't flinch but straightened, my back muscles relieved by shifting in my chair.

"She stumbled as she ran and waved. Do you stop? It's the gunner's job to eliminate a threat. What do you tell the gunner, Tom? You have less than five seconds to make the call. In the time it took to ask this, it's too late."

Tom exhaled and slumped in his chair, horrified.

"The woman realized the vehicles were past her and weren't going to stop." Emotions felt so real as if it were occurring again. I looked over Tom's shoulder at Hartford's skyline—I needed to be reminded of where I was. "As she looked at our Humvee, I was sure she looked directly into my eyes as we passed. Her abaya was torn. She stumbled, losing a sandal before dropping to her knees. There had only been an illusion of hope. The gunner hesitated. What are you going to do, Tom?"

The classroom suddenly felt frigid. I shivered. My teeth chattered and my lip quivered. One of the students gasped and left the room, holding it in before bursting into tears when she stepped into the hall. Her sobs faded as she moved down the hall. I shivered uncontrollably. Tom stared at me, wordlessly, seeming to forget we were in front of the class.

"I... I don't know." Tom looked at the course facilitator, showing the palms of his hands. "I don't know what to do."

"Okay, okay. Can we call a time out?" another student asked, weeping. "Please, can we stop? I think that's enough."

My hands trembled and my fingers felt frozen as I wiped sweat from my forehead.

* * *

Maybe she had waited in the shadows until she heard vehicles. Her running became disjointed as if her mind knew her last attempt had passed but told her to keep running. Her slight shoulders dropped but she stared straight ahead as her kneeling image faded into the darkness.

Her fate was sealed. We were supposed to help Iraqis, yet no regulation allowed aid for that desperate young woman, who soon after may have fallen as an honor killing, possibly before the sounds of our vehicles faded. Stopping could have created an international incident with our team accused of kidnapping the woman at the very least.

* * *

As I sat in front of Tom, I felt the planet's most powerful military was helpless and had been left with no alternatives.

* * *

Throughout the summer, convoys passed the site where her body lay for days, blood and fluids eventually absorbed into the dirt, leaving what appeared to be a hole in the ground, right near the solitary highway light and within view of her murderers.

The explanation was she was denied a traditional Muslim burial and left outside the town. Instead, she was left to the elements. But our souls were also stained. Accountability and responsibility can never be delegated.

* * *

The teacher felt it was necessary to debrief the sixteen remaining students of the class. I apologized to Tom, who seemed the most interested in what he could have done.

When asked, I explained that they could be on one end of a telephone call from any of the members of my unit. I would want the best for them. They were good men and women, and they were dear to me.

That phone call could possibly have come from me.

Chapter Five

The Young Lieutenant

ABOUT SEVEN WEEKS AFTER LANDING at Providence Airport, our Education and Training Department found out one of the officers would be assigned to act as Division Officer.

Education and Training had been relatively autonomous previously but having a division officer in our area brought the benefit of a higher profile to our jobs, especially if we were doing well.

I'd known the lieutenant before my deployment and she'd just returned from her own tour with the Marines, a young and up-and-coming officer, ambitious and looking to impress her chain-of-command.

Before she was entirely moved into the office, I was told to report at the end of the day on a Friday.

Walking into her office, I stood until told to sit. I felt I had adjusted well into the desk job routine. She seemed preoccupied and continued to move papers on her desk, before explaining that the two people in our department, HM2 Mikki

Jefferson, and HM3 Jermaine English, were ter-
rific performers.

I knew that to be true. Before I left for Iraq, I'd
worked in Radiology. Only when I returned did
I move to Education and Training. The learning
curve was steep. Whatever progress I'd made in the
new department had been through their patience
and willingness to bring me up to speed. They
were doing their jobs and mine in the meantime.

The lieutenant wasted little time, explaining I was
the weak link, and the troubles of the department
were because of my lack of leadership.

I was unprepared for her statement. I had focused
on deadlines for initiating a new program, the Tactical Combat Casualty Care (TCCC) that had begun
in Newport, Rhode Island, designed for Corpsmen
deploying to Marine or Army combat units. The
initial feedback had been excellent. Jefferson and
English, both Fleet Marine Force-qualified, were
driving positive changes before I'd even reported
to the department.

"I've been sent here to keep an eye on you, and I
think I've already seen enough."

Even in stunned silence, I delineated five stages
of death within seconds of each other. Denial. Bargaining. Anger. Depression. Acceptance. During
the bargaining stage, I had a desperate thought.
I had left for the deployment as the *Sailor of the
Year* for the Atlantic Fleet Shore Commands. The
lieutenant knew of what I had been capable—
maybe I could parlay that credit to level things.
I launched into my plea.

"I should have taken some time after Iraq, ma'am. My transition has been harder than I could have imagined." My voice was scratchy, my brain spoke before my vocal cords were ready. In a first attempt to blurt out an explanation aloud, I felt like my words overlapped before she interrupted me, without looking up from her paperwork.

"If that's the case, I could process you out of the Navy within a week. That's easy if that's what you want," she said, dropping her pen in frustration—as if that conversation was pushing her past a deadline.

"Ma'am, that's not what I want. I'm just—"

"Then you better get your crap together, and quick. You're dismissed."

Something. Think of something.

The lieutenant was going to send me home on a Friday afternoon after that conversation? She and those with like minds sent me to Iraq, and I wasn't worth a complete sentence when their attention was required?

The darkness in the room became an angry red. Not lighter. The corners were not more visible, just red. After a few seconds, she picked up and dropped her pen, still without looking up. Her body language was increasingly angry.

"You're... dismissed." She enunciated each letter. She'd been sent on a mission with the same mentality I'd exhibited in Iraq. She was just doing her job—unemotional, detached. It was the mission she'd been sold.

I stood there, mouth agape, without a sound. I thought maybe she would look up and say it was all a bad joke.

I slowly turned around and hesitated before I continued into the brightened hallway. I numbly walked out to my car. I had difficulty understanding how departmental metrics held the same sense of urgency as a combat situation. The enemy was not kicking down the gates of Submarine Base New London while military personnel waited for my training report which surely would have saved us all.

I wished I had a gun, but weapons and bluffs were a horrible combination. I imagined walking back into her office and making her *look* at me. *Look* at me! I wanted to be seen. She had looked right through me.

Maybe Manuwwar hated me in the same way—a man following orders with little or no regard for him. I suddenly wished I had closed Manuwwar's eyes or faced him toward Mecca...something. Maybe that was why I sat there in an empty parking lot late on a Friday afternoon. Because I hadn't been empathetic enough.

The lieutenant was simply doing what had to be done. She had the luxury of dealing in a reasonable world with deadlines, planning, thinking, and talking it over in the Officer's Club.

It was logical to assume I had put Iraq behind me. No matter how hard I had tried since I landed in Providence, I hated the part of me who couldn't bury the deployment.

Where a ride in the country had been comforting before, I found myself scanning the sides of the road for freshly-dug dirt, trash piles, or dead animals—all of which could be a sign of IEDs. Open spaces felt anxiety-inducing. That part of me found it impossible to complete the simple task of shopping in a supermarket—they weren't designed for me to find a place where everyone in the store is in my view with none behind me.

* * *

Ahead of me in the parking lot was a tranquil view of the Thames River, but not a single iota of serenity reached me. The lieutenant could have been cannon fodder, and that realization sickened and repulsed me. I needed help.

The command almost learned that doing the hard thing the easy way was disastrous. People would have responded that I was the least likely person in the world to do such a horrific thing. And of the tragedy. And I would have served a horrible and dark purpose.

What seemed worse than any trauma of war was that my own side treated me as expendable. I had grown accustomed to the breathless feeling. I needed to go for a drive.

* * *

"I'll ask one last time, what are you doing here?"

Six al-Qaeda insurgents dressed in black in the darkness. Behind them were three black vehicles parked haphazardly, the beams only illuminating the shadowy outlines of night. A small hill rolled downward behind me and I backed up, keeping all of them in my view while trying to find ground level enough to pounce.

Because my weight was shifted on the gentle slope, the enemy had a huge center of mass advantage—above mine with their weight aided exponentially by gravity. I was in trouble, desperate trouble, outnumbered with every law of physics against me.

The sound in my head was Camp Bucca's megawatt diesel generators used to power the base every second of that twelve-month Iraq deployment. I couldn't be far from help.

My weapon, where's my weapon? Think! Someone has to know I'm missing. No landmarks, am I out of the wire? Was the convoy attacked?

My eyes darted from side to side, blinking away stinging sweat. Palpable heartbeats and breath dominated my eardrums. The six figures shifted in the night, like a kaleidoscope with only gray and black fragments. Four of them clicked flashlights and directed the blinding light into my eyes, disorienting me. My universe had shrunk into about ten square yards.

No matter what pain I'm about to endure, if it takes all the energy I have, I will look into the eyes of my killer. Like Manuwwar and Abdul-Hayy did and the bastards pulled me into Hell right with them. That must be why they're here, to avenge their deaths. No prisoners of war in Iraq. Maybe if I stall as long as possible...

"I'm visiting a friend," I said, steadying my voice. He asked a stupid question. I gave him a stupid answer.

I backed into something knife-like, tearing the skin near my right shoulder blade as I inched backward on some form of shrubbery.

The only direction was forward. Thoughts came in staccato bursts.

There are six of them. Am I imagining things? Where the hell am I? No weapons drawn yet. Four flashlights, so I know where four are. Look away from the flashlights. My eyes won't be used to the dark. What are they waiting for? The ringleader speaks English. Kill the guy who's doing the talking first. That's my chance.

"What's your friend's name?" the leader asked, his voice somehow smiling, almost gleeful. *How does a voice smile?*

The four flashlights inched toward me with an alluring, mesmerizing quality. Yet the world was compressing like an object sinking to the bottom of the Marianas Trench, the kind of pressure that can turn a submarine into a five-foot square cube of scrap metal.

Involuntary tears streamed, my breath had a haltering, quivering feeling. My teeth clenched, but I consciously made an effort to relax muscle groups, one at a time. I would need my strength.

The flashlights encroached to within less than ten feet.

Jim Enderle

Why do I feel fear? I welcomed death during the rocket attack, didn't even move, fight back, run— nothing. I'll feign cooperation, disarm the ringleader. The longer I wait, the less my chances.

"Um, her name is Cindy," I said using my wife's name.

As I heard my voice speak her name, I tried one final time to envision her in crystal clear detail, smiling at me, her image oblivious to my predicament. I had forfeited the right in one single, life-changing day. It brought calm, but no comfort. All that was left was more death.

This is useless. At the count of three...

"Would you like us to call Cindy?" the ringleader blurted. "We can call her on your phone."

"Go to Hell, I don't have a phone."

Manuwwar was right, other militants have my family's address. I'll kill all of them. One... two...

"Is this your phone? You must have dropped it. It's going to be okay. Let's call her." A hand from behind a flashlight suddenly extended a cell phone. It looked like my phone. It *was* my phone with the same cracked glass.

I can't be home, I can't go home. Cindy will know in a microsecond, she'll know...

The flashlights' beams dropped away from my eyes and revealed uniforms—police uniforms. I stood on the grass. My sense of smell abruptly returned.

An all-consuming focus on survival was replaced with my five physical senses.

They were Waterford, Connecticut policemen. I stood on a patch of land a couple of miles from my home.

"Here, do you want to talk to her?" The policeman pulled up the contact list on my unlocked phone.

Everything was a blur. At what point did I have no realization of where I was?

"I, uh..." It was too surreal to process. It could have sworn I sensed the smells, sounds, everything from Iraq. I was *there*.

It's been almost a year since the deaths of Manu-wwar and Abdul-Hayy, nine months since certain death in the rocket and mortar attack, six months since calling in air-support...

I stared at the phone, still in the officer's hand with Cindy's name and our phone number, humiliated and unable to speak. My quivering fingers, rather than reaching for the phone, covered my mouth. The officer held the phone in front of me as it rang on speaker mode until I heard Cindy's voice on the phone.

"Jim, what happened? Where are you?" Her voice was panicked. She bypassed the usual phone courtesies. She knew.

My military wife, over the years, had developed a keen awareness for variation to a savant level. Cindy had learned the routine over fifteen years— it seemed every military wife laughed at the "as the brow goes up, everything at home goes down" stories. "Everything" included any mechanical or natural catastrophe one could imagine. Cindy's had no choice but to accept every challenge of Murphy's Law, a humorous law of nature where anything that can go wrong, does. Since my return from Iraq in 2008, it became an impending sense of doom.

I shook my head as if the cobwebs could be cleared and stared at the phone with no capacity for words.

"Hello, Mrs. Enderle? This is..." The officer turned and walked away, speaking in hushed tones for a few seconds.

There was some stranger talking on my phone to my wife about my future. More and more, conversations about me began when I left.

"She's on her way. Just relax, we'll figure this out."

Within seconds it seemed, there Cindy was, parking behind the squad cars. She'd always been a beauty, the kind that never fades. *Good old Cindy! She'll know what to do, it will all be okay now.* But it was a melancholy relief I felt, just before a feeling of dread. I still stood about twenty feet from the group, not a part of the conversation and unsure where I would be spending the night, or what it would mean to my military enlistment. I had just been selected as Navy Chief.

The beginning of my most recent spiral was my department's young lieutenant, with her shiny new Fleet Marine Force device earlier in the day. She explained how easily she could process me out of the military after I'd confided my struggles with the transition home. In all the world, I had chosen her as the person who would help, one more time than many other combat veterans would ask. Many veterans don't approach a second person for help.

Within a few minutes, I was released to Cindy who had convinced the officers I was not a threat to myself nor my family. I felt the spongy grass under my feet, smelled the exhaust of an oil delivery truck, heard the sounds of traffic on Interstate 95 about a block away.

How could I have not realized where I was? How can I explain this? It was a misunderstanding and the police over-reacted, that's what it was. If I say anything else, I know how Cindy is, she hates loose ends. She'll find out.

We drove the first four blocks in complete silence, with only the headlights revealing the turning, unlit road. The radio was off, but the silence was thunderous. I had not been drinking and, if not for a randomly passing police car, it was doubtful anyone would have noticed. Odd behavior attracts its own reaction with equal force. I was horrified that I was seen as dangerous to the point of requiring overwhelming force, and relieved at the restraint shown by the Waterford Police Department.

Finally, Cindy took a deep breath.

"Jim," she said. Her face looked tired in the dim interior lights. "You have got to get help. You know I would do anything for you, but I don't know how much more of this we can take. I just don't understand." Cindy's voice faltered. "I don't want you to feel bad. You're surrounded by people who love you. Let us in."

My hands were folded in my lap. My head hung in abject remorse. *When does she ever get to decompress? Where does Cindy go for strength? It should be me who provides a reprieve.*

I should never have come home, but now that I have, I can at least salvage their lives. It's the only meaningful goal I have. What a relief she asked a different question than the one I feared. *If she asks what happened in Iraq, I'll lie. No way I bring war into my home.*

"Okay. I'll talk to Behavioral Health tomorrow. I'm so sorry, Cindy. I didn't know where I was."

Chapter Six

Gonna Wash That Man
Right Outta My Hair

15 February 2009

O VER THE FOLLOWING DAYS I assumed that since
Waterford Police Department released me to
Cindy, they didn't consider me dangerous to my
family. I wouldn't be charged with any crimes and
no report would be sent to my command. But I
made a promise to try counseling and met with a
first counselor, a personable young psychologist.

The random subject of running marathons came
up I revealed I had finished thirteen marathons,
many as a member of the Navy Running Team. The
psychologist explained that he held the goal of
completing at least one marathon in his life with
a profound, nodding look.

"It's a type of *hajj* for you, then," I said, thinking
of Sayyed's explanation of a mandatory pilgrim-
age to the sacred ground of Mecca at least once
in a lifetime for all able-bodied Muslims. Sayyed
counted it among the greatest demonstrations of

solidarity among the faithful. I wasn't entirely comfortable with the idea of comparing a run along the shores of Lake Michigan, stocked with water and snacks, with a hajj.

"Yeah, like that. Well, maybe I should say more of a bucket list item. I wouldn't want to diminish one of the Five Pillars by comparing it to running a marathon."

I liked his graceful and polite correction to what I had said. He segued from that to my military career's best and worst moments. It was easy for me, both questions had the same answer.

I had been selected to represent the Atlantic Fleet in a worldwide *Sailor of the Year* competition. The majority of accolades revolved around a mentorship program written for junior enlisted and commissioned personnel. In the form of essays, articles consisted of low-cost or free family activities, college transcript analysis and applications, advancement study materials, and any other topic of which young sailors would ask.

"Success leads to the greatest failure, that of pride." I explained WWII war correspondent Ernie Pyle said that in a call for humility after a great and costly victory, for the world to be worthy of peace. So maybe success itself could lead us to a bad end if the accolades became position or authority or reputation we had to either preserve or forfeit.

"Can you help connect the dots? How could a program for the benefit of young people and their families be a bad thing?" From the counselor's vantage point, he saw what the senior administration of our clinic seemed to believe. On paper, the program was beyond reproach.

In 2005, I was self-appointed as the mentorship coordinator at a time the Navy was emphasizing "intrusive leadership"—the military equivalent of a village raising our young. Within a year or so, some of the articles caught the New England Commanding Officer's attention. She created a new duty and placed me in charge of all clinics in New England.

"It wasn't a bad thing, but I wasn't the best person for that job. I'd never been in charge of anything in my life." Proof could be found in other facets of my life. On construction sites, I dug ditches. In sports, I was the guy who did the intangible things. I blocked, passed, played defense, and tried hard.

Sometimes our strongest qualities were our greatest weaknesses. I had such conviction in that mentorship program that I was doing the right thing, and I'd ignored some of the resistance against my ideas. I'd never recruited allies that could have advanced the program for everyone's benefit.

Isolation was at the top of unintended consequences, but people deferred to me and I was uncomfortable. I just wanted to be creative and funny without scrutiny. I kept no records of the program's effectiveness. My reputation had become an obstacle. The support of the highest echelon muffled any criticism.

I returned from the competition in Washington, D.C. and felt I needed to live up to the accolades, so I pushed even harder. In the process of doing all that high-profile work, those in my department were left with handling all the responsibilities, including covering my duties as a technologist.

One of the technologists, Will, was in the process of transitioning out of the Navy because he hadn't done well enough on his advancement exam to advance within the Navy's allotted time. What I didn't understand was his career and life was at a stressful crossroads, a time where many aspects of his life were in transition.

It's tradition to have a going-away luncheon on a person's last day. Usually, the person organizing the event asked if the person departing had anything they'd like to say. When Will was asked, he mused mischievously with a grin spreading across his face. The twenty or so people packed into the break room leaned forward.

"Sure Will, anything. You have one foot out the door." The lead tech responded.

"Okay." Will seemed to relish his moment. He turned away from me before pivoting back. Facing me, he raised both middle fingers. "Fuck you, Enderle." It was an undeniable double-barrel salute.

I was the only person in the room who was surprised. I had an achievement for being in touch with others' needs. Right there in my own department was a man with his life on fire and I wasn't available to him. I admitted to myself that I'd known he was going through some difficulties but left that uncomfortable conversation to others.

"So, I guess that explains it. I rarely thought of those accolades again. It may have been possible that many people felt that way and just weren't in a position to confront me with it. No awards provided comfort after that."

I was in the process of preparing for the Iraq deployment and I wondered if another person or group would undertake the program. I had the criteria for a moratorium on the mentorship program.

After I deployed, the program died a rapid death with no fanfare.

* * *

The counseling session hadn't gone well. I didn't need a reminder that even the high points of my Navy career were humiliating.

Just off base was a lounge with table tennis and pool tables. I pulled in without a second thought.

By beer three, I had a pleasant thought of physical violence. I just wanted to identify some threat and destroy it, then beat it into the dirt, until I realized I would probably cry at the thought of unleashing my anger on something other than the subject of my rage—which I didn't even understand and couldn't name.

A guy at the end of the bar thanked me for my service with another round of Guinness. I wondered if counseling was necessary. Maybe I was better for the experience in some way and just needed to believe it.

I felt less hopeful after the counseling session. Entirely possible was my new "*mission*" was illusory, a continuing yearning for purpose and belonging I'd taken for granted in Iraq.

An exchanged glance among the unit spoke its own language, a forced smile when one struggles brought the questions which seemed obvious. The lack of communication between Will and I would've never happened if we were deployed together. I would've caught it and reached out in his time of need, at least acknowledged him. I had ignored Will's needs. And I felt grateful it was pointed out.

Being deployed brought a connection I missed. Maybe those in my unit shared my feeling of isolation. Depression set in. Back in America, I had a smaller chance of explaining my predicament. I pushed my Guinness aside and it slid on the melted frost further than I expected on the dark wooden counter. I needed to be alone, and the time had come to go home.

An odd mix of rage and the urge to simultaneously break down and cry passed. I went where I was told and followed orders and found the very people who sent me to Iraq referred to me as "brother" or "warrior." They really had no idea what to do or say and threw those words out as a replacement for real conversation. I had become an American equivalent of Iraqi women and children with weighted gaits. I got to the car, wept, and then collected myself.

Getting home and walking in the door, dinner was cold, and the boys still worked on homework. Cindy walked with an armful of laundry and tripped on the top stair—the stair she'd asked me to fix for months. I'd been working twelve hours to finish an eight-hour day's work. I fell further behind in every aspect of my life, every day. Cindy rose from the floor, picking up what had been a neatly folded pile of clothes.

"You couldn't have called? Dinner's cold. You're on your own."

I had often stayed late under the guise of having to work but mostly stayed late just to sit in a quiet office. Often, I'd look on the computer for the latest news on Iraq.

"I'm more tired than anything, I just need to try to sleep." I hoped maybe we could defer an argument to another day. With my sleep difficulties, the topic had been a sore point. Cindy was awakened when I had a nightmare or was restless.

"You and your precious sleep. Have you been drinking? So, you come home late and go to bed early? I'm in the middle of five different things and you're out tying one on." Cindy often said how little she could do to stop me from drinking besides voice her frustrations. I had never consumed much alcohol.

"I've had enough of this," I said, shutting off the conversation before it really started. In my mind, I was angry that I hadn't said I was sick and stayed out of range where Cindy might smell booze on my breath. "Besides, I wasn't tying one on."

Jim Enderle

In our relationship, the three beers I'd consumed would have fit Cindy's definition of overdoing it. The food she'd prepared sat in the kitchen and there was laundry to refold.

"I need to talk to you, let's not do this. Come and have something to eat. Please?"

"Goodnight," I said, as I headed up the stairs, under the guise of avoiding an argument, but we were in the midst of an argument without end.

"Fine, you go to sleep then. I'll be right here singing show tunes until you're ready to talk."

Cindy and I both knew that could last until Armageddon and beyond if possible. I changed for bed and pulled back the covers.

"Brand new state, brand new state, gonna treat you great!" Cindy sat at the top of the stairs, before changing of the musical's words. "Not like Jim, who didn't call and came home late!"

Determined not to give in, I turned out the light and took deep breaths. I felt the tension abate. Maybe Cindy would realize her attempts were futile.

"Ooooo-klahoma, where the wind comes sweepin' down the plain... "

I laid in bed staring into the dark. Fifteen or so minutes passed. Breathing exercises didn't take away the breathlessness of my accumulating fury. Finishing the Oklahoma soundtrack, Cindy moved seamlessly to South Pacific but singing louder.

"I'm gonna wash that man right outta my hair... "

Anger welled inside and I rolled over, striking the mattress with both arms up to the elbows. Throwing the pillow hard at the floor, I got up and did as many push-ups in the dark as I could. It was desperate, but maybe I could have expended my wrath with exertion. I thought again how closely exertion and uncontrollable sobbing were related. Fifty-two, fifty-three...

"Wash him out, dry him out, push him out, fly him out, cancel him, and let him go! Yeah, sister!" Cindy deliberately picked songs with a message.

"Okay, you want a fight? Let's do this." I sprung up from my push-ups and knocked over the ironing board in the dark. Cindy stopped singing. "Let's go. I've got all night. Bring it!"

I walked quickly and was startled to find Cindy standing in the corner at the top of the stairs. We stood by the window with the view of my sanctuary—the river and island to the left. To my right were my combat boots.

I didn't need lights to see the blood under the layers of southern Iraq's silt-like dirt.

"All I wanted to do was talk and you..." Cindy leaned against the corner. She reached out as if asking for my help or forgiveness. I wasn't sure which.

"No, you just wanted a fight. Well, here I am," I roared. "You know what, I'm leaving. I need to go for a drive."

I heard movement downstairs. I had awakened Alfonso and Lorenzo. Cindy moved from the corner to the edge of the top stair.

"You've been drinking. You're not leaving until we talk. There's one way out. What are you going to do, push me down the stairs?"

Footsteps ran up the stairs in the dark, two at a time, before Lorenzo's small frame stood in front of Cindy at the top of the stairs. I saw his arms extended to either side.

"No!" My voice broke at the thought of my thirteen-year-old having to stare down his angry monster of a father.

I had to find a way out of the house. After taking a step back, I dove over the bookshelf landing about halfway down the flight of stairs before stumbling through the darkened house. Alfonso, who had been standing in the living room, listening, was startled and cowered behind the dining room table.

I sobbed as I reached the car, still imagining Cindy's outstretched hand. As anger subsided, I realized she wanted to make peace. But she was not supportive of my *mission* to leave Iraq where it was on the map. She was unable to fathom what I was tasked to carry out. If she was to be a member of the unit, she had to go along with the plan. Not knowing what that plan was, wasn't an excuse. I never knew what the plan was either.

I straightened in my car seat. Executing the plan was hard enough without her doubting questions.

Cindy had to understand there was one way to show love and dedication toward my family. Over time, those who loved me would come to understand even if the specifics weren't clear.

Everyone knew there was a dangerous world out there, but somewhere else.

Not in our home. At least until tonight.

Chapter Seven

The Restaurant

16 February 2012

CINDY AND I WERE FURTHER apart than when we first met and would stare at the same moon and pretend we weren't over a thousand miles apart. She was convinced of my needing help and was angered that I hadn't been ordered into counseling.

"I can't believe they're watching you die of torture and won't do anything. I'm going to your command. You never talk to me. Has it occurred to you that my imagination is probably worse than the secrets you've kept?"

Cindy had underestimated my survival instincts. There were no anger outbursts at work and, over the last year, I had re-established myself—at least in all outward appearances. About the worst thing I'd been called was "enigmatic," primarily because I spoke little about anything outside of work. When I did, the family tale was endearing or funny. I'd state we remained a committed, loving couple who loved talking to each other.

Meanwhile, I had a self-preservation contingency plan in place. The only people who had seen my meltdowns were the same ones who could be obligated not to say anything. Previously, I explained that for Cindy to say anything, she would be damaging my chances for advancement—which would hurt her and the boys. I needed to amend the strategy.

Cindy felt my anger was damaging and dangerous, more so than any promotion. The next time she was in the clinic, she saw an officer she trusted and approached him. She explained her desire for me to attend mandated counseling with landmarks of my progress. She was bounced from one department to another and eventually was told to speak with the officer with whom she started.

"Jim, I've gone to the command for the last month," Cindy said. From both her sentence and disposition, I was certain little had come of it.

"Oh, what did they say?" My posture didn't change, and the fact I wasn't alarmed seemed to deflate Cindy even more.

"Anything from maybe I was over-reacting in a condescending way to the fact that I might be the problem. You have them completely fooled. They think you're Mr. Perfect. I don't know what to do..." Her last word trailed, utterly demoralized.

"If it's one person, you could be right. But if it's everyone, maybe it *is* you, Cindy." Immediately, I knew that was a lie, but a falsehood that greatly benefited me. I had to stay the course. Maybe Cindy would accept the untruth and move on.

"Maybe it is me. You look exhausted. Maybe you should get some sleep. I'll join you in a little while." Cindy's words were barely audible.

My heart sank. The result I had prayed for had just dropped in my lap, but no achievement could have possibly felt worse.

We had become a series of broken sentences. A simple question of how my day went brought dread. Once, Cindy even had played a most melancholy version of the "why" game.

"Jim, you had a bad day because you're not sleeping."

"Why?"

"You're not sleeping because you have recurring nightmares."

"Why?"

"You're having nightmares because you're tormented."

"Why?"

"You are tormented because you won't talk to anyone."

"Why?"

"You won't talk because you don't trust me."

"Why?"

"You don't trust because you're operating in a vacuum."

"Why?"

"Because I'm powerless to stop it."

"Why?"

"Because God said so."

I thought maybe a shower, dim lights, and fresh sheets would have provided a smooth transition to slumber. I climbed out of the shower and heard a distant, muffled sound from the top of the stairs. No lights were on, but I heard Cindy in the middle of a cleansing cry—the sound of utter helplessness.

I quietly walked down the stairs, feeling as though I were invading a private mourning. I reached the bottom of the stairs and the crying quieted.

I silently moved into the living room and when my eyes adjusted to the dark, I saw Cindy's small frame in the fetal position on the couch, facing away from me.

Maybe the boys had fallen into an uneasy sleep. The house was silent.

I stepped toward Cindy, maybe ten feet away.

Do something.

I thought of reaching and gently touching her shoulder or whispering that I loved her. I only had undertaken the *mission* because I loved her. I was a good person for bearing the weight of my memories alone. I was. I was not going to allow her to experience the pain I couldn't escape.

Say something.

Maybe she could feel as though I would protect her. I hoped she was relieved from any aching she'd ever felt. She'd been required to forfeit so much of what she believed and if she could do so, I felt she would've been freed. Her world was changing; she'd never asked for that.

I stood in the dark room staring at Cindy, who seemed to drift off restlessly, stirring every minute or so and mumbling something.

Do something, anything.

I wanted so badly to reach out, but she would awaken with new optimism that we could talk about Iraq. I could not drag her through that again. My hands were extended in front of me, as if an explanation were forthcoming, before they dropped to my side. I prayed an Act of Contrition, unable to take a step toward Cindy. I loved her. I could do anything for her except take a single step.

Cindy had waited for me to come home. I realized I wanted her to accept an untruth and move on. I thought of our earliest telephone calls. After the story of her waiting for that package, I told her I would never allow her to be left in the darkness. I had become that package and didn't have the heart to tell her—an unintended, mean-spirited joke.

* * *

After a few hours of fitful sleep, I awakened from a nightmare. It was 1:30 AM. Unable to sleep, I decided to go to an all-night diner. Most likely, the alcohol I drank neutralized the sleeping medications.

Rather than the quiet corner booth I had hoped for, I was seated next to a table of four people.

As I walked through the restaurant where one young man—maybe in his early thirties, built like an offensive lineman with an oversized t-shirt and Patriots cap worn backward—was doing most of the talking. A man with thick dark hair and sweats and two young women were engrossed in his explanation of military strategy.

"So, first they identify the front line, see, then they bomb the crap out of 'em. You know, submarines, Air Force, whatever. So, then the enemy's all disorganized, right? Then, they send in the ground troops."

I'd grabbed a newspaper and looked through the International News section. The high humidity in the night made the stale, breeze-free air seem warmer.

As a new arrival in Iraq, I'd believed it was some sort of initiation joke when I was told it rained sideways there and planks were placed across ditches as bridges. A bunch of funny guys, I thought. Months later, I realized they were correct. Seasons vacillated between Hades and a cold version of monsoon. The bitter winds rivaled those of the Chicago waterfront.

"When they send in the ground troops, they know there'll be losses, you know? And I hate to say it this way, but they're expendable."

As he spoke, I read of an EFP roadside bomb striking a convoy in As Salam, Iraq—a town within sight of our convoy route on February 15th, 2009. One American soldier from the 610 ESC, 14th Engineer Battalion, 555 Engineer Brigade was killed.

It had been a convoy, just like mine. Perhaps the chances were slim, but I could have known him and heard stories of his family members, his hobbies, his loves.

I looked at the man sitting across the aisle.

"Excuse me," I said, interrupting his presentation. "Did you just say you hate to say it that way?"

"Yeah, I mean it sucks, but it has to be that—"

"Then don't say it that way." In a calmer moment, I'd be curious in hearing an explanation of why a mother's son was expendable.

"What?" The man squinted at me.

He rose from his seat, took two steps toward me, towering over my left shoulder. He stood close enough to punch me with either hand. But he wasn't going to punch me. If he had blood on his hands, he would've known better to back a person into a corner with no choices. I was unable to get out of the booth, which meant he was in more trouble than he thought.

He most likely believed in some movie-like, hermetically sealed violence. His savagery was complacent and safe, a kind of brutality that never existed anywhere on earth.

Time slowed. I felt betrayed by his arrogance; his disrespect for all I'd endured. It was impossible anyone understood when they've never known or faced the consequences. His bluff to me was going to cost him. He was one of *them*, the same people who spoke of war like the build-up before a sporting event or boxing's tale of the tape. He would have sent me to Iraq without a second thought. He was going to pay.

I sat at that small table for two and placed my right hand under the tabletop and lifted. Luckily, the table wasn't bolted to the floor. I could get up quickly, after all. By overturning the table.

"You want to say that again, smart ass?" he said with a bit of a growl. The man leaned further over me.

I had his answer. I thought of that moment in Atlanta's airport when I'd been uncomfortable with the idea of the Magician's Choice. But then, when it benefited me, I hadn't a second thought. There were no more prisoners of war there than in Iraq. The real choice seemed apparent.

My right hand grabbed the fork from my place setting and slid it to the middle of the table as my left hand performed a sleight of hand, wiping the side of my face. From where he stood, he didn't seem to notice my left hand dropping back to the table. Once I held the fork in my left hand, it was a short, unobstructed shot from jabbing the fork tines into his groin before his excursion to the nearest hospital.

There was no training on handling a threat to my life any other way. I was following my last lawful order: To subdue the enemy. I reached for the fork with my left hand, still staring straight ahead. I saw a Connecticut State Trooper approaching the table.

"Hey, guys. Is there a problem here?" Another State Trooper was a couple of steps behind him.

My empty left hand slid back down under the table. If it came to it, I would have simply explained that I had eliminated or neutralized the threat. That was my universal language—one everyone understood—some the hard way. It had kept me alive, brought life and awareness and purpose and meaning. I feared my old complacent and un-suspecting life. I was more comfortable in war's more linear world where a limited and predictable number of things invariably occurred. I wished marriage were so rational.

"Come on. Let's all go for a walk. Let's go."

"There's no problem here, officer. We were just leaving, right guys?" The man's whole demeanor changed. He sounded downright jovial.

"Great, we'll be right back in then. Let's go," said the second officer.

The four of us walked outside and one officer asked what had happened. The man said I had an-tagonized him. His conversation with his friends was none of my business.

The officer turned to me and asked what he had said that angered me to the point of interjecting.

"When you spoke of troops being expendable, you were talking about everyone I served with. Look into the eyes of one of your 'expendables.'" It was exactly what I wanted to say. A look into the eyes of another human, a veteran, had power. I couldn't bear the feeling from one more person that I was consumable and thrown in the regular trash, not even meriting the recyclable bin.

"Hey, I'm sorry, dude. I didn't mean for it to come out that way."

When the man heard the explanation, he extended his hand to apologize, and I immediately felt shame I had been a split-second from badly injuring him.

One officer stayed near me and, as the man walked away with his friends, he spoke to me.

"When did you get back?"

"January of 2008. I'm not sure I'm back yet."

"It gets better, brother. Not sleeping well?"

"No."

"What have you got going on today? Can you go home and get some rest?"

"Maybe, I start work in a few hours. I'm okay. Thanks."

I doubted sleep was possible. I was appalled with the thought of injuring the man without a thought. I couldn't think of a time before the lieutenant and that restaurant, when seeing a problem and resolving to correct it had been enough to learn what those moments taught me.

The state troopers lingered for a couple of minutes. They expressed concern that I was out in town at just after 2:30 AM with the strip club down the block closing soon. They had likely concluded my frame of mind might not blend well with a rowdy gentleman's club mentality.

Soon thereafter, they were on their way and I walked toward my car. I thought maybe I'd decompress for a few minutes and sat on a curb. I wondered what life would look like if things worsened. Out of the corner of my eye, I saw a stray dog moving under the parking lot lights.

The dog (I thought it was a Labrador) approached me with his tail between his legs. He was very skittish, as if he had been physically abused. He looked drastically underfed.

What horrible person could have done that to one of God's creatures? For a moment, I saw a glimpse of myself over the person with violent impulses only moments earlier.

Over fifteen minutes, I was able to lure the dog by whispering nice things and putting my hand out in a non-threatening manner. He circled around, took a step toward me, and then back again—unsure if he should come closer. I slowly gained the dog's trust. He saw me as one of the pack.

There we were, my new friend and I, both on the outside looking in, unable to know who was trustworthy enough to approach. Both of us missed our respective packs. I petted the dog and he eventually licked my hand. Satisfied to have met a friend, the dog walked off, looking back one time. I looked back like a dear friend.

Then it occurred to me that the dog maybe licked my hand because there was food residue on it. It may not have been me at all. I laughed so hard at the thought that I rolled in the grass—an odd sight to the people parking their car at almost 3:00 AM.

Sometimes people just needed to laugh, I supposed. A rowdy group leaving the strip club wanted no part of me.

Chapter Eight

Breakdown

17 October 2012

FELLOW CHIEF HOSPITAL CORPSMAN DESTINY Lee had asked a dozen times.

"Jim, are you sure? We could scale things back, but you should have a retirement ceremony. You'll regret not having one. I'll help."

"I appreciate that Destiny, but no. There are just too many things going on right now."

My dad had told me about a cancer diagnosis, so my parents traveling from Chicago was out of the question. Cindy recently spoke of going to Miami to be with her parents for a while.

I watched Cindy once toward the end of the summer pace the deck as she spoke with her cousin in Miami. In the previous months, subtle signs appeared. She stopped greeting me at the door or she and the boys were frequently out running errands. We slept separately.

On the deck that day she wore a peach top and jeans as she paced. She was so feminine and light on her feet, I thought. I didn't remember the last time I had brought out an optimistic bounce from her. I would have wished that bounce for anyone I ever loved.

But Cindy and I had adapted to having conversations by text or electronically chatting, as it seemed any real-time conversation triggered an exhausting *déjà vu*. We couldn't get out of the whirlpool of maybe five perpetually revolving arguments, all of them equally interminable.

"Letting it go is just not in your vernacular," was one of my more creative statements, which even impressed Cindy.

"Vernacular, good one." She nodded in approval in mid-argument.

For that moment, Cindy's sense of irony showed through. She had that knack, the woman on the back of my motorcycle singing Little Peggy March's classic *I Will Follow Him!* at the top of her lungs. I yearned to feel that way again. Everything seemed so far away.

"I've been waiting for fifty years to use vernacular in a sentence." Even as we argued, I wanted to say I could be wrong, that I needed her love and wanted to share our lives as we had in a past life.

But I'd invested too much in her protection. If I admitted that, I would surrender all the energy I had devoted to sparing them from the war experience. No, that must have been a test of my conviction. It was critical to be resolute for everyone's good.

The levity was short-lived. From Cindy's perspective, for a person who'd faced a traumatic experience, I wasn't very empathetic to her ordeal and distress. I hadn't done what it took to make our family unit function.

She stated, more frequently as time passed, that our family deserved the same level of dedication I'd shown to my battalion. For me not to speak honestly with her was an act of betrayal and not up to her family "code."

"For all your pontificating about group cohesion and loyalty, I'll bet you communicated with those in your unit. I bet you talked to them."

It was her personality and naiveté which greatly contributed to our difficulties and I often said if she were to accept that I was the only person who could be trusted with whether to divulge the story. Those were the very qualities I held dear when we met. It followed the logical conclusion that I knew what was best. I hadn't come to unilaterally deciding to evade her questions. If I were to relent and tell Cindy everything, I would have felt responsible for the loss of the innocence and optimism I cherished about her. If she would have just given in.

I stood at the kitchen counter preparing dinner with Cindy nearby. In a good mood, her hair bounced like a gentle, coiled spring. She strode rather than walked. I couldn't help but think it was in spite of me rather than because of me.

"You're going to leave me, aren't you?" I seemed incapable of putting the right combination of words together.

"No, Jim. Why would you even say that?" Cindy was taken aback.

"I saw you walking on the deck this afternoon talking to Sandy, that's all." The resentment that saturated my soul burned.

Why can't she just let it go?

Cindy didn't respond and continued collecting ingredients. My job was to read the amount on the recipe and mix everything together.

"Oh, be careful with the salt. You were a little heavy-handed last time," Cindy said without looking away from ingredients.

In a split second, my eyes widened, and my right arm tightened like a spasm, my foot dropped back. My arm drew forcefully against my chest like a tennis backhand. With no conscious thought, I was one second away from striking Cindy. My unsuspecting wife would have been the only person more surprised than me.

I turned away from the counter pretending to be in pain with something in my eye and left the room. I'd never felt more repulsed and disgusted with myself.

Running up the stairs, my tears flowed. Something had grabbed a hold of me. Cindy and I were at a bitter end. I could not have sunk further.

When I returned to the counter, I answered Cindy's questions by saying I thought I got some black pepper in my eyes.

"Well here, let me rinse your eyes over the sink."

"No, I'm fine. The tears will wash it away just as fast." I wasn't able to bear the thought Cindy wanted to do something kind for me. I was sickened with regret.

"Come on, I'll just—"

"No!" I screamed. Cindy blinked and recoiled, putting her hands up in self-defense. "No, I have to leave, I'm going for a walk."

"What's wrong? Jim, come back. What's the matter?"

I quickly walked through the house and felt as though the walls would close in if I didn't hurry. I walked down our block, unsure where I was going to go.

Cindy followed, leaving the front door ajar.

"Can't we just talk? What did I do?" Cindy yelled after me while trying to catch up.

I didn't answer. There was no answer.

"Please, let's just talk." Cindy caught up to me and grabbed my arm by the elbow, trying to slow me down.

"No! No talking!" I pulled my arm away from her and walked down toward the highway at the end of the block.

Cindy tried to grab my arm but again I pulled away, stumbling off-balance for a second. Running out the front door, leaving both doors wide open, I ran down the highway. Cindy ran after me, down the block, calling to me.

"Can we just... no! No-ooooo!" Cindy let out a scream, a long, agonizing shriek. She collapsed on the side of the highway and fell hard to her knees. Cindy drew in a breath as if she took in all the air in the world and let out a prolonged scream until her voice trailed.

"Noooooo!" she sobbed.

Cars along the highway slowed, but no one stopped. A neighbor stood on his porch and watched. I stopped running and went back. I had only heard that scream once before.

All my thoughts on leaving the war in Iraq and not bringing it home hung in the air but I hand-delivered it right into my house, into my family's lives.

"I'm sorry, maybe we can talk." I reached for Cindy's hand.

"Get away from me! Get... away from me!"

Why wouldn't she just give in? I had to do it. I could only think of my reaction to the blindfolded man with the picture of his daughter, the little girl in the dress.

Why couldn't Cindy just get it into her head? My intentions were pure. I only had to maintain for that moment. It was for the greater good—an ultimate act of enduring love. My quest at dispiriting

Cindy was slower and so much more agonizing than the story of the interrogator in the *Incident at Vichy*.

I recognized the familiar intersection at which I stood. There had never been victory there. One could have charged into battle and been responsible for the agony or death of others, been captured and killed, or fled and been labeled a deserter. It was a coin flip.

Through Cindy's pain, she couldn't yet see what I was doing provided her with the best option, while I carried the burden of my unending interrogation.

There were consequences for my behavior. I had to believe they were worth it if it saved her. I hadn't retreated yet, and there was no victory or glory. I was an outcast by my own hand.

* * *

The man who stood on his porch walked down the steps, apparently wrestling with the idea of approaching us. I moved away from Cindy and sat on the highway guardrail as she continued a cleansing cry, muttering something unintelligible. Within a few minutes, the man climbed his stairs again and looked back, as if he was planning on keeping an eye on us.

Cindy eventually sat back up. On the ground against the same guardrail, she tried to collect herself. The time for regret, I had learned, was later. Right then, I had to complete that empty mission. The only alternative was to provide hope, lift Cindy up and earning her trust, only to drop her again. Neither of us was capable of going through another cycle—we had neither the energy nor the stamina.

Cindy slowly climbed from the highway shoulder and dusted herself off. We walked without a word up the gentle slope of our street. The man only went inside when he saw Cindy on her feet, walking with me.

I thought of all the subtle ways we had moved apart in the past three-and-a-half years.

"I'm buying the tickets tonight. You can ride the train that carries the car for a good part of the trip to Miami." My voice sounded more detached than I had planned.

Cindy walked alongside on the dark street. I knew our relationship had been teetering. She stared ahead as if she were comatose. I saw her head nod in the moonlight. I got what I wanted and felt miserable, but my family was safer in Miami. Deep down, I wanted to remove any responsibility from her shoulders. The only way to save her was to make her feel unloved with the hope truth would eventually reveal itself.

"You understand this is the only way? I'll load the car tomorrow."

"I understand," Cindy said. Her posture changed but her eyes stared straight ahead.

We walked along a row of recently planted forsythia. In our long Sunday morning drives to nowhere in particular, she pointed out each optimistic bright yellow bloom in the Spring. Later in the year, we drove past the same bushes, which stood out with equally brilliant orangish-red leaves.

I wondered if Cindy and I had taken our last ride together through Connecticut's back roads, drinking hot coffee, and singing along with whatever songs blared from the car stereo.

If it were true, so many times in our lives had passed without my attaching the proper reverence to them.

I was on the verge of ending a lifelong love to save her from the world outside our doors, to save her from me. Was that what I was being asked to do?

As we walked, I reflexively reached out for her hand and without a thought, Cindy held my hand.

Maybe we both felt peace at the same time in memory.

Chapter Nine

Separation

19 October 2012

I LEFT THE CLINIC EARLY BECAUSE there was packing to do, a task harder and more draining than digging ditches. So much was left unsaid with Cindy, but it was the weightiest day of my lifetime. I looked at the clear sky in mid-day. The sun shone as if filtered through a lens seemingly designed to remove the sharpness of a color's hues.

Cindy milled around the kitchen. Probably neither of us knew why. She washed dishes she planned to never use again. She watered a plant before excusing herself when she saw me come in the door. As she went upstairs, I pretended to need something from the basement and stifled my sobs.

Recovering, I climbed the stairs and took Cindy's luggage to the car. The hours were excruciating with only "excuse me" politely exchanged if we found each other. Our eyes didn't meet and at one point I wondered if Cindy had been thinking, *look at me*. Maybe if she had a gun, she would have pointed it at me and said, *look at me*. And if I did, she would just put the gun down. It was one final insult to that *mission* of mine. One final thing I had brought home and inflicted upon my family.

At one point, a strap broke off a bag Cindy carried, spilling its contents onto the floor. I habitually moved toward her to help, but she emphatically put up her hand. I stopped in my tracks and went back to what I was doing.

* * *

Well after midnight, the car was packed and the GPS set. I even started the car. I didn't want the moment of her departure to last.

Over the previous week, I summoned all menacing and hateful intent, so there would be no doubt in her mind that leaving was the right choice. I had finally done something good; I wanted unencumbered freedom for anyone I loved. Maybe she would never look back.

Likely, I was the only person in the history of mankind with a long-term goal to scare the love of a lifetime into the concept of abandonment as progress. I even feigned abject rejection as an act of love. I alone had decided that treatment was heartrendingly acceptable. Confused and broken-hearted, Cindy and the boys were denied the benefit of prescience.

On our last day, I wondered about the man I confronted in the restaurant. It seemed so impossible when he stated some waste of human lives was suitable to achieve victory. I'd rejected his expression of that, then had done exactly that—I'd expected Cindy to go along with the decimation of our marriage with no explanations.

Cindy and I stood together, numb in the chill of autumn past midnight. Like any married couple, we found ourselves at the crossroads before, but with no ostensible chance of salvation. Over Cindy's shoulder, I saw headlights of passing traffic through the leafless trees. After a long moment of silence, we hugged so tightly that I felt her exhale. I breathed deeply, trying to hold the torrent of tears.

Hang on, just a couple of minutes longer. Please don't ask the question on both of our minds. Please, God, let me live up to the task before me.

"Are you sure this is the right thing to do?" That was not the real question Cindy was asking. She wanted to know if I loved her, I thought.

Even then. All I had prepared to do was try to convince her she had done all she could. As Sayyed had told me many years before. It made as little sense to Cindy, too, in all likelihood. We had somehow gotten through the discussion of the boys being able to stay with both of us and shuttle between Miami and Connecticut. I was grateful we had jointly decided not to put them or our families in the middle. Choosing sides would only add to the complications of our reunion if one ever happened. We only sensed those chances were greater than minuscule.

Cindy still seemed to be confused about why I was so steadfast in wanting her to leave, but if she didn't believe it, she would stay. Any longer, one more cycle through my apologies and outbursts, more apologies and more outbursts, our love would be utterly extinguished. Besides, my apologies may have been terrifying to Cindy and possibly represented broken trust and the foolishness of love. She would have believed me, almost certainly. At least she would have wanted to. I was just as likely to repeat my behavior.

"Yes, I'm sure." My detachment added to the heaviness.

I didn't say I loved Cindy. The cycle inevitably would have started again. I couldn't bear it. Despair invariably trounced hope at the end of every cycle. Yet, I was doing that for nothing but love.

Cindy got into the car, seeming to steel herself for the drive from Connecticut to Miami. Maybe she really was concerned with the seat adjustment, the GPS, the radio, the inventory packed into the car. Or maybe she was stalling before realizing it was futile, just when my own resolve was withering.

Without looking back after our hug, she slowly drove down to the corner and used her directional.

I'll bet she stops at that crazy stop sign.

We'd laughed dozens of times that the stop-sign at the end of the block served no purpose. I could never understand why it was there, I would say, maybe it was a prank or a social experiment to see who would stop there. There were never, not once, any cars there.

But like every other time before, Cindy came to a complete stop and looked both ways. Even at 2:00 AM, she used her turn signals. Some traits were so integral to one's character that they simply couldn't be deprogrammed, no matter if there wasn't a car within five miles. Some characteristics were so innate, to change them would've been impossible.

Just days after our 21st anniversary. I'd seen Cindy act that way since we married. But on that night, I felt I looked into her soul and it seemed so profound that I felt I needed to know nothing else about her. No further explanations were required.

I thought of running to the bottom of the hill. I knew what we both were thinking—maybe counseling could have saved us, we could really have applied ourselves. For what seemed like the first time, I instinctively took a decisive step and sprinted down the hill.

But the traffic light turned green and Cindy pulled away without looking to her left. Maybe she could have seen me if I'd gotten there a split second earlier.

No sound came from my mouth.

With a left turn onto the highway, she started her long trip to Miami only glancing as she passed our house. I wasn't there because I had run halfway down the block. Maybe she was sure I had gone inside the house already, one last sign to her, her one final hesitation at the same time I finally did something. I stopped short as the car pulled away, just in front of the stop sign. I felt a melancholy affection for the stop sign at that moment. It was useless no more. It had tried one last time to hold Cindy up for me. If only I'd acted sooner, I could've caught her. It wasn't the stop sign's fault. No, it was meant to be that way.

I felt elated grief, elation at making the right choice with no understanding of the ramifications and the grief of the fears of the same unknown.

I slowly walked back to the house, its lights appeared less warm and welcoming. Walking back into the house, the warmth in the room lifted the cold from my clothes. I looked around our home and saw every reminder and memory, each with a plan of how they would make our house a home. Each had its own dream at one time.

Now they were popsicle sticks and soccer balls.

I walked into the kitchen in the back of the house, its window looking at Mamacoke Island and the Thames River.

Earlier in the day, I noticed the autumn wind had turned fall foliage into an outdoor carpet of bright yellows, reds, and oranges, with a smattering of browns. I was a stranger there. I felt as though the place, the spot on which I stood, was somewhere I'd only visited in a recurring dream—enough to be familiar, but unsure how to get from one place to another. I stood in a house that wasn't quite my own. Cindy had taken the home's permanence to Miami.

Leaning against the kitchen counter with nobody else there, the necessity to hold everything in receded. From numbness, a feeling rolled like an unstoppable rogue wave. I ran upstairs to the bedroom, not quite making it to the bed before collapsing on the carpet in heaving sobs, my cell phone fell from my pocket.

Cindy can't even be in Old Saybrook, I can call her. No, this is the hardest part. I can't call. It's not fair to her.

Memories of conversations with Cindy replayed in my mind, but more recent recollections played loudest.

About two weeks prior, Cindy said in a voice that dripped with pain and dejection, "You have changed the rules and definitions without telling me."

Life had played the meanest trick on me. I couldn't think of a moment of an entire year in Iraq, the trauma and fear and vulnerability that I hadn't brought with equal strength into Cindy's life. I was the hapless fool who believed I could will my way through the self-imposed assignment. My conviction, determination, and discipline had taken me away from all I loved.

I dried my eyes with my shirt and raised to all fours when another emotional wave rolled over the top of me.

"Nooooo! God damn it, noooooo! What... have... I... dooonnnnee?" My voice trailed and I took in a breath so the ensuing agonized scream would have blown out all the windows of our house. "Noooooooooooo!"

Jim Enderle

Maybe it was my imagination, but I heard the faint reverberations of an empty house. Sitting in the dark, I heard my own quivering, hyperventilating breaths. It was no use. Nobody was there by my own design.

Maybe five silent minutes later, I stood up and looked around. There was suddenly so much space that I felt claustrophobic, and the whispering sounds of the one-hundred-year-old house were like a blackened theater.

A sound came from downstairs—a creaking sound like stepping on the floorboards just inside the front door. It could have been Cindy. Or, it could have been terrorists who finally tracked me down.

Thank God Cindy was gone before they finally found me.

The house wasn't safe. The sound of my heart beat in my ears. I picked up a t-shirt and realized how noisy it was at that moment. Moving like a shadow, I reached into the closet. My uniform hung there, with Sayyed's translations of Manuwwar and Abdul-Hayy's correspondence. I cursed, thinking I should've thrown them away.

On the belt of the uniform was a Ka-bar, or "Kill a Bear," knife. I gripped the leather-washed handle, the serrated edge of the knife down, and moved soundlessly to the stairs. The blade of the knife was blackened, so the chance of reflecting light was negligible.

If it were Cindy, she would have called out by now.

Leaning against the wall, I slid down the carpeted stairs while breathing into my t-shirt. At the bottom of the stairs were the bathroom and bedroom door, both closed. I felt a superhuman ability to see in the darkness.

The third opening to the right entered the living room. On the far side of the living and front rooms were three sets of two windows. I saw the bare trees rustling in the moonlight. No moving shadows within the house could be seen. No sounds of movement.

What were they afraid of? They have the weapons.

Quickly reaching around a corner, I turned on the living room light and ducked back into a corner. No sound of an alarmed and exposed intruder. With the Ka-bar still raised, I walked into the living room and checked every door, suddenly confident that any trespasser wasn't armed. Few armed interlopers break in only to hide.

I decided to check the basement. Still, I briskly swung the door open, with a posture and facial expression meant to intimidate. I was in my element.

After I turned on the basement lights, I paused, and once again, no sounds. I had an upper hand over my environment. Still, the knife remained raised over my shoulder, but a sly smile crept over my face. The back basement door was locked. My anxiety ebbed, and I turned back toward the stairs before I met my match.

There, on the washer, were clothes waiting to be washed. On the top of the clothes was Cindy's Christmas sweater with an endearing stitched reindeer with a big Cheshire cat smile. It was so Cindy. She had worn it and maybe had pulled it out of storage for the Christmas we would never have had the chance to share.

God, that woman loved Christmas. To her, there was the Christmas season and two weeks of summer. I smiled, but tears flowed. I imagined she was approaching New York City. Cindy planned on driving straight to Washington, D.C. area. The car would be loaded in a boxcar and Cindy and the boys would move to the passenger train forward the boxcar and ride almost to Miami.

I walked to the dryer, putting my Ka-bar down. Sunlight would have soon peeked through the windows on the back of the house. Part of me wanted to empty the house, the other half wanted to leave everything the way it was—all Cindy's clothes left behind, every remnant of our plans and dreams.

I picked up the black sweater and held it before slowly bringing it to my nose and drawing in a breath. The faint smell of her perfume and powder rose from the sweater. I sat on the stairs and wept into it.

Recovering again, I stood up. And tenderly put the sweater where it had been. I tried to recall an adage by Anaïs Nin hanging over one of our marriage counselor's chairs. "*Love never dies a natural death. It dies because we don't know how to replenish its source. It dies of blindness and errors and betrayals. It dies of illness and wounds; it dies of weariness, of witherings, of tarnishings.*"

I played with the words and tried to make them my own. Emotionally exhausted, I decided to try and sleep. It was early on a Saturday morning.

When do package stores open?

Bringing the Ka-bar from the basement to the upstairs bedroom, I suddenly became focused on the quiet in the house and obsessed with the idea of being found by insurgents. Somewhere in the world, my address had been put into a database or Excel spreadsheet. Or, for all I knew, it'd been buried in the shifting sands of southern Iraq or never survived the rainy season.

They're patient, I know. They'll never forget. Only we knew what exactly happened to Manuwwar and Abdul-Hayy.

Maybe insurgent's imaginations were as active as my family's and what they saw in their minds was much worse than what really happened?

Sleep was impossible, and each day's nightfall came with an attached dread. Getting a cup of coffee had seemed like a good idea when washed down by my package store cache, then sleep.

I walked onto our front lawn. Tread marks remained in the lawn from Cindy's departure. The street I'd sprinted down hours before seemed washed by early morning dew. Something caught my eye on the lawn. The metallic-looking glimmer shined brighter than the frosty dew.

Bending to take a closer look, I picked up one of Cindy's trinkets—a necklace with the words emblazoned: I WILL LOVE YOU FOREVER.

Chapter Ten

The Spider and
Archimedes' Principle

E VERY YEAR AS A KID, our family planned a one-
week family vacation, usually to either Wis-
consin or Minnesota. In the six months prior, we
looked at brochures for various places, activities,
and prospects for catching lots of fish. Since I
loved maps, I looked up the lake, the nearest city,
and the terrain around the destination.

Most of the time, I imagined myself as a secret
agent about to save the world. I spent that time
imagining what the place would be like, formulat-
ing a type of pre-memory of the place. But every
time, once we got there, it was entirely different
than anything I had imagined.

By the time the week was over, Dad, who worked
two full-time jobs for most of those years, was
just beginning to find his new rhythm. Even as he
relaxed, his sense of discipline never waned. He
still awakened at 4:30, subjecting us to his list of
things to methodically accomplish before the day
was over. That was just Dad being Dad.

Being a bit of a daydreamer, my imagination was integrated into our segmented schedule. On one cast, I imagined batting in the bottom of the ninth in the seventh game of the World Series in Wrigley Field. Down one run with runners on second and third and two outs, I battled to a full count. As I cast my rod, I released early, and the reel whipped from the end of the rod. I heard the cheers of the crowd as I laced an opposite-field single, the game, and World Series-winning hit.

If my brother Norm (an avid White Sox fan) could have intruded in my daydream, he would have plainly stated "...and the world ended."

One time, to Dad's chagrin, we were ready to pull up the anchor of our fishing boat and try another location when I swung my fishing rod and struck a series of branches, dropping an unsuspecting spider to the calm, shaded surface of the lake. The spider furiously kicked its legs. I had disturbed his carefully crafted web.

I dropped my fishing pole under the spider and lifted the tip, thinking if I did it gently, the spider could climb onto the pole and I'd pull it safely into the boat.

But the tip of the rod, about five feet away, was hard to control. I only managed to throw the spider further off balance. Even more panicked, it struggled.

With a sense of urgency, I moved the rod and tried to steady it but couldn't keep the tip still. The more I tried to save the unfortunate arachnid, the more I'd lessened its chances of survival.

Jim Enderle

Within a long minute, the spider stopped struggling and I lost track of it. My Dad and brother waited to pull anchor until I reeled in my line. I silently sat there, not wanting them to know I was crying. Despite my best efforts, I contributed to drowning the desperate spider.

Unbeknownst to me, spiders could stay floating on the water by instinctively spreading out their legs and therefore, their surface area. As much as a spider can think, it may have wondered what it had done to deserve its fate.

I looked again as the boat motor revved.

There was no sign of the spider.

Chapter Eleven

Last Day in the Navy

November 2012

I SAT IN MY OFFICE ON my last workday, never imagining the view of the end of twenty years in the Navy. By then, everything had been cleaned, drawers in my cabinets and desk drawers emptied. My computer chair sat in the middle of an office that seemed much bigger.

My mind wandered to a framed version of the *Desiderata* which still hung from the door. It was an ode of comfort to people during uncertain times.

I particularly enjoyed introducing the *Desiderata* to those who had never read its enlightened message. As I sat there, I tried to remember what I could, muttering the words audible only to me: *Nurture strength of spirit to shield you in sudden misfortune. But do not distress yourself with dark imaginings. Many fears are born of fatigue and loneliness.*

I thought I should have read it more frequently. Just then, I heard footsteps coming down the quiet hallway of the clinic, two hours after the workday. Likely, it was the duty crew ensuring the office doors were locked. I quickly jumped from the seat and turned off the lights and sat in the dark in my locked office.

...And whether or not it is clear to you, no doubt the universe is unfolding as it should.

Yes, it was. The final days of my career were marked by an attempt to save my doomed *mission*. The harder I'd tried, the further behind I seemed to fall. I'd been taught when results weren't there, work harder, and press even more beyond that. Willpower previously had been enough. At that time, it was a curse. I became the boxer who never learned to tie up an opponent while staggering into more blows.

Under the door, I saw the shadow of footsteps, pausing for a moment, pivoting, and checking the door before moving down the hall. I had one final task to complete my twenty years. There would be no speeches, no passing of the flag, "Old Glory" would not be read, and I would not be whistled ashore—the traditional and symbolic way of returning to civilian life.

Maybe my retirement speech could have just been anecdotes, refined and rewritten countless times. No rough drafts there. Retirement speeches seemed to contain a common thread: the inspiration of a loved one, the resilience of a loving family, stories of shipmates who mentored and circled back around the slowest team member to lead the way to the finish line. These were my fondest memories, but I felt separated from them. I couldn't have spoken of them with conviction.

Among my favorites was a retiring admiral who portrayed himself in his final speech as the Navy's version of Olympian Dick Fosbury, the man who revolutionized track's high jump event, the "Fosbury Flop."

After a series of sports setbacks and failures throughout his athletic life, Fosbury, described as without the pure physical ability to compete with world-class high-jumpers, felt he had little to lose but to shatter norms. Perhaps a great athlete would never have found it necessary to do so. At the end of the story, the admiral had an emotional pause when speaking of Fosbury's answer to how his unconventional approach earned a Gold Medal in 1968.

"All he had to do," he responded, "was get his head over the bar and the rest followed accordingly."

The footsteps faded toward the elevator. I sat a moment longer in the dark. I stood, turned on the light, and looked around the office one final time before walking to the back steps and following them to the basement.

I cracked open the basement door at the end of a long passageway. There was no sign of life. I moved down the hallway, checking for noise and came to an office I knew had no lock. It was the lieutenant's old office, which since belonged to the facilities manager.

I stepped into the office and felt a swirling of unresolved emotion. The office was a symbol of all left unsaid. It was fitting in that office that I remembered I couldn't look up at Cindy. I understood then I was setting things in motion. Each of those actions had consequences.

Part of me wished the lieutenant felt as badly as I did—we were equally guilty of similar insults to those loyal to us. My *mission*, like the lieutenant's, had to take priority. Neither of us could have afforded to think about the ramifications of those affected.

I thought again of the main point of my retirement speech. The one old Marine I had seen in that volunteer activity for homeless veterans in Boston. Lance Corporal Coleman, who waited for his Corpsman to get there, never doubting for a second we'd arrive. Another young Marine on the *USS Wasp* beautifully answered a Dear John letter. We spent the night sitting on the flight deck until the sun peeked over the horizon.

* * *

Reaching into my pocket, I grabbed my office key and placed it on the desk, which had the same fluorescent lights on under the shelving. The only difference was that the coat rack in the corner to my right was empty. No enemies staring back at me. There were papers on the desk, but different papers—reports, for the latest deadlines with the perceived urgency necessary to single-handedly avoid a nuclear holocaust.

I stepped into the doorway, pausing to hear only a couple of pipes swishing. Someone in a bathroom had just flushed. Otherwise, there were only distant echoes of the clinic's duty crew, a waiting room television, and the swishing of automatic doors. Making it to the back stairwell was easy, I thought. But getting out of the building without being seen was a challenge and included walking by Medical Records.

There were so many people I had learned to love and care about in the clinic. I was certain it would only be uncomfortable for both sides to stop and say goodbye. It was easier for everyone. I'd never meant to cause problems. Maybe like the hapless spider, my career and life had been doomed to good intentions.

* * *

Cracking open the door into the elevator lobby within sight of the Medical Records office, I peeked. Although the copier was whirring away, I saw nobody manned it, so I quickly walked past. I made it out of the building and walked out to my car with a sense of relief.

I turned the ignition. The car started and all I wanted to do was decompress, but drinks would have to wait. I couldn't chance going somewhere and being recognized.

The air just before dusk had a chilling edge. From where the car sat, there once again was a serene view of the Thames River. On either side of the river were railways, although they weren't extensively used. Across the river, moving southward was a long freight train. It was a picturesque view.

Jim Enderle

I truly appreciated the beauty of the world but was unsure of where in the snapshot I was supposed to stand.

"And whether or not it is clear to you, no doubt the universe is unfolding as it should," I whispered to myself again.

I needed a drink.

Chapter Twelve

Suicide Contagion

FOR WAR VETERANS, THERE NEVER is a bad time to catch up with an old friend. Jim and I could miss months or more and touch base as if no time had passed. One day, I looked at the phone and saw his number and let it go to voicemail. We would catch up, we always did, because we always had time. Until then, *always* meant *forever*. I would learn. Iraq had changed yet another definition.

"Why don't you come to Connecticut?" I asked once. His answer was Connecticut was not far enough for his wanderlust from his native upstate New York.

We were an odd pairing when traveling together while the ship was in a foreign port. Jim told me I should have taken more pictures so I'd have the memories I might have forgotten.

"I have them all stored, right up here." I said, with my forefinger jabbing just above my temple.

I told Jim he took so many pictures that he lost the experience of seeing the country as it unfolded.

He did enjoy my idea that when we left the ship while visiting a foreign port, I wanted to get away from anyone who spoke English and take in the smells and sounds of a sidewalk café.

* * *

Once Jim moved to Washington State for a three-year assignment, I left a message and got a call within the next few weeks. Maybe it took a couple more weeks before I returned that call.

All I had was a phone message—to give him a call, *please*. No particular urgency in his voice exactly, but I'd missed the clue in the word 'please.'

Three days later, I called and left a message. One week later, I left another message, and one week after that, I heard a recording that the number was out of service.

I sent an email. Still not in a panic, I searched the Internet to see if I could find his number. Cindy used to say anything could be found if one was persistent enough. My search appeared on the screen and I looked through.

The very first file was an obituary. I looked past it. A minute later, I scrolled to the top and clicked on the link. My heart pounded. It was Jim's obituary with his picture in uniform.

I was too late.

I'd played the voicemail dozens of times since, each a lash of penance. I should have answered, should have called. If only I had known, I would have called. But that thought provided no comfort. Pain hung like a persistent fog.

I repeatedly listened to the message, hoping for a clue. I missed something. Nothing was worse than being a liability to my unit of close friends. In my selfishness, I hadn't listened.

If I were hanging from a rope by my last finger-nail, it had just been ripped from its nail bed.

* * *

Reverberations of Jim's death were profound and few things in life were as they appeared. Only when I decided to call and couldn't get through did I investigate. A short Internet search later, I found an obituary dated the day after his phone call.

In spite of appearances, everyone in the world was in such pain.

Sitting at a traffic light on the way to my second appointment with a new counselor, I looked into my rear-view mirror and saw a young woman in the car behind me, the same attractive young woman who was talking with the cashier at the coffee stand minutes before. They exchanged a couple of witty remarks and laughed. She had a nice laugh, and one of those genuine smiles that makes it impos-sible not to smile back. The corners of her eyes crinkled, and it seemed every muscle of her face smiled, yet she seemed unsettled somehow—as if she had awakened too late and spent the time since chasing those precious minutes.

Minutes later she was behind me at the red light. As I looked, she swayed in her seat like she was in a rocking boat. Her face dropped into her hands and she wept, oblivious to where she was. The wrinkles on the corner of her eyes transferred to her forehead and she looked up, her face awash in tears, not realizing I was watching her. I sat frozen, afraid that approaching her would have proven me a voyeur, but I continued to watch.

I suddenly looked away, feeling no right to observe. We missed an entire green light with neither of us noticing. She *felt* something and whatever vexed her may have lost its hold. I was convinced a cleansing weeping would save her. Perhaps she would be redeemed and comforted and cleansed by her tears. Her plight elicited empathy and hope.

So long ago, I had felt like stopping halfway through the Chicago Marathon, but just around the next corner was the elation of resilience. Possibly, her fate had yet to be determined. I prayed her chances were better than mine.

* * *

The cool office contained shadeless, high-reaching windows that stopped just beneath a brown water-stained ceiling. The therapist's working space resembled that of a mad scientist with papers sticking out of folders on shelves everywhere, except his large oak desk. I wondered if the building had been built around that desk or how many people it would take to move it.

Without outward emotion, I explained I had thought long and hard and it would be best to end my life.

My words seemed clumsy and didn't match their meaning. I wasn't deciding to take the Merritt Expressway rather than Route 95, which ran parallel to it, but it felt that way.

Rather than object, the counselor's blue eyes peered over the top of his silver horn-rimmed glasses and folded hands, and he nodded. He wore a crimson pull-over sweater over a mismatched blue shirt. The therapist and I looked at each other. My fingers tapped the right arm of my college chair. Robert's fingers tapped on his tarmac of a desk, out of sync with mine.

"Okay, Jim. Can you tell me why, today, you've chosen to commit suicide?" he asked, after a deep, thoughtful inhale.

"Because then it would be over."

I'd surrendered any points for creativity. It was almost two weeks after Jim had ended his life, so as not to have burdened anyone (I guessed). Psychologists had long known suicide among military units was infectious. There was even a term for it: suicide contagion.

I had little interest in speaking with a civilian counselor. There were twenty-two veterans a day who committed suicide. I was certain one could not be proficient about suicide from a distance.

Cindy and I had been separated for just over a year. Since then, I'd deliberately chosen a job where I worked independently and alone and was self-medicating with slurries of nightmares, sleep, anxiety, pain meds, chased with copious amounts of alcohol.

Jim Enderle

I had seen Jim's suicide as tragically honorable, even profoundly admirable. He had found some expression that matched the pain he felt, a way to achieve balance. He was the fifth person with whom I had served who had chosen to end their lives, maybe each of them for different renditions of the same song—it was addition by subtraction.

I thought again of the young sailor who'd committed suicide in the unit we'd replaced. His loss seemed so senseless then.

"I never understood the glamorization and glorification of war." The words came out as I had thought them. An absence of malevolence was different than therapeutic forgiveness, merely blocking out enmity didn't constitute love. A lack of conflict and destruction was not peace. I failed at doing so. Definitions of the words I used and the associations with which I had insidiously changed.

"Are you planning on writing a suicide note?" The therapist asked questions without breaking eye contact.

"I hadn't thought of that." The question was unexpected. "I guess so."

To earn and build trust with the person on either side of you was any military unit's training objective. That element was necessary whether it was Marine General James Mattis or *M*A*S*H*'s cross-dressing Sergeant Maxwell Klinger. That was an ultimate goal—to have felt that level of trust under the most arduous circumstances.

My purpose had passed in a blur. Everything I had learned to belong to such a meaningful endeavor was suddenly unneeded, even intimidating to others. The very things I used to garner the respect of the unit were a millstone in my new world. I wondered how many country boys in the unit who had found comfort in the woods fly fishing, spent more time checking the tree line.

"To whom?"

"I'd write to Cindy, my sons, my parents, brother, and sister."

The thought entered my mind that in my last phone call with Cindy, she asked me to at least call to say goodbye in moments she feared the worst.

People were misspoken when they had said a combat veteran misses combat. I missed the talking and forming a tribal connection. We were accountable to one another. The trust wasn't blind but on faith. People had their agendas outside of that, but that was understandable. A man wouldn't cry alone in his bunk at night without someone asking about it, maybe right then or later, depending on how well we knew each other. Feelings and emotions weren't a scary thing back then.

"What would it say?"

"I... this is nobody's fault. That I would hope they would not see my actions as suicide, but euthanasia."

I had had pictures in my mind of the total devastation after WWII. Then I imagined the scope and magnitude of effort and resources required to rebuild huge parts of two continents in northern Africa and Asia, and almost all of Europe. But the world did it—it could have been done. But there was no Marshall Plan for suicidal veterans.

Instead, after I was gone there would be the predictable self-protective words of those wondering why I hadn't called them. In truth, I would have called any or all of them, exhausted every opportunity, if I believed answers were available.

"Would you tell any of them in person?"

Historically, the concept of honorable suicide was found across almost any culture. Samarai, kamikaze, insurgent Jews at Masada, the Romans had "patriotic suicide," Stoics in ancient Greece believed that death was a guarantee of personal freedom. Sayyed explained the belief of some who believed they were born dead and all that determined our afterlife was living and dying with conviction.

In Iraq, those fighting against our occupation were not found in the obituaries, but in sections announcing celebration and weddings. Their respective communities rallied around the family to ensure their needs were met and their status was raised to one of respect.

"I understand where you're going, Doc. You might be assuming suicide is always irrational or impulsive. But answer this: what is so wrong with not wanting to live long enough to extinguish and obliterate every good memory in my family?" I had thought about that from as many angles as I could, trying to think of other options. "Wouldn't you wish for them the opportunity to recover and have a sense of nostalgia or the possibility of a fond memory? Right now, they're left to grieve every time they look at me for the rest of our lives."

The counselor looked back at me and adjusted his wedding band. Something about the grim conversation was empowering. No human being had a real way of talking me out of it.

"Only from the outside looking in does that seem like a good idea. Try to convince me you would do something different." I sat back in a wooden chair with armrests. I had more ammunition that I'd recently read.

The human body was a miracle of creation. In order to protect and preserve itself, it raised and lowered blood pressure and temperature, constricted and dilated blood vessels, released adrenaline, endorphins, or anything else it had at its disposal in order to survive. But the war experience somehow took all those characteristics and turned them inward, like an auto-immune disease, where everything designed to protect us began eating away from the inside? Maybe that was what had happened, it had all been turned inward.

The therapist said again that he held no judgment in any decision I made. In truth, he admitted, he had no idea what decision he would have made.

"Will you say a final prayer? Do you want to say it now?" He once again answered a question with another question.

"That's simple. If there is a God, that he will present a sign—some kind of miracle."

Fortunately for me, I felt I had borne witness to a number of miracles. I had believed each of the many cycles of energy during a twenty-six-mile marathon was an inexplicable phenomenon. It made no physical sense that a person's energy level could have been depleted then reset as if one hadn't run a step. I had to admit there were others if I thought about it.

"Okay, how long are you willing to wait for a miracle, Jim? I mean, say you witnessed a miracle before our next appointment. How would that change your life?"

"I don't know... I think I would just like to feel like something I do has meaning. It's not that I want to die. It's just that I don't know how to live anymore." I just didn't have the social skills to climb out of a quarry of greased marbles.

"You will have the same choices a week from now. How about if we talk more then? You have my number already. We can make appointments before then as necessary. Let's give it time, okay? Then we'll see where you are."

"Uh, okay." I had been given an alternative which didn't lessen my sense of agency.

"I've probably asked enough questions today, but I have one more: Why, Jim, today, are you deciding *not* to commit suicide?"

"Because then it would be over."

Chapter Thirteen

The Bar Scene

October 2013

THE LAST WEEK OF OCTOBER brought an end to God's fireworks show, New England fall, where around every corner was a more spectacular view of Connecticut's rolling hills. As I walked through the woods in the back of our house, I felt bad that a view of the river through bright yellows, oranges, and reds, was being wasted on one who hadn't appreciated the view.

Against the blue sky, I noticed one tree in particular. On the tree, only one yellow leaf waved, barely clinging to its branch. I double-checked. Sure enough, just one maple leaf fluttered like an over-sized butterfly. One would have thought the gale force winds earlier in the week would have removed its will. But there it hung, unable to prevent the tree's winter slumber alone. A single leaf only provided a negligible amount of nourishment. I stared.

There's no hope, just give up.

As if it heard me, the leaf playfully fluttered, without nature's acknowledgment that life eventually forced numbed compliance to its whims.

A cold and unexpected cross-breeze whipped from the north and the leaf couldn't hang on any longer. It was life as it was meant to be.

* * *

That night, I sat in my chair—the one I'd been sleeping in for months. Lying in bed brought a terrible, alcohol-soaked sensation, as if consumed drinks would pour back out from my throat. There were too many windows on the house to monitor in our dark and quiet neighborhood. In a darkness-induced fit of anxiety, I unblinkingly stared toward the back stairs.

The trap was meticulously set. A blinding 2500-watt bulb faced the carpeted stairs. I faced toward the back of the house in my chair, just past the uniform with the brown leather sheathe for the Ka-bar I held and the letters in its pocket.

Just beyond the closet, on the lowest of the bookshelves, were my combat boots. I was certain I saw the blood under layers of dirt in the dark. I envisioned my dog tag interlaced on my left boot as though grayish mud had baked dry over its raised letters.

The moment insurgents walked out from the shadows had been played out in my mind so often that I wondered if it had happened already.

If it were yet to happen, I could stand and lean into the clothes hanging to my right.

Were insurgents afraid of monsters in their closets when they were children?

* * *

On the verge of a delirious dream, I imagined standing on New York City's George Washington Bridge. I felt remorse, a sadness of all-consuming depth. My focus was on finding a place where I didn't have to be aware of everything around me, so I could collapse into it, relish being deprived, even if for a second.

Looking southward, I scanned the skyline and smiled. A warm, almost tropical breeze felt like a soft kiss. I remembered my childhood fascination of the world as I looked from my apartment building rooftop toward Cabrini Green. For that moment, the greatness and resilience of humanity were in good hands. It was a perfect scenario— nobody would find, look for, or miss me. No tears would be shed.

To my surprise, I perfectly balanced on the rounded rails of the bridge. The darkness of the Hudson River, two hundred and thirteen feet below, welcomed me. I could finally conquer darkness. Empowered, I leaned forward, no longer worried about balancing the world on my shoulders.

Maybe there was another soft and affectionate caress for me. It was all I had wanted, a gentle stroking of my brow as I dozed.

Being oblivious to my surroundings and yet safety was possible. My feet left the rail of the George Washington Bridge like a bird leaving its nest.

Jim Enderle

It seemed that was all I had ever wanted—to feel that way. I fell, finally freed of any constraints. In one instant, Iraq was behind me.

Maybe that was what Jim and others felt, a joining of the Communion of Saints. We veterans would have had our own corner of the party in a better place.

Then my reverie turned for the worse as gravity took over and I didn't soar or hover. Rather, I was as heavy as a boulder of lead. In that instant, I tried to whirl around and grab the rail.

I had changed my mind, but it was too late.

The warm breeze was overblown by a cold wind from the north. But I had already let go, falling so fast that it didn't feel like freedom anymore. Jumping off the George Washington Bridge was not a dramatic cry for help.

I awakened with a start, convinced most people regretted suicide before they hit the water.

* * *

I clumsily sprung from my chair, stepping on the extension cord to which my spotlight was connected, sending the light crashing to the carpeted floor. I still gripped the Ka-bar in my right hand. Realizing again I was home, I stopped and listened.

Nothing.

The occasional sound of cars passing on the highway returned. It was almost one o'clock in the morning.

I had heard the screams and wails of loved ones as I awakened. Suicide was no longer an option. I knew then what had to be done.

* * *

Within fifteen minutes, I got dressed and drove to a local bar. A popular local band had finished playing at about midnight and maybe twenty people remained. Passing my usual stool at the end of the bar, I sat in front of a wall of televisions playing replays of the Saturday college football games.

At one end of the bar, a woman sat in a part of the bar that looked at the rest of the place. Although she had been there since I arrived, she continued to look over the ads on the paper place mat in front of her.

Maybe she wished she'd brought a good book, but I thought it was more likely she was waiting for someone. It was possible, too, that her date had been there and abandoned her. Her hands moved without conviction and she avoided eye contact. I wondered if maybe she wished she were somewhere else or if she had been saddened by the fact that on that night, the emptying bar was as good as it got.

At the other end of the bar were three loud and rowdy men whose voices and laughs were easily heard above the conversational din of other patrons.

There was a particular criterion for the *mission* before me, more of what I wasn't looking for. Being a black belt in martial arts caused no consternation. An expert with a rifle or pistol hadn't scared me in the least. In fact, none of the qualities that made a person dangerous concerned me. Pistols, rifles, and black belts were not at all what made a person deadly.

The three men were well past their alcohol-saturation mark and kidded with one another. Two of the men were tall and muscular with black lumberjack beards and teased the smallest of the three. Seemingly, they just met him, and he felt hanging with them raised his profile. His ironed yellow button-down shirt with a pen in the pocket contrasted sharply with the pullover sweaters of the other two. Between ribbings, they gladly accepted his offer to buy the next round.

"Since when does a 'suit' give me more than a hard time?" one asked the man with the button-down shirt, the two laughing harder than he did. "Hey, the little lady down there is wondering when you're going to ask her out."

"What's that, she's not pretty enough?" the other bearded man quipped, ignoring the man's embarrassed response that he was engaged.

I looked away from the football highlights at the lone woman. She shifted nervously and rubbed her hands as if they were suddenly cold.

"Don't worry brother, by the time the place closes, she'll be freaking gorgeous."

Why doesn't she just leave?

I found myself angry with her. She lowered her head and put her shoulder-length brown hair behind her right ear. She looked back at her ads. She didn't appear angry, she was hurt. I saw a subtle biting of her lower lip.

Don't sit there and take it. Leave.

"Hell, another forty-five minutes and I'll take her home myself." In no part of the man's calculus included how the young woman felt about it.

I looked at her for a moment but could only see the young Iraqi woman left on the side of the road with no choice but to accept whatever treatment cold, callous men had in mind. In my memory, she had looked right at me, her last hope gone before falling to her knees in her torn abaya. I couldn't bear for it to happen again.

I looked at the mahogany bar for a moment before standing up as if a hand had picked me up from the stool by my shirt collar. She would endure no more abuse that night.

None of the three men noticed me before I slowly walked into their field of vision and stood so they would have to look over or around me to see the young woman.

The young man with the pen in his pocket had been closest to me and moved to the other side of the bearded men. If he wasn't uncomfortable enough with the insults cast toward the woman, he was obviously more uneasy with their consequences.

"You are going to apologize to her," I said, as I walked toward them from about ten feet away.

One of the bearded smiled awkwardly, unsure what to think, and deferred to the other bearded man. The second man returned his glance as if he were entertained.

And then I saw him, the one I had looked for. There was no change in his expression, the muscles in his face clenched like a fist. He turned his head toward me like a cornered apex predator. The top of the food chain turn their eyes, they turn their entire head. I was certain he possessed the intangible I sought—he had blood on his hands. He said nothing because we both knew that moment had little to do with words.

I was finished with words and their changing definitions.

"You heard what I said. Apologize to her." I was within five feet.

I smelled the unforgettable stench of burnt flesh and evisceration, smoke hung in the air. Was I imagining things? The man's sweater had the sleeves cut off and showcased his muscular, tattooed arms. His breathing didn't seem to quicken, but he stood ready to pounce.

I stood there, bloated from months of medications and alcohol. A few years prior, he may have turned and apologized. By then, I was winded walking up a flight of stairs. I was no physical match. I had seen plenty of pretenders in my days. That man was not one of them.

Just then, four policemen bolted in the front door and two others came through the back entrance. All fear was stuffed down their throats and swallowed.

Make eye contact with everyone in the room with a furrowed brow. Don't think of messing with us.

The bearded man held his stare for a moment before turning to the police. The bartender had apparently seen trouble brewing and wasted no time calling for help.

"I don't know what his problem is, this guy here saw everything," he said pointing to the man with a pen in his button-down shirt pocket. He used the presence of the "suit" to his advantage. His disposition changed quickly.

"All I said was to apologize to her," I said, without breaking my stare. The policeman standing in front of me formed a barrier between us.

"To who, dude? There's nobody in here but us. Dude's crazy, officer."

"To her..."

The woman was gone.

* * *

The police officers had listened to my explanation and called a court-ordered counselor on the following day, ensuring I had the Veteran's Crisis Line number. Thinking I had a choice, I told the officer I'd go to jail before seeing another counselor. Each therapist was a validation of the previous one—I was incurable. I couldn't bear it. But the officer wasn't giving me a choice.

The counselor called late Sunday morning and said we could meet that afternoon. I obliged.

"Jim, I'm going to start today with something, and I hope you see that it's sincere. Is that okay?"

"Sure." For most of my life, I had avoided hearing the most dreaded word—disappointment. My behavior as a child had been molded by hoping to never hear the word from my loved ones.

"I want to thank you, for serving, for enduring."

Unsure what to say, I didn't respond.

"Now, I just said that. What went through your mind the other night? What did you think it meant?"

"That you're disappointed."

The counselor seemed uplifted by my answer. "It just means we have work to do. But we'll figure this out, okay?"

We spoke of what had precipitated the previous night's events. I was sure he had attached that night to notes of my previous conversation about suicide, and that I had broken my promise to mix prescription drugs with alcohol. But he never mentioned it, instead focusing on that night and how it advanced my goals. He didn't seem as interested in what was said over what my motivations were.

"What did you hope to gain from confronting those men? I'm trying to understand."

My first answer was that I was upset that those men felt they could speak to the woman that way.

Questioning me further, I relented. Maybe the whole episode had been a breaking through the veneer of something else. I felt like I used to when Cindy and I argued.

While I reacted, I didn't even see her face and lost the ability to see emotions. Later, I was able to recall facial expressions clearly. Only later did I realize that she was hurt or afraid.

Anger boiled over, and it felt good only at that moment to release it. It was like something that itched so badly I would deliberately scratch it until it hurt. Next to itching, the pain was a relief. It was not a matter of reasoning or rationale. That had nothing to do with it. If it did, there would be no such thing as destructive anger.

"Jim, it's okay. This is why we're here." Robert paused, picking through his choice of words. "Last night, or later when you thought about it, what did you hope to gain from approaching those men?"

"I hoped they would kill me."

PART THREE

Chapter One

Mothers

August 2013

O UR HOME DURING DAYLIGHT HOURS had a serene charm. The windows on the north side overlooked rooftops of houses along the Thames River, a veritable daily postcard. There were a few times that I walked from one end of the house to the other and didn't take in the view.

But there was one room in the back of our house, just off the kitchen, which I resisted even the thought of entering. It was our overflow room, filled with some boxes, an extra freezer, and anything else that didn't have a place elsewhere. In one corner, on the top of a black file cabinet sat a teapot, rope for a clothesline I had promised to build for Cindy from our shed to the back deck, and miscellaneous tools to aid in its completion.

To anyone else, teapots were simply an innocent vessel for boiling water. To me, it would only be symbolic of the blindfolded detainee's picture of his daughter in front of the rubble of a home, a fragment of the teapot catching the sunlight and reflecting just to her left side.

I felt a sense of gratitude that I allowed the father his keepsake, but I was tormented by a place-setting lovingly left for the homecoming of a loved one, who would see a home amid the rubble. Just as I would see IEDs whenever I saw varying shades of dirt, trash alongside the road, or dead animals.

Since September of 2007, I'd carried the translations of two Iraqis who died on the 9th of June, 2007. Each of their eyes offered a profound view of their spirits, freed of any pretense. They only had seconds of life—no time left to pursue any agenda. I certainly wasn't evolved enough to understand the investment that eye contact required, nor would I have chosen the moment.

Awakening the morning after the bar incident, I knew there was a rationale to keeping the letters through the dozens of times I thought of igniting them. Somewhere within was the answer. Maybe reading the entries meant some cosmic tribute to Sayyed, with whom I'd lost touch. I felt unreasonable anger toward Sayyed, then an equal level of guilt when one of my emails was returned. Sayyed's account had been disabled. From one day to the next, he existed only in my memory.

I walked upstairs, past the mostly empty bookshelf with the combat boots. A small speck from the dog tag shone through in mid-morning. The tag held a morbid purpose: to identify a military member's parts after explosions. I almost walked past the closet when a waking nightmare vividly struck me.

Teapots. Blindfolds. Smells and sounds. Rubble. Roadside litter. I had become a series of associations with Iraq. Within the last day, I preferred death over confronting them.

Little was left to lose. Nothing I could have read in them was worse than being bludgeoned to death.

I impulsively pulled the letters from the cargo pocket. The paper grudgingly unfolded, having been creased for so long. I heard the faint sound of sand sifting down the crease onto my skin.

Even in an empty house, I felt like a voyeur, undeserving of the writings of these men to their loved ones. I had only known their first names—Munawwar [Well-lit, Radiant] and Abdul-Hayy [Servant of the Living]. The more I ignored them, the more power they held.

My fears in opening the letters became clear, at that moment the letters would validate Munawwar's hatred toward me and predict a pleading, outstretched hand to an enemy who stood stoically by. Abdul-Hayy would explain why his final look over his father's shoulder was of terror at a man who could not have been conceived as a helping hand. If I knew their perceptions of our mission, and of me specifically, I dreaded unworthiness of being my parents' son or the man Cindy married or an example to my sons. I'd contributed to their distaste.

* * *

One of Abdul-Hayy's letters was the first to be unfolded. At the top of the letter, Sayyed had written as much vital information as he could find. At first, Sayyed said he would read them to me, but eventually offered to translate the letters once he'd been given permission.

I'd told Sayyed I would read them mostly because I appreciated his sincerity and faith in my interest.

Perhaps for the first time in military history, the men I understood best in my new life were my enemies. Maybe Munawwar would wish to kill me if he knew I held innocent and poetic letters to their loved ones, just the way he had mine, fearing they were in danger.

* * *

Abdul-Hayy's family resided in Yusufiyah, Iraq, just over twenty miles southwest of Baghdad. Abdul-Hayy was seventeen at the time of his death, with four younger sisters, Filza [Rose from Heaven] 15, Alaa [Beautiful, Pure, Caring] 14, Samaah [Bounty, Generosity] 10, and Heba [Gift from God] 8.

Sayyed had explained once that children in Iraq commonly refer to their mothers as "Mama" and fathers as "Baba" because these are the first words infants pronounce and the first faces they recognize.

Before reading a word of the letter, I put it down, believing I wasn't prepared to read further. "Mama" was also Abdul-Hayy's final word before his right hand dropped limply to southern Iraq's steamy desert floor.

Sayyed held each man's personal effects in his hands in the days following their deaths and I glimpsed at them. Abdul-Hayy's handwriting resembled artistic Arabic calligraphy. Abdul-Hayy had kept a journal into which he had jotted down notes and essays as long as a few pages going back to the end of 2003. He would've been thirteen then, within a year of each of my sons.

Although many Yusufiyah residents traveled to Baghdad for work or to bring goods to an open market, Abdul-Hayy's family had no car, making visitation all but impossible to Camp Bucca almost three hundred miles away. They had already networked with neighbors to travel to Baghdad if and when Abdul-Hayy and his father would be brought to Baghdad for trial. Abdul-Hayy felt remorseful that he and Baba were detained, and their small, single-level home was occupied by Mama and three daughters.

Abdul-Hayy's fears were well-grounded. Yusufiyah was a mostly rural area about twenty-five miles southeast of Baghdad in a region dubbed the Triangle of Death. The area had a mixed population of the two major sects of Islam, Sunnis and Shi'ites. Citizens coexisted before circumstances made the area a tinder box for sectarian violence.

Even before Americans established their presence in 2005, tensions were high. The cross-section of Shi'ite militias like the Mahdi Army, sectarian death squads, and Sunni al-Qaeda militants falling back to the Triangle. Al-Qaeda had lost its previous strongholds in Fallujah and the large parts of al-Anbar Province—a wide expanse of desert from west of Baghdad to the Syrian border.

Tensions were further exacerbated by nationalists, off-shoots, and splinter groups from both sects. Home invasions, beatings, and executions occurred on streets in broad daylight. I was certain Baba and Abdul-Hayy feared the possibility of crimes perpetrated on a young woman and three girls living in a home alone.

If Saddam Hussein realized the importance of the strategic area, he was not alone. "The Gateway to Baghdad," as the area was also known, was comprised of Mahmuhdiyah, Yusufiyah, and Lat-ifiyah, and a checkerboard of fields and irriga-tion canals. They connected the Euphrates Valley, through which insurgents from Northern Africa and other Middle Eastern countries flowed relatively easily to Baghdad. Since the invasion, the Triangle became the largest dispatching point for suicide bombers and IED manufacturing used against both American forces and Iraqi civilians.

The most prevalent and recurring topic in Ab-dul-Hayy's journal was the 2006 rape and murder of fourteen-year-old Abeer [Fragrance of Flowers] Qassim Hamza al-Janabi and murders of her par-ents and younger sister by four American soldiers.

The murders set off a wave of retaliatory killings and the numbers of militants swelled with the promises of revenge in the girl's name. Abdul-Hayy recounted the death of his eldest sister, fifteen-year-old Filza in the crossfire of one subsequent firefight.

After Filza's death, Abdul-Hayy expressed guilt. He had been inadequate in protecting her, and rather than say or do anything, he stood unable to move. Abdul-Hayy hadn't inherited Baba's construction workers' hands or thick physique. What could he have done? His answer was clear. *Something.*

Samaah was the most precocious of his sisters but she had gone from a confident demeanor, Abdul-Hayy wrote, with every plan to attend college to carefully walking as if each floor tile were a trap door. She compulsively had to have both of her feet on two tiles at any given moment lest she fell through.

Alaa expressed the Arabic greeting from *"As-salam alaykom"* [peace be upon you] as too lofty of a request and began wishing merely for one's safety although security was certainly as equally unattainable.

Heba was healthy but described constant pain and clung to whoever was closest. Abdul-Hayy wrote of an immeasurable adoration for Mama, who carried the self-imposed, cumulative grief of the family. They hadn't shared a book, their favorite pastime, since Filza's death.

Abdul-Hayy believed Mama had died with Filza. Silence had become a form of expression. A hopeful horizon figuratively arrived at their front door. Once fascinated with flight, Abdul-Hayy stopped wondering what birds viewed as they soared above.

* * *

On the night of the arrest of Baba and Abdul-Hayy, Americans knocked, and seconds later kicked the door in. Baba had ordered Mama to never answer the door without the man of the house present. They had no understanding of the words barked by the soldiers. Mama wept and screamed at them and Abdul-Hayy moved between the soldiers and Mama and his sisters, writing of his shame that he had wet his pants.

Mama kept crying until one of the soldiers yelled for her to be quiet. She did, as if she held her breath in mid-cry. Heba twitched involuntarily as if an electric shock had run through her little body, too frightened to make a sound, her mouth agape in a silent scream.

As the soldiers inspected the home, Abdul-Hayy comforted Mama as if she were a child. The family was moved to the front of the house feeling like they would be shot. Mama beat her chest, grief, and terror indistinguishable. It was the first and last time Abdul-Hayy would speak for his mother and he felt unworthy.

When Baba returned from his bakery, he and Abdul-Hayy were arrested. Baba pleaded for an explanation then wept. Their only crime was stripping broken electric generators to barter for food. Mama, further traumatized, watched helplessly and without expression as Baba and Abdul-Hayy were bound and detained.

By then, a few neighbors had come in front of their homes and protested. Abdul-Hayy and Mama heard them. She only stared with a haunting look he had never seen before—the look of a mother who might never see them again.

* * *

I put Sayyed's translations of the journal entries down. Abdul-Hayy had placed words on my own mother's look as I stood at the airport terminal with sea bags in hand at O'Hare Airport, three connecting flights from Iraq.

The writing brought a vivid memory of my own.

* * *

In 1969 or so, my entire world was contained within a couple of Chicago city blocks. Our residential neighborhood had clear demarcations. If I were looking from our rooftop southward, I saw the high-rise Cabrini Green housing project. Turning to the west, just beyond the railroad tracks, were the Stewart-Warner and Appleton Electric factory and headquarter complexes which employed over 10,000 people.

Pivoting toward the northeast, I saw the towering steeple of St. Alphonsus church. Beyond the church, the top of the Wrigley Field grandstands peeked over the apartment buildings. Straight east stood the lakefront condominiums looking out at the skyline and Lake Michigan.

The most impactful memories of life occurred within five hundred feet or so from my bedroom. From our apartment, just past our neighbor's three-flat was a vacant lot where groups of neighborhood kids converged to play baseball. If one just sat there long enough, there would be enough of us kids to have a game.

We played so often that we knew all the tricks. If you directed the ball to right-center the ball rolled under or between the parked cars on Oakdale Street, greatly improving the chances of a home run.

The bases, unevenly spaced, required adaptations. The first base was a rock, protruding just on the other side of the sidewalk. Second base was a young sapling, perfect for grabbing with the left hand as we ran, whipping us toward third base like a slingshot. Third base was a large oak tree with its roots angled and if one hit the tree just right, they could turn the corner, almost parallel to the ground, toward home plate with no loss of speed.

Across the street from the lot was St. Alphonsus' convent. And, adjacent to that three-story brick building were walls that surrounded the entire block and encapsulated the grammar school, rectory, and athenaeum. It was on that wall that we drew chalk strike zones for past-pitch and again, we had to adapt.

If the batter hit the ball and it was caught in the vacant lot, it was an out. The first yard beyond the lot was a double, the second yard was a triple, and the fourth yard was a home run. Celebrations, however, were short-lived.

In that fourth yard was a hungry-looking Dobermann Pinscher, which meant buying another rubber ball. If we fouled the ball to the right, across the alley, it went into the yards of the "coalition" of women who would take the ball and go inside, despite our pleas. They just wanted to clothespin their laundry in peace.

The negotiating process sometimes included the School Sisters of Notre Dame who lived in the convent. If we fouled a pitch straight back, the top-spin would almost assuredly take the ball straight into Sister Fabiola's flowers in the courtyard between the convent and the school. The batter was responsible for the top-secret mission into the yard to recover the ball. I, among others, often opted to just come back after dark rather than face the wrath of the Sisters, who also acted as our teachers once the school year started. The School Sisters of Notre Dame's flawless memories were never in doubt.

If Chicago in the late 1960s was a turbulent place, it seemed less so in our predominantly German neighborhood. Ann Landers columns detailed the ongoing and passionate debate over whether toilet paper should be dispensed over the top or from underneath. Young baseball fans debated sports columns over the impossibility that Mets shortstop Bud Harrelson was better than the Cubs' Don Kessinger. Four wood-framed houses down the block from our apartment building, where I once consoled my best friend Bill Wambach after he found he didn't make our seventh-grade basketball team. It seemed to both of us to be a life-changing intersection.

Within the following days, I helped Bill deliver the *Booster* [a neighborhood paper] and his route included Mrs. Schmidt, who treated us to one of her homemade candied apples each. Just like that, as we leaned on black railings of her wooden stairs, munching away, life moved forward.

That weekend, I carried my baseball mitt to the Cubs game, convinced I would catch a foul ball for sure. There was no reason or rationale to the odds between a slim chance and less than none, I just felt I was due.

Alongside the convent and wall by the vacant lot was a half-block of concrete brick walls. It was possible someone from outside the city would look at the landscape near our apartment building and see nothing but a concrete wasteland, perhaps wondering who could happily live there.

Often, I would walk Mom to her work at the rectory, passing one of our "clubhouses" in the thick bushes alongside the school. One day as Mom and I held hands, I saw some grade school classmates and, for the first time in my life, withdrew my hand, suddenly afraid of what they might think. Mom maybe even wondered each time we held hands or when I ran with that joyous skip only children are capable of, as if it were the last cherished time.

Another time on the way to the rectory, Mom issued a spontaneous challenge of a race to the corner. City races were like that, from light pole to light pole, to the end of the green Ford, or to a sewer cover if it were visible. These were important details in any city race. The dare came so suddenly that Mom had a head start of a couple of steps, and with all the dancing and running in place she did, I would have to make time. She was already on the second set of green iron bars between cement-capped brick posts.

I sprinted ahead—seeing the bottoms of Mom's white canvas walkers kicking up—and smiled, feeling the rubber bottoms of my Converse All-Stars gripping the sidewalk. I moved closer as we ran and if I continued gaining ground at that rate, I had a good chance of getting to the corner first. At almost twelve, I was in perpetual athletic motion, with enough stamina to heat our home through a winter night if it were converted into burning wood. At five-and-a-half feet tall, I already towered over Mom.

The green iron bars were a blur and two more brick posts later, we were neck and neck. Mom laughed, perhaps anticipating when I would catch up. I surged forward and almost pulled even. She ran along the wall and was gaining on the street side of the sidewalk.

I had a split-second notion that somewhere Mom must have taught me that gentlemen walk on the outside of the sidewalk, that every person on earth values manners and considerate behavior toward others. I couldn't think of a single instance where those exact words were used, but I was convinced beyond any doubt they were true.

My life had the luxury of happy mediums.

We were maybe five steps from the corner, Mom and I pulled to a stop before the four-way stop sign intersection of Greenview and Wellington Avenues. We finished in a tie, both laughing.

It was a satisfying competition and I had achieved two goals. First, I ran quickly enough for Mom to be proud, and secondly, I did not win. I hadn't earned the right to surpass her. It was *Mom*. Mom and I hugged and walked the rest of the way to the rectory.

In my mind, I went back to an idyllic childhood. I saw myself climbing to the roof of the apartment and looking toward where Cabrini Green, that place beyond my imagination, once stood. It just as easily could have been Yusufiyah.

Abdul-Hayy's notes expressed a sense of hope after American forces invaded in 2003. America's reputation had preceded her. The majority of perceptions were that Americans were capable of anything in mythical proportions. Abdul-Hayy's final entries added a caveat: America could have worked a miracle of her choosing if that were what she wanted.

If the turmoil had worsened after the occupation, it was because the welfare and safety of civilians were not a priority.

Chapter Two

Robert

August 2013

M Y HOUSE RESEMBLED A BATTLEFIELD, not a place anymore where people were invited to share meals, play board games, or feel comfortable. Each window had spent x-ray film resting on the inside of the sill. If an intruder opened a window, the film would crackle as it hit the wood floors. I had double-checked.

A tripwire designed to alert me of intruders was attached to a switch linked to a remote alarm. My blinding light with the cord to the chair where I slept positioned to buy me and my Ka-bar the split second we required. With the lunacy of a mad scientist, the various contraptions represented a person with an ironic will to live. The rooms were rigged for every contingency except happiness.

I picked up the Ka-bar from the floor. It felt so much heavier than the previous night. I had backed into a proverbial wall, but it wasn't enough. I slid with my back scratching against bricks until I reached a corner. And that wasn't enough either.

Between the night in the bar and the next afternoon, I had figuratively covered all four corners without finding a door, window, shaft, ductwork, transom, or hatch. I had surrounded myself with brick and concrete. Not even an Iraqi Muqanni, those brilliant tunnel diggers, could have helped me escape that predicament.

I fumbled through a pocket to find the name of a highly recommended counselor, perhaps my fifteenth since the deployment. I negotiated with the policeman, a former Marine, outside the bar. He wouldn't arrest me if I promised to go to counseling. The police would have no leeway the next time I was involved in a fray.

"Highly recommended" counselor was a very subjective term, but that was a recommendation from a sergeant in one of the Submarine Base's TBI/PTSD clinics.

The first sign of hope was our immediate bonding and the way we processed our deployment experiences.

* * *

Robert, the counselor, looked over his horn-rimmed glasses and seemed preoccupied with clearing his desk as if he were behind schedule.

I took the opportunity to look around. The shadeless windows were powerless to filter the late afternoon sunlight, which revealed stacks of manila envelopes. There appeared to be enough paper in the office to collapse the inner floors while building held firm.

With the incident at the bar, the counselor saw fit to schedule daily appointments for the entire week. After feeling rested first thing in the morning, optimism quickly dissipated. I then had the luxury of having two excuses to start the day with a drink: the fact that I had an affinity for Cape Codders and the dread I had reported to the principal's office daily for the next six days. I had no idea how my life had unfolded the way it had.

"I was pronounced cured of my post-deployment symptoms two months ago, so I don't know why I'm here."

More than a dozen counselors had come and gone before Robert, and each had invariably been delegated my file by the most recent therapist. I honestly felt as though, in my own language, I had asked for help from each therapist. Each had seemed to confirm my hopelessness.

I sat in the counselor's drafty office and the sunshine in the windows belied the frigid, windy reality of a wintry afternoon in New England. The man in the bar had the eyes of a killer and the incident still resonated two days later. Steam radiators clinked and clanked.

After a minute or so of milling around, Robert made a sweeping motion, sliding all his stuffed manila folders to the far side of the desk. Maybe the movement was a dramatic message that he cleared everything aside to focus on me, but I remained cynical.

How long before he's looking at his watch as I'm mid-sentence, while wondering if the daily special will run out before he gets to the cafeteria?

After five years, the rhythms of therapy were all too familiar. There had originally been the usual talk of hope and positive outcomes. The counselor and I both smiled and nodded at the appropriate times before inevitably the conversations were stunted. I was a modern Sisyphus, condemned to roll a huge rock up a steep hill, only to have it roll back down and have to start over until the end of time. Sisyphus had often been seen as mythology's personification of war. I was Sisyphus. I was war.

"Well, that's..." Doc said without so much as a blink at my sarcasm.

"This is our first appointment. Will I have to fill out all the forms and checklists again?"

"Why, what would they tell me?" Robert had the demeanor of a guy who enjoyed wordplay and humorous repartee. He folded his hands on the mahogany desk.

"That there is no checklist for me."

My face felt flush, reliving the embarrassment of yet another confrontation with the police two nights before. There were a number of factors that may have increased the likelihood of Post-Traumatic Stress Disorder or moral injury.

The man who deployed was forty-nine years old, had a graduate degree, children, an intact marriage, an excellent relationship with his parents, brother, and sister, had no history of abuse, abandonment, or neglect, and on and on it went.

I continued, "The last counselor looked through the checklist and wondered why I was taking an appointment of someone who needed therapy more than I did."

"Well, I'm not much of a checklist person."

"You have about six sessions left, so you'd better be a miracle worker."

Robert wasn't thrown off by my sarcasm. He read of the numerous therapies to which I had been introduced and explained there were a number of components to our working together. He asked what my expectations were and if I had had any counselors I responded well to.

I responded I had seen Dr. Daly, a Navy psychologist, and loved how she used my love of reading as an extension to therapy and as a method of goal setting, of seeing past the present.

I was impressed by the question, but hope was something I felt in restrained proportions. Being Sisyphus was enough of a burden, but I was also Odysseus, eternally in the process of returning home, but sabotaging himself at every turn, and telling every lie that the moment demanded.

Dr. Daly made an appointment feel like a continuous story. Her love of reading about the Middle East reminded me of my dear interpreter Sayyed. Before I retired, she dealt with my incessant debate on whether medications were addictive with great patience.

I had worried and argued that if I couldn't get through a day without taking them, I was addicted. Dependence was an addiction to me. I felt sad that just over a year later, I was often inebriated, sometimes twice in the same day.

"When you were young, what was the worst punishment you received for misbehaving?"

"Being grounded. The feeling I let my Mom or Dad down was worse than punishment though."

"Did you just take it all in or talk to anyone?"

"I just felt badly and tried to never be disappointing again."

"Are you like that now, do you think?"

"I guess so. Other people have their own problems." I leaned back in the wooden college chair and tapped the arms, afraid to feel hopeful with another provider, I consciously fought the idea that Robert seemed to be a caring provider.

He will abandon me as soon as I begin to divulge the truth. I'm not impressed. Being here three months from now will impress me.

The cursory introduction revealed the doctor's impressive resume: Harvard, board director of this, consultant for that. That made counseling all the more dispiriting, the therapists were qualified and pursuing their life's work. Not long afterward, they were added to the long list of providers, who seemed to me, there was no way there from here. *Here* was both in Connecticut and Iraq, my brain flitting between the two. *There* was a subjective illustration that might have implied some goal or arrival.

Only with a great answer does one realize the genius of a good question. The previous night, I had been fortunate enough to be escorted from the bar by a policeman who completed two Marine tours in Afghanistan. We had a similar language of our traumas, like an encrypted message or an inside joke. It was important, he said, to open my mind and accept help in any of its forms. One never knew where the pearls of wisdom were.

I nodded at the policeman. It had been me who shared my version with patients at the PTSD/TBI clinic. Do not discount people who hadn't "been there." We, as traumatized veterans, couldn't afford to be choosy about where our lessons sprout, was what I told them. I barely remembered those days.

Those days, I felt incapable of working a job other than the one I had—as an independent x-ray technologist—working alone and driving to various homes for the elderly. I loved conversations about their histories and all they had known and seen. Their only agenda was human interaction. I suppose it was mine, also. When I wasn't working, I once went three or four days without uttering a word to anyone. The sound of my own voice startled me.

One moment stood frozen in my head. Back in my first incident with the police when Cindy told me I was surrounded by people who loved me. "Let us in" was what she said. It was that simplified kind of life view and maybe it was that simple. A few in my unit enlisted after Hurricane Katrina struck the Gulf Coast in 2005. Their alternative was homelessness.

I had such admiration for those who came back and never seemed shaken. One sergeant in the Traumatic Brain Injury Clinic had to learn all over again how to button his shirt. At first, I felt like the most selfish person in the world to have been uncomfortable with his struggles while he diligently practiced a task he'd done thousands of times without a thought over the last forty-five years.

"Pull the button-hole shirt edge to the left," he said out loud. Completed as if he were moving a lead-weighted sliding door. "Okay, grab the inside of the button with the right hand and aim toward the button slot." The task became complicated as it required working with both hands.

"Now turn the hands as if you're snapping a tooth-pick..." he hesitated, knowing he had come to the tough part and took a breath, as he'd been taught. He was so close. I didn't want him to feel more pressured, so I stood just behind him. I felt my teeth gritting. His shoulders moved with each inhale, one breath, then another without moving his hands. He nervously licked his lips.

Come on, Wilson, you can do it.

I snapped back into the moment. The therapist asked if I had concerns and I expressed that I didn't want to continue to be bounced from one provider to another.

I had pulled every self-defeating and self-medicating habit one could imagine into a life. But it had to be that way. And so, it was.

"You've said writing is the way you express yourself best. Write anything, it's called free writing. If you don't like it, cross-shred it. When you spoke of that night in the bar, I want you to write a letter to a loved one about your thoughts."

"There are almost no traumas," he added, "that are singular or linear."

It was more comfortable to talk about what I remembered about other parts of my life.

"Can we do something here, Jim?" Doc hesitated momentarily, before going on without my answer. "Iraq has given you an education that wasn't covered in Harvard, so I listen, deal?"

If he said one meaningful thing in our time together that helped me, I would be one detail better than I was before seeing him.

Maybe I was speaking with a person who understood a different trauma, domestic violence, rape, or any other hellish experience.

Chapter Three

Munawwar's Letter

I TOLD NOBODY OF MUNAWWAR AND Abdul's letters, but I had time before an appointment with Robert.

I had decided to space reading the letters to process what I'd read—a task which required self-discipline I was unsure I possessed. When it came to Munawwar's letters, the man who gleefully held my family's address that night, I tried to imagine what he would write.

I pulled out the remaining letters, only to find they had all been written by Munawwar, apparently, the more prolific writer of the two men, most likely because he had been detained much earlier that Abdul-Hayy and his father. Or, perhaps Abdul-Hayy was more diligent at sending his letters. It seemed odd Munawwar, for all his letters, only held one addressed to him—from his mother in 2004.

Sayyed outlined Munawwar's family life, written in the margins like afterthoughts, but I read those notes first—they were the details of which I was most curious.

Twenty-Seven at the time of his death, he was born and raised in Hit [pronounced Heet], an ancient, walled city along the Euphrates River in Iraq's al-Anbar Province. For over three millennia, Hit was famous for its naturally occurring bitumen [asphalt] wells, starting as far back as Babylon to the present day.

I looked up Hit's location on a map. Like many other Americans, I'd only heard of the cities in Iraq in which notable battles were fought (that included the majority of Iraq's larger cities). That acknowledgment brought melancholy of so many fascinating history lessons lost.

It turned out a battle in Hit was the first time of two times. Munawwar had become a refugee in the Iraq War. He and his father fled after his mother and sister were killed in crossfire in the streets of Hit.

I thought, *Munawwar had kept his mother's final letter. Maybe all his letters were written to ghosts.*

Munawwar's mother, a biologist, had instilled a love of plants and an appreciation for the Euphrates River's fertile mud. Most entries were written to a woman Sayyed presumed was Munawwar's fiancée Ameena [Honest, Trustworthy]. Munawwar expressed a great love of writing and a passion for biology, particularly heliotropic plants.

The plants, like the sunflower, had leaves that follow the path of the sun in order to maximize their exposure. Something about that daily routine was optimistic and he compared that to having a love for a woman which never fades. *Was his love for Ameena unrequited? Had she also been killed?*

I'd picked up that blistering hot rebar and sought to kill that man who spoke in such poetic subtleties that I was certain he deserved love more than I did. All he had desired, I had run out of my life. I left the letters on a nightstand nearby bed, deliberately wanting them to become a part of the room. I read slowly in a reclining chair when I had a quiet moment, narrating them aloud.

Munawwar lived in an area among the poorest just outside the city limits of Hit, but it came with a splendid view of the Euphrates River and was within sight of both the river and the American airbase in the distance.

Munawwar wrote of a comparison between the relative squalor in which he lived and the ever-expanding amenities of theaters, a pool, and streets lined with fast-food restaurants and outside vendors—all the comforts of home.

Convoy after convoy brought truckloads of air-conditioning ducts and equipment, along with living quarters. That was as close as his community got to the billions of dollars flowing into Iraq which brought frustration and bitterness to those originally supporting the Americans' arrival.

Watching Americans move about confounded Munawwar. Americans, he wrote to his Ameena, must have felt they were too good to swim in the river like the rest of the world. Instead, they chose sterilized swimming pools. They used almost limitless resources to guarantee their comfort, so much so that it exhibited wastefulness. Americans must have never put their hands in the earth from which every beautiful thing he grew and touched had sprouted. They were too separated from the ground to believe in God.

In early 2004, Al-Anbar Province was drawing the attention of American planners, with a major battle looming in the restive city of Fallujah. U.S. Marines virtually surrounded the city, sending families scampering to both Baghdad and nearby cities in the province.

Soon thereafter, insurgents sought to break the siege by launching an attack on Ramadi and war inched closer to Hit. Munawwar's father decided on a move to Husaybah to live with his brother, describing Hit in that time as standing before a firing squad before a wall with no end, no corners to safety.

An attack and killing of seventeen civilian contractors on an American convoy settled the issue. Munawwar and his father fled the city with about twenty other refugees toward an ever-dwindling number of safe havens in al-Anbar Province. If Munawwar's father was confident of anything, it was Americans didn't just respond to an attack but were sure to send a message while they did.

As I read, I thought they may not have been militants at all as Munawwar described having only knives, fishing poles, and a slingshot with which to defend themselves.

Within weeks of their arrival in Husaybah, however, insurgents fleeing Fallujah and Ramadi still seeking to relieve pressure elsewhere, attacked a Marine convoy as they left their base near Husaybah, on the Iraq border with Syria.

After a full day of fierce fighting, reports stated a hundred and fifty insurgents had been killed. Among the civilians killed was Munawwar's father. Munawwar had been identified when he remained with his stricken father. Munawwar couldn't bear for his father to die alone—"A fate," Munawwar wrote, "no human should face."

Munawwar resisted joining the insurgency. From his letters, it appeared his father was his last surviving family member. Munawwar was compelled to join the insurgency in some way and decided to use his knowledge of the Euphrates to help militants transition into Iraq from Syria, other parts of the Middle East, and northern Africa.

I had wondered if something in the letters would reveal his hatred, but Munawwar never used the word. He described what he'd wished for me. As his most bitter enemy, as the person who embodied all he felt compelled to fight against, he had only a few heartbreaking words. That I was raised by parent who loved me as he was loved by his parents. Love was the only way out of war. Otherwise, we were instrument in its perpetuation.

I stopped reading.

Munawwar was detained almost immediately in a sweep of the city after the battle and sent to Camp Bucca in May of 2004. Munawwar described himself as having never even been in a fistfight. With a paper clip, Sayyed had attached an essay as if Munawwar's thoughts should be distinct from Sayyed's translation.

I put the pages down and took a deep breath, my thoughts shifting from any certainty of what that man was capable of writing. His last moments replayed as they had for the last five years. Picking up the pages, I read Munawwar's words.

"I heard once that anything can be taken from me but my thoughts. They were my own. But gradually, I stood in a gentle tide and jumped up to be seen and yelled to be heard. I wanted these things so badly that I was oblivious to landing further from the shore each time, and with every jump, I could only wish I was in the spot I just forfeited. Now, I only have the dirt on which I stand, and the realization that I'm far removed occurs when I refer to myself as "he" as if it were someone else.

"My convictions were borne of good intent, from a minimum of anger and hatred, its posture erect and honorable. The lines I've crossed since are not found on any map. These convictions, like bravery or profound love, lose their meaning in an attempt at defining them—they are only understood by witnesses.

"For example, this freedom word; the uninitiated believe the sacrifice and costs are the same, yet I'm doomed from outliving my shackles and I've subscribed my death in just the hope of a glimpse, while elsewhere the complacent are endowed freedom as a birthright. But blessings are mine, and they are plentiful, for struggles are a privilege,

given only to those who can bear the weight by God. Yet I am still the fearful young tree bending in a howling wind, without the foresight to understand my roots are stronger as a result.

"I remember one teacher explaining that my writing brought a perspective that cannot be taught. But I believe she's mistaken: this trait was indeed taught. I've remembered the smallest kindnesses ever extended to me. I clearly recall my mother serving the humblest of meals, her hands swinging away from the dish, like a magician at the end of a most intriguing trick. Magic indeed.

"My dear God and my dear parents, judge me harshly. Give me no consideration for the choices and judgments I've made in this war, for all goes badly when you do. Please let me live up to the task before me. Lines become blurred or removed entirely. It's when the stakes are highest that rules are hardest to follow and this sad world needs rules, they are meaningless if judgment preempts them, another consequence of war.

"They are coming for me, I know, but I am encouraged. The future has hope if a man like me, with nothing notable in my favor, has attracted the competitive spirit of those who write and rewrite our definitions and our history at their whim. I have reached them. I will continue to tell the stories of extinguished lives, extending them in the annals of history. They will find me, and I will die, but until then, I only long to hear the words of my beloved youngest sister who wrote that my held hand acts as her worry stones when I see her

again. I am loved, it raises me above the outgoing tide and brings me home."

* * *

I put the pages down after reading them aloud three times. I picked out words I had used myself repeatedly and at times I looked away from the page and completed the sentence as if it wasn't necessary to read.

Munawwar seemed to have addressed me and all I represented, trying to understand the convictions of an occupation directed from halfway across the world, at one time describing the occupation as an invasive species of plant. Once they take root, they required more water and grew faster than the plants around them. Even that was not enough, their leaves denied sunlight to the other plants. In Munawwar's words, these invasive species absorb all the natural resources for themselves, throwing everything else out of balance, killing surrounding vegetation and eventually stripping the soil of its nutrients.

The beautiful expressions of both men, Munawwar and Abdul-Hayy, seemed devoid of hate. I'd read them repeatedly to the point of almost memorizing and found an odd comfort in them.

Conflicted, I was going to counseling under the guise of looking for answers while the very possibility of it was terrifying. Some of these perspectives were found in the writing of my rivals, repeated in my mind often enough I wasn't sure whose words belonged to whom. Words were keys to a locked door with no idea where they would lead—possibly that I had become an accessory to my suffering. Maybe that had little to do with Iraq at all.

I'd been relieved that Robert didn't seem to press, at least in the first five sessions, about Iraq. He seemed content to allow me to pick topics. At the same time, I felt pressurized anger just under my skin, just as Cindy used to describe. I felt an odd resentment toward Robert, the one person committed to helping. I found it wasn't uncommon for a traumatized person to direct their anger at their rescuer. I wished I had the sense of purpose I found in the readings of Munawwar's and Abdul-Hayy's letters. I regretted that I hadn't rewarded Cindy for never seeing me as a finished product.

In over five years of therapy, I understood what made me an almost impossible patient. I had expected an almost impossible level of loyalty, to an extent that maybe even my unit was incapable of. A look at one's watch or a shrug at the wrong time and I would never return.

The way I heard words and saw actions were encrypted and only I held the code. I often felt that I only had the energy to speak with one person about Iraq, so it was intentional that I chose carefully.

Was that what war entailed, what I had been trained to believe? Was that blind patriotism? I didn't know what was real, I didn't know who I was. Since Iraq, it had become impossible to discern the passage of time, which folded into experiences until threats were indistinguishable from surrounding patterns of safety. My failings in previous counseling involved my propensity to use whatever words were necessary to avoid having a deeper discussion with Robert. I felt like I'd come from the pressurized depths of the ocean too quickly without being treated for the bends. Divers know the body must have time to be acclimated to such dramatic changes in environment.

After reading Munawwar's letter, I decided to share what I'd read with both Robert and Cindy. That little voice inside me told me to wait until my optimism materialized, but I felt I couldn't wait.

I dialed Cindy's number, hoping she would answer.

The last time I called, my words slurred after front-loading three stiff drinks. Cindy asked me to take a cold shower, sober up, and call again later.

When she answered, she sounded like she didn't recognize me for a few seconds.

"Are you okay, Jim?"

"I'm better than okay. I have to talk to you, Cindy. I think I've made a breakthrough." The phone went silent for the next few seconds. "Cindy?"

"I'm here." Cindy's tone was non-committal, maybe even a little shell-shocked after our last call. In almost a year, there were precious few phone calls that didn't pivot unpredictably from one moment to the next.

I'd been selfish to call. Just once I could have asked her how she was.

"Well, I'll call you back, Cindy, I'm on the way to an appointment. Is everything going okay with you?"

"Yeah, I'm going to work, then to my parents' house."

"Okay... uh, I love you," I said habitually.

Love is a funny thing. As I felt optimistic, I wanted to express grief. I felt thankful we had kept in regular touch, but also so close and distant simultaneously.

"Okay, be safe," Cindy responded as if she believed I said it without a thought, so often over the years that they were just words.

The tide had taken me away from home.

Chapter Four

From Girls Scouts to
Twelve Angry Men

September 2013

"I WISH YOU SAFETY," ROBERT SAID at the beginning of a session about one month after the police incident.

As I listened to the first three words of his statement, I anticipated hearing the word "peace." Since reading Abdul-Hayy's letter, the word safety carried a profound meaning.

Robert had no way of connecting words with Abdul-Hayy's. I had carefully not mentioned what I had read in Abdul-Hayy's letter. I wondered where Abdul-Hayy's mother and sisters were or whether Baba had returned home after Camp Bucca closed on September 17th, 2009.

Robert seemed to have a well-developed knack for drawing stories from grade school years through my Navy career and threadimg to the present. Moments after he had wished me safety, I explained I had no interest in talking. I would have preferred to listen to the clinking and clanging of the radiators in his office.

Robert didn't flinch, making a suggestion he referred to as narrative therapy. As Robert explained it, that would entail talking about my parents, brother Norm, and sister Julie—really, anything I was comfortable talking about. We could just tell what I figured would be like old sea stories, but I suggested he tell me something about himself instead. I asked how he wound up attending Harvard.

"I have another idea, say I had you step into the hall and your mother was sitting in your chair. I explained to her she can only tell me one story. What story do you think she would tell?" Robert shifted the discussion's choice back to me, denying my attempt to talk about him until our time ran out.

I felt disengaged from my memories of a charmed youth.

"Okay." It took me a few seconds to think of a story, a perfectly harmless tale that seemed to have no connection whatsoever to my deployment to Iraq. To Mom, it was an endearing part of our family lore. In visits to Chicago, especially in the company of friends who'd never heard it before, I usually got around to recounting it.

* * *

I had been in the Navy for just over one year when I struck up a conversation with a woman who'd brought her daughter into the clinic for an appointment. The little girl was still in her Girl

Scout uniform. The Navy wife and mother admitted she was having a hard time.

About that time, the Girl Scouts had a new policy that without 24-hour medical coverage, they wouldn't be able to have their three-week summer camp in southern Maine. The costs were prohibitive to have that kind of round-the-clock medical coverage and she was desperately trying to come up with alternatives.

I suggested I could ask the clinic's Corpsmen, all of whom were Emergency Medical Technician (EMT) qualified. The Girl Scout's mom was breathless, and by the end of the afternoon, seven other Corpsmen besides me volunteered.

The camp was set on an island in one of Maine's countless back bays, with a clear view of lobster boats hitched to floating docks that lowered or rose with the tide. Across the water, three tents housed about ten Girl Scouts apiece. A soft, spongy path of brown pine needles led to a log cabin which served as a headquarters, activities center, dining hall, sickbay and medical treatment area, and den mother headquarters. A phone sat on the desk for girls who found their time away from home too much to bear.

On one of my early twenty-four-hour shifts, I walked around the island with the team leaders. The island teemed with screaming sounds of thirty-eight ten-year-old girls.

One of the girls stood on the fringe of the activity and watched. Sometimes when the other girls ran, she ran and skipped alongside them, not quite part of the fun, but perhaps wishing to be. If either group scored, she jumped and celebrated with them. When she looked my way, I smiled but she avoided eye contact, before glancing at me again when she thought I wasn't looking in her direction.

"Poor thing," the Den mother commented, "She's never been away from home. A few of the girls are having such a hard time, but especially her."

One of the girls in the middle of the action fell and scratched her elbow. I sprang to the crying girl's aid with disinfectant, a band-aid, and an Ace elastic bandage. Rebounding in miraculous fashion, the girl rushed back to the middle of the fray, no worse for the wear. The emergency had passed, and I returned to the cabin.

Within minutes, the shy girl who had been on the edge of the activities came in with a friend, apparently acting as the shy girl's spokesman.

"Sir, Gina hurt her right wrist. I think she fell." The two girls exchanged glances. "Yeah, she fell."

"Hmm, let me take a look at that." Gina started to lift her left arm before catching herself and extending her right arm. I grabbed her arm and manipulated her hand downward at the wrist. Did that hurt? Gina shook her head. Negative. Over the next minute, I moved her hand in every conceivable direction and asked if there was any pain. Each time, she shook her head. No. I leaned back on the wooden chair in deep thought. But it still hurts? Gina's lip quivered and, finally, I got an affirmative nod. I brightened.

"I've got it. Just in case, I think I need to wrap your wrist, if that's okay. Do you think that would help?" Gina tried to hide her excitement and glanced at her friend.

"I'm sure that would help," said Gina's spokesperson.

Once the bandage was applied, Gina skipped out the door but her friend, in running after her, suddenly developed a sharp pain in the ankle she twisted. Maybe it happened during the school year, she said. Or maybe not.

Within minutes, a line of girls as far as the eye could see lined up patiently with a full assortment of musculoskeletal injuries, so much so that I had to dash back to the base for more bandages, where my supervisor laughed. I'd been at the camp for about three hours and the walking wounded included an entire Girl Scout pack.

From that day and for the rest of the three weeks, Gina was involved in activities with the others, sang songs by the campfire, helping volunteers cook, hiking. The changes were subtle, but the Girl Scout team leaders noted the change and noticed she hadn't required as many tearful calls home.

* * *

"You like that story yourself, don't you? Why do you think your mother would choose that story?"

"Mom taught us empathy for others was among the most admirable traits." It was an answer that required little thought at all, but I felt a sense of panic. "I mean, I don't think Mom ever said that exactly, we all knew it was how she lived. If we were called considerate, that was the highest compliment."

Robert asked what Gina represented to me. He seemed to believe he was onto something while I insisted it was simply a good story to tell.

Since it was the end of the appointment, my assignment was to reflect on the story but with a twist. I could retell the tale, replacing each of the characters in the story with me. He was curious of the criteria. If I could pick anyone in my life, for example, who would I have selected as my advocate to speak for me when I was unsure how to ask for help?

By the time I walked back to my car, one single thought made me want to run back into Robert's office. I tried to put words to the thought or feeling, so waiting a week wasn't a bad thing. I had trouble putting words to thoughts, but the feelings were revelatory.

Since the deployment, one of the common themes of my struggles was my sense of lost identity. I had described the feeling of not living up to all I had been taught, but that description seemed to lack depth. I wondered if I ever had an identity of my own.

When I first saw the Gina at the Girl Scout camp, she participated alongside but not a part of either group. Like her, I realized the sense of not quite belonging to any one group. Few things were lonelier than remaining so neutral or afraid to commit that I wasn't noticed by either side. I had tried so often to fit in that I felt like tofu, which assumes the taste of that with which it is cooked. And within that context, I could only guess at who I was. My attention would be drawn to others in similar circumstances to see how they had dealt with being an outsider.

"Maybe this sounds different than Gina's story, but I've thought a lot about this over the past week," I said. Telling the story set another thought in motion. Robert listened attentively with hands folded.

* * *

Just before I met Cindy, I asked a different woman out. I saw Liz at work, then left that job for another and ran into her there. Finally, I asked her out, certain she would decline. But Liz said yes, and I meticulously covered everything a perfect first date entails. Piano-side seats to Ramsey Lewis, her favorite. Flowers delivered during dinner at the best fondue place I could find, also her favorite. My truck cleaned and detailed. New clothes and a haircut.

After a great night, I dropped her off at home, even stopping at the twenty-four-hour grocery market for a couple of items. That gave me a few extra minutes to think of my answer to an age-old question. Do I try to kiss her on the first date? There was no algorithm for something with so many variables.

On the way out of the store just after midnight, rain began to fall and I used my jacket to shield her from the rain, put the groceries in the truck, and hesitated before moving to return the cart.

"Just leave the cart, someone will come grab it."

I stood there in the rain for a second, thinking someone else would have to make a trip to the cart, then back. Then I ran the cart back to the rack in the front of the store and sprinted back.

Drenched by the time I got to the truck, I got in and noticed her smiling, before laughing at the torrential downpour.

After a few dates, she admitted she had fallen in love that first night in my moment of hesitation. After all my preparation and planning had failed, it was all I could have done just to be myself and act intuitively, and at that moment, she found a quality she sought beyond my ability to plan.

I feared the person unsure of what to do, or which side to take, was as definitive as my endearing views of Gina at the Girl Scout Camp. Or Cindy at that ridiculous stop sign. Or the looks of Ab-dul-Hayy and Munawwar. I had somehow failed everyone, unable to take a stand. I felt in Iraq I'd been given a choice of two elements of character so closely related, protection of my family and behaving in a humane manner. Choosing one meant a character split I thought was unresolvable.

I admitted to Robert I had a great deal of affection for Gina's Girl Scout camp story. Throughout my life, I seemed to notice people who figured things out somehow, people like me. I'd witnessed cer-tain bravery in her endearing humanity and I felt warmness. Maybe if I contributed to a transition from the fringe into a group for Gina, maybe that meant I was okay. Even if nobody noticed, I felt that constituted belonging.

Robert had spoken of finding a purpose through activity, like returning to school. By midweek, I had enrolled in a college course just to get used to the school environment again, a class entitled "Attention and Perception," about how we perceived the world around us and, in miraculous fashion, how often and how easily our senses could have been fooled. In the world of magic, any trick took advantage of what the audience was allowed to believe and what the performer knew.

As a class assignment, we watched the movie *Twelve Angry Men*. The movie told of a jury deliberating over a murder case in which the evidence necessary to convict was all but irrefutable. Except for one juror, who over the course of the movie, brilliantly changed the minds of each juror one at a time.

In the end, the man accused of murder was acquitted. Eleven people with the obvious and easy answers were overcome by the one person brave enough to ask critical questions.

Robert had asked about picking an advocate. Maybe he expected I would name myself.

"I guess you, you would be my spokesman."

Robert nodded. I was certain he'd heard enough over the last dozen sessions that I had good options within my family, but he didn't pursue it, deciding it was more important to ask what I wanted him to ask for on my behalf.

I would have asked him to advocate for me to be safe and likable. "Safe and likable" probably seemed like an odd pairing.

The present sense of identity, or lack of one, seemed disconnected to any past expectations. If I hadn't lived up to those ideals for whatever reason, Robert wondered why it wasn't a relief to have had a chance to reset my identity, almost as if anything were possible. I was freed from that burden.

By the end of our reenactment, some new ideas cropped up in a cascade of memories. In one conversation I expressed one of the worst punishments from my parents was to have felt I disappointed them. The fear, even paralyzing dread, of disappointment was a recurring theme but the resolutions were equally prevalent, if less obvious.

I'd witnessed something profound in the discussion. I had observed Gina and felt connected to some facet of myself, Cindy at that silly stop sign, Munawwar or Abdul-Hayy in their final moments. I hadn't considered that Liz, or anyone else, had seen something in me that was lovable, a miraculous awareness.

The satisfaction the story brought was a possible acknowledgment of a legacy. I was satisfied with the only inkling of me a century from then would be a thought, with no indication of its source, of a kindness disguised and folded into the characteristics around it, virtually indistinguishable from the rest.

Jim Enderle

I had valued moments while observing others which seemed irrefutable. But at that moment, when Munawwar's life hung in the balance, my response was dictated only by who I really was.

Chapter Five

Answering the Right Question

November 2013

T HERE WERE SOME TREES HANGING onto copper-col-
ored leaves after a brilliant fall foliage season.
In one letter to his fiancé, Munawwar had described
plants as having a variety of circadian rhythms.
For some, a daily one, as evidenced by their closing up nightly only to open again each morning.
In the fall, most plants drifted into hibernation
at one end of the annual rhythm. Munawwar rec-
onciled human beings and world history through
the lens of the plant world and found comfort in
its consistency and order. He would have been
astounded by a New England autumn.

I had progressed with abstaining from alcohol and
painkillers for the previous two months. Robert
reasonably connected my love of reading to a feeling of investment in my own well-being. Alcohol,
painkillers, and other self-medicating behaviors
that made emotional and physical pain bearable
were exchanged with activities that involved any

combination of motion, sunlight, and fresh, crisp November air.

I finally applied Robert's sleep hygiene concept, which included a number of elements and required an investment on my part. At the top of the human body's miracles was its circadian rhythm. Robert had introduced a multi-pronged approach to sleep difficulties, starting with mindfulness as a mitigating tool.

Darkness came to represent danger and alarm while during the day, nothing was as it appeared. I saw bombs behind posters, in hollowed trees, dead animals, and litter on the side of the road. A change in soil color indicated freshly dug IEDs, which Robert countered with planted aloe plants.

While Robert might be thankful for overpasses eliminating the need for a traffic stop, I saw an ambush. I was suspicious of third part nationals after Munawwar obtained my family's address, while Robert felt their exposure to Americans would humanize us in their minds.

That countered a visual concept introduced by trauma with a new association for discolored earth. Memories of the past skipped directly to the seeming invariability of the future. By practicing Robert's mindfulness exercises and staying in the present moment, I felt a safety in my environment I had forgotten was possible.

Scheduling a nightly routine included each of sleep hygiene components and was a natural activity for a twenty-year military veteran. Starting at 8:00 PM, I dimmed lights throughout the house, showered, turned off all electronics, and either read or wrote until bedtime at 10:00 PM.

My bedroom had a soft light that I turned on earlier. The room was only used for sleeping and maybe reading the last few pages of my latest book.

My unit hadn't been taught to alleviate the unique experience of combat when it no longer required. The very trait that made us trusted, productive members of our unit had been keeping me awake in my own home.

"I want you to know I appreciate your investment in your well-being," Robert said. I thought at first it was just a joke and let out a half-laugh snort.

The medications I took did not stop the brain from revealing images it had conjured in the most alarming way. Robert believed there were messages within the details. Without medications, I was tasked with writing every element, including colors, how I felt, and if I remembered smells or touch.

* * *

In one recurring nightmare, I was in the middle of a rocket attack. I ran toward an area with a large group of people, congregated beneath white-colored tents. I yelled for them to move to a safer area, but before I arrived, an explosion rocked the area and I heard panicked and agonizing screams.

Next, in the fragmented nightmare, was a funeral. I stood and wept among the mourners and listened to the eulogies—many dedicating their lives to the memories of those lost. Others started non-profits to benefit those who'd lost limbs or were paralyzed. Some raised funds for the children who'd been orphaned by the senseless violence. I wondered how I had managed to attend funeral services for the Connecticut Newtown massacre of December in 2012. At the end of the service, I realized I was in my camouflaged uniform and went to hug one of the parents whose child had been killed. I wondered about the appropriate thing to say.

To my horror as I approached, I saw I was in the middle of an Iraqi town and the casualties were the result of American bombs. Almost ready to embrace the bereaved parents, the mother saw me and shrieked and pointed at me. All the attendees, dozens of Iraqis, turned toward me.

"He is the start of our suffering. Him! He threw the rock."

The mob of angry people ran toward me. As I turned to run, I found myself in a walled city with the crowd closing in on me. I was tired and lost. Then I hit a dead end and was surrounded by high walls. I awakened before the crowd murdered me.

* * *

After describing the recurring nightmare as descriptively as possible, we went element-by-element and documented the emotions and their corresponding meanings. In one instance, I wrote of two times in the dream I felt particularly fearful: When the mother identified me as the man personally responsible for the attack which killed her son, and when the angry throng had trapped me in the walled, dead-end alleyway.

"Which time between them brought more terror for you?"

"When the woman identified me. It's not even close." I said, suddenly realizing that the look of a mother who'd lost her son at my hands scared me more than being killed by a crowd bent on revenge.

"Why do you think that is?" Robert asked. He twirled his yellow pencil in his right hand.

"Looking at that woman, that mother, it was being held responsible to another human being. I think the way she looked at me was especially haunting." I said, with the sudden urge to test how sturdy the arms of the chair were. I gave a gentle tug.

"How do you think it compares to the look of your own mother at the airport. You also described that as haunting." Robert said, tapping the pencil on its eraser.

"Her looking into my eyes was about the only detail I could describe clearly. She said I threw that rock that started everything. I believed in the dream that I did."

With the dream, I also felt times of high energy during times of moving purposefully, cycled with deep exhaustion. The tiredness came in periods of mourning, when grief overwhelmed all else. I described running a marathon, and an innate ability to relax during exertion, and in the natural cycle of running, a second wind always felt imminent. Every breakthrough was another step toward achievement, feeling completely spent was not unnerving to me.

Our talk of nightmares shifted to what I felt the revelations meant for my present life. My first thought was of my son, Alfonso.

One of the treatments to help ground a child on the autism spectrum was something called joint compressions or activity on something like a trampoline to relieve the accumulated energy. The idea was that built-up force manifested in overwhelming physical energy and a thought-process racing too quickly to grasp.

"I think I should start to exercise again," I said. Resilience was found in those moments where I kept trying, when all my energy had been spent. Each time, I seemed capable of more than I believed.

"Move a muscle, change a thought," Robert said, using one of Alcoholics Anonymous' oldest slogans.

There was an unspoken benefit to long-distance running. It wasn't unusual for me, in a run of more than ten miles to spontaneously burst into tears as I ran—which occurred in every marathon I ran. Crying, for me, was a solitary enterprise.

"Let's talk about determination. I believe you have exactly the same level of dedication as before." Robert said.

My first instinct was, that was a debate I could win. Certainly, to me, that was untrue.

"What do you think as you hear me say that?"

I didn't think what he said was true, that one's determination was likely decided by the circumstances. Robert gave credit where it was due but had two questions.

He asked how I had just spoken about the cycles of a marathon and times that I had all but decided to stop. But something just kicked in, he said, and I decided to keep running. Multiple times in the course of a marathon, I would decide I'd had enough but didn't stop. Each time, I confirmed I was capable of more than I'd imagined. Robert's assignment was to think of moments along that theme.

"Isn't your commitment to be prompt each week for our appointments along the lines of running daily?"

I hadn't answered but supposed it was true.

Secondly, Robert had another analogy and gave me a week to think about it. Wasn't it at least possible that I did have that level of determination and self-discipline throughout the time since Cindy left for Florida?

"There's no way. No. I don't see how that's possible." I shook my head, not able to see how the person who had enlisted in the military and had worked within its rigid structures and rules, was comparable to the raging, drinking, isolated person I had become.

The second part of the assignment started with a statement. My self-discipline and determination had indeed been equal. Robert's reconciliation of those seemingly opposed two phases of my life was a description of an auto-immune disease, where my own cells couldn't tell the difference between good and bad cells and turned on itself, and its own innate design became the enemy.

I nodded, remembering another of Munawwar's entries.

In the plant world, some plants were known to commit tactical suicide when infected, killing the part that prevented the infection from killing the rest of the plant. It was a natural process similar to shedding leaves in autumn, or the cycle of forest fires. Periodically, it was the natural order of life for the forest to burn to the ground, its ashes becoming the finest fertilizer for the birth of the next woodland.

* * *

The next appointment, Robert told the story of a Native American medicine man. When a tribe member was ill or troubled, he approached the medicine man, who asked the series of four questions.

"When was the last time you felt such joy that you danced?" Robert spoke slowly, enunciating each word. "Secondly, when was the last time you felt no inhibition and you sang out loud?"

I nodded with each question.

"Third," Robert held up three fingers for emphasis. "When was the last time you felt comfortable in the sweet territory of silence?"

Robert waited. I had no answers for each of the questions so far.

"Fourth, when did you cease to be enchanted by the stories around you?"

Depending upon the answers to the questions, the medicine man formulated a plan with little regard to symptoms or any diagnosis. Robert asked me to tell a story that would answer any of the medicine man's questions.

I recounted the story of a Vietnam veteran named Pete who I met at a veterans' luncheon. Before Pete had been drafted, he couldn't spell or find Vietnam on a map. By the end of his second one-year tour, he hated the place. It was hotter than Hades. When it did rain, it came sideways in sheets. Pete saw insects there larger than anything he'd seen in his native Brooklyn, NY, outside of a zoo. The foliage was so thick, he leaned against it as if it were a brick wall. Vietnam had no redeeming qualities for Pete.

The Army went to surrounding communities under the pretext of offering security and gaining enemy movement intelligence. One time, Pete went because a team member became ill. Before that, he'd only observed Vietnamese villages from a distance, barely able to view smoke from a pit in the middle of a series of huts.

Moving alongside the first lieutenant and the unit's interpreter, they moved into the village, where a young woman, about Pete's age, stepped out of one of the huts. He stared longer than was polite, but she was beautiful and graceful.

She looked away, but just as Pete looked back toward the lieutenant, he thought she may have glanced back at him. Between them, their eyes danced like those of two young people. He noticed his posture straightened and his stomach instinctively pulled in. Pete wondered if she walked by a few times with nothing in her hands was because she may have thought he was attractive.

Immediately, Pete's command sensed a whole new *esprit de corps*. He offered to participate in any movement going near that village. Perhaps they'd exchange a glimpse. Even more so, their eyes might meet. He had heard her speak that first day and Vietnamese sounded romantic, even poetic. He developed a love for the variety of greens in Vietnam and was curious to taste the food and asked an interpreter if he could learn some rudimentary conversational Vietnamese.

On each of his three trips into the village, they exchanged glances at a distance and she eventually smiled shyly. It wasn't appropriate for Pete to approach the young woman without consent from the village elder.

Unable to communicate, Pete harvested lemongrass, ginger, cinnamon, and Thai basil leaves in a wicker basket. With the herbs, Pete wrote in imperfect Vietnamese, "*Toi chuc ban binh an,*" Which translated to "I wish you peace." He left it in the middle of the village and, as Pete's team pulled away from the last visit to the village, he saw the young woman walking with a shy wave of her hand toward the basket.

* * *

Robert and I sat there in thought. I thought I'd learned everything possible from Pete's story. I felt I had told a story which answered some of the medicine man's questions.

"I love that story," Robert said. "I would like you to tell the story of your convoy to Baghdad, with the blindfolded man."

I saw little connection between Pete's story and mine, but I relented and told an abbreviated of the man I allowed to keep his daughter's picture.

"Set the story for me this time. Do you remember how you felt that night?"

"I was tired of Iraq. Even camel spiders and scorpions seemed miserable there." I said, looking at my hands on the arms of the chair. "You know what I remember now? The man's daughter wore a dress that maybe had been new when she put it on, but I imagine a bombing came right after and her yellow dress was dirty."

I recounted the whole story as Robert listened, only occasionally bobbing his head. As I finished, he asked, "Why did you let him keep the picture, Jim?"

"I felt sorry for him," I said with barely a thought.

The obvious answer for why detainees wore blindfolds was so they couldn't communicate with each other. I ignored how the detainee had communicated in a different way with me.

"I'd like you to think a little deeper, Jim. I think there's more."

A blindfold is not a thin veil, but a brick wall. Looking at the humanity of detainees on a tight schedule was a distraction we couldn't afford.

As the line of detainees walked up to the steep ramp and into the back of a C-130 Hercules transport plane, I had watched the man, only detained for stripping generators of metals to feed his family. At the end of the line, he tried to regain his composure after his begging for his picture.

Stepping into a lighted area, he white-knuckled the baggie. When a man in front of him lost his balance, he had a choice of letting go of the picture and breaking his fall or holding that precious picture and landing face-first on the rough surface of the ramp. A second later, his forehead thudded on the ramp, a detainee fell on top of him. As much as he could, he held the picture aloft.

"When I saw him fall with his precious picture, I felt I made the correct decision. You should have seen him." I thought of losing the picture I had carried of Cindy and how precious it was.

"Good. But that didn't answer my question. Walk around if you have to. Go get a cup of coffee. Then let's talk." Robert leaned forward.

I was at a loss for words. He seemed to be looking for a specific answer. I looked out the window for a long minute and leaned on what I'd learned from Pete's story.

I explained the beautiful young Vietnamese woman came to represent humanity which obliterated Pete's sense of otherness. In the middle of all the death, destruction, pain, and human suffering had soared above the worst circumstances we could imagine. One woman with whom he'd never spoken had changed his entire perspective of Vietnam. It had taken one look into the eyes of "those people."

"Very good." I thought Robert might applaud but he stopped short. "That is, if your friend Pete were here for counseling. I want you to think about it, take as long as you need."

Robert was pressing me. I asked to walk down the hall and smell the fresh varnish on the new hallway baseboards. Suddenly, an idea struck. I quickly walked back into the office and sat down, leaning forward on the edge of the chair. I held one finger up, pointing with a wave.

"What..." No words came out. I felt a tear run alongside my nose.

"Take your time, Jim, as much as you need."

I breathed deeply, then slowly exhaled. The sound of the breath trembled.

"Maybe he was a person who had done something unforgivable, so much so that he couldn't picture his daughter without the aid of a picture. And as hard as he'd stare at it, he couldn't hold that dear image in his heart."

I hadn't fully realized how sad I had been when Cindy's image faded. I wouldn't wish that on any husband or father in the world.

Robert was moved and ran his index fingers along the bottoms of his eyes.

"Maybe he was a guy like me, just trying to be worthy of his suffering, to find his way home."

Chapter Six

Forgiveness 101

December 2013

IT SEEMED TO ME THINGS were going so well that I'd decided to contact Cindy. She'd been non-committal, my 'I love you' just hung on the phone lines between Connecticut and Florida. I felt I understood her hesitance and wanted to finish our telephone call from the previous week.

I wanted Cindy to say she loved me and if she said it, it could only mean she truly did. Besides, there were a number of updates of which she needed to be aware. I hadn't had a drink in four months, could walk up the stairs and not be winded, and had proven to be a good client under a good therapist.

I dialed Cindy after work and asked if she'd had a chance to unwind or if I should call back. She had stopped by Trader Joe's and Pollo Tropical on her way home and was in for the night.

"Look, I'd really like to talk about something."

I'd been receptive to anything that seemed necessary to work things out. All the responsibility I had in dismantling my family could be erased if we could just work everything out.

Cindy and I had been married for almost twenty-two years and had been through many rough times, I told her. And many of them we would sit together in a room wondering if that was it, the one obstacle we couldn't scale together. That struggle had been the toughest challenge and after eleven months apart, I was beginning to see my way.

One call, she felt like that woman I hadn't yet met back when we met. I asked if she remembered the time I asked her to say something in Spanish, anything.

"That was one of the most beautiful things I'd ever heard," I told her, asking what she said. Cindy said she didn't know what to say so she read the contents from a recipe she was going to try. I asked if she remembered how hard we laughed.

"Yeah, I remember. That was funny." But Cindy's tone was tense.

I asked why we couldn't try to work things out. I felt there were so many reasons to be optimistic.

A long, uncomfortable moment of quiet followed.

"I never had a say in the way things unfolded." As Cindy's words were spoken, I easily remembered times she pressed me for something to share.

"Those were my questions last year."

My chest tightened. Even though Cindy was correct, I resisted admitting it. It was a habit developed after Iraq. I had accused Cindy of being manipulative in order to get me to talk about the deployment when we'd had those conversations before.

"Your answer was always about me having to leave as if I were the problem."

To admit she was right would negate anything I had said previously, and I felt a blaming finger pointed at me. I had forfeited my relationship in exchange for a sense of protection. I often thought that protection was of my family. Maybe it had more to do with protecting me.

"Okay, here we go with the 'always' and 'nevers.'" I retorted before catching myself. I followed the old script, expecting a different result. I felt Cindy's implication was that I'd taken the easiest path I could find, and the response burst out. "I'm sorry. Cindy, I didn't mean... Damn it!"

"I'm not listening to this. You haven't changed a bit. The same old Jim!" Upset, Cindy wanted to hang up while I begged her to hear me out.

I had been facing my struggles head-on and I probably would have those deficits for the rest of my life. But I knew that I loved her and wanted to be a family again. She waited but I was on a short leash.

"I mean, what do I have to do to have my life back?" I asked. "I feel like I will be swimming upstream for the rest of my life. I'll never outlive the mistakes I've made and the flaws I have.

What do I have to do? Tell me and I'll do it!" I was willing, at that moment, to negotiate talking about the war. I had to be willing to do something different.

Just in the time it took to ask that question, two profound thoughts occurred to me.

For one, the way Cindy phrased that sentence, maybe she was hoping the progress I had made was real. Secondly, I had made myself the center of the universe and determined what was necessary. When I felt I had suffered an appropriate amount of pain, it seemed fair to me to expect forgiveness from others. But I, as the perpetrator or abuser, did not have a right to establish the criteria for forgiveness.

I tried to express that to Cindy, who had given me a lot of latitude in explaining myself.

"You know what I've learned, Cindy? You're right. If I still believe I'm the person who decides I've done enough to be forgiven, then I still have a lot of work to do." I felt as though it was a breakthrough. "You're right."

Cindy waited for a second, gathering her nerve and apparently realizing the words she thought wouldn't sound as well out loud.

"What is it?" I asked, feeling a cold sweat and tightness in my chest. It was the undeniable sense of impending doom. In twenty-one years of marriage, my instincts had improved.

"Jim, I think we should file for divorce. You know I don't just throw that word out there." Cindy said.

I felt dizzy. In all our arguments, our separation, everything, the word divorce had never been spoken aloud. Even the night Cindy left, the idea had never crossed my mind. How stupid could I have been to put us at that intersection?

"Let's just end this, so maybe we can forge something else together. Let's just rip off the bandage and put this behind us. We've ruined everything." Cindy's voice had been steeled by months of reflection in Florida. She had every right and I wanted to show some respect for her thoughts. It was that magician's advantage again. I knew what I had allowed her to believe over what she hoped to see.

"You're the boys' father, you'll always be in my life. You know how much I care about and love you."

Somehow, I'd believed we would be married long enough to see these struggles as a rough. I had placed my boundaries around my experience, and Cindy had done the same thing. My sadness stemmed from my desire to figure the deployment out for myself, with the assumption that Cindy wouldn't do the same. If I'd demanded the ability to resolve things, it was impossible to begrudge her. The idea had only hit me then. I'd been so blind.

I could imagine her phone was moved far from her ears, expecting anger, but I didn't answer. Part of me just heard that she loved me, but I thought mostly of how tragic it was that she had to be 1500 miles away to speak without fear of me. It was still stressful. I could tell by the exhale I heard on the phone.

There were only two times I'd heard that exhale—upon deaths of Munawwar and Abdul-Hayy and, apparently then, as I had inflicted a final blow to our marriage.

"Can you understand why I would say this?" Cindy asked softly. I remained silent.

Right in the middle of the discussion with Cindy, I thought of touching Abdul-Hayy's father's shoulder in the worst moment of his life, as his only son died. He understood and reciprocated. Abdul-Hayy's father and Cindy were right. Everything that needed to be said had been verbalized.

"Yes, I understand." I fell silent, purposely leaving her more uncomfortable in the space between words. I realized how manipulative that was. "I understand. Okay, I'll do it."

There was a long moment of quiet. We both stifled our sniffs. It was too much to absorb.

I had asked for too much for too long. I had told people I wanted Cindy to feel healthy and walk with a bounce, but maybe that was all talk. Now, I hoped I could not make her feel badly for thinking of her self-determination for once among the few times in our twenty-two-year marriage. She'd been terrified of me. What courage it took? More bravery than I saw when I looked in the mirror.

I must have felt it was a part of our marital contract. I had used manipulation to prevent Cindy from leaving earlier, then used other forms to arrange for her to leave. In the meantime, she found it difficult to escape her duty to the family. She was trapped.

At that moment we were both free. I hadn't been that relieved since Cindy left.

If I had said that out loud, one could reasonably conclude I was not in love with her, but it was the opposite. In the absence of any way out of my spiral, I recognized how trauma had a special ability to turn anything inside out.

"Are you okay, Jim? Do you know that I love you? I always will."

"I love you, too, Cindy. I'm okay." I felt pressure building in my chest that I'd never felt before, in an inverse proportion to any relief I felt. Explode from the inside, scream at Cindy, curse God, cry, destroy something, overdose, or drink. I had no idea what that pressure meant. "Well, I guess I'm going to hang up. We can talk more later about what to do."

"I don't want anything from you. I don't want to do anything that would hurt you. Do you believe that?"

"Yes, I believe that. Maybe this is for the better. I love you and I would never complicate your life. I'll talk to you tomorrow?"

"Okay, I love you."

And with that, we hung up.

I sat numbly on the edge of the bed with no clue of what would happen within seconds. After a few minutes, I slowly got up. Oddly, I was back in Iraq, walking through the rocket and mortar attack in a straight line. It made no difference if I were to duck, either the mortar landed on my head or it missed. Running or caring if I lived faded into the night, the ground quivered under my feet. My fate had no connection to my will.

I slowly walked down the stairs and, without hesitating, walked into the back room, calmly turning on the light. There it was, the damn teapot which had been sitting innocently since before Cindy left. *Innocently haunting me is more like it.* Picking it up, I burst through the door which had uncooperatively closed, knocking it loose from its hinges as if I had superhuman strength. Fragments from the door landed in a couple of places in the room. Whipping the sliding glass door open to the back deck, I ran and launched the teapot, hoping it would crash on the street a couple hundred feet down the hill.

Hyperventilating, I grabbed all my recently washed uniforms, anything Navy related, and threw them into an olive-green seabag, so furiously that I fell to the basement floor. Half-running to the car, I threw it onto the back seat and started the car, making it roar and squeal as I'd unnecessarily floored the gas pedal before I slammed it into gear.

A few miles down the road, with my face clenched like a fist, I threw the uniforms into a dumpster as if I wanted to dent the dumpster's sides. I picked up the seabag and spiked it to the bottom of the dumpster twice, anger spewed like a steam valve, before bursting into tears. The Navy had cost me everything.

I returned home, consciously slowing down to avoid a ticket.

Back in the house, I walked through the living room—which had a bottle of wine. I stopped. If ever there was a reason to imbibe—I thought of how drowning my sorrows would mitigate the enormous pain. Strangely, I picked up the bottle and held it before I threw it off the front porch. It crashed on the street, the momentum of the shards carrying into the shrubbery. I'd turned a corner.

I knew I had a large number of options. Suicide crossed my mind for a moment but passed quickly. I honored Cindy's honesty and the only purpose I could think for ending my life was to freeze her decision in time for the rest of her life, so much different than my thoughts of being honorable and lovable. That was not addition by subtraction and the thought's manipulative nature repulsed me, yet each microsecond seemed to announce another miracle.

At least for that night, I didn't give in to vices that held me in place and without movement.

I had followed the therapeutic design, but medications were not enough. Exercise wasn't enough. Therapy, where I faced adversity in a clinical setting, wasn't enough. Even the recent feeling of safety in my own body wasn't enough. Dream and nightmare reconstruction fell short. Suicide intervention wasn't enough. There was something missing.

Once again, I'd gone through the checklists of life and had hoped I would get full credit, yet I'd fallen flat. Making progress and some level of understanding wasn't enough. For some reason, I still stood there, in the ashes of my marriage, feeling something possible in the worst of moments.

I thought of something Abdul-Hayy had written, and once I decided to continue ahead, I had suddenly become worthy of my suffering. I had hoped for that chance and only through my failings was I given that opportunity.

I reflected on how I'd spent a lot of my energy toward staying the same and wasted all that energy. Staying the same was an invariable slide backward. I had known some people who seemed to be exactly the same person throughout their lives—what discipline. Maybe they had failed much less than I did or were less flawed.

Using the words of others, even words as beautiful as the *Desiderata* or Shakespeare just didn't carry the weight second-hand. I needed my own words again.

But another catalyst was like nothing else I'd experienced in our marriage. After twenty-two years, both of us knew the buttons to push to get a reaction or make the other feel something.

Why hadn't I tried to make Cindy feel bad, to attempt to keep her down when she finally found her voice? If it were done right, I knew she would have felt, regardless of everything, as though the separation were her fault and her decision. I could have relieved myself of the responsibility, even though in my heart the truth was clear, guaranteeing my continued downward spiral.

It was the moment I had prayed for, but not in the form I'd imagined. I realized that even if we didn't get back together, I would still forge ahead. I didn't want her to feel guilty.

That was the moment something changed.

I didn't even want to tell her what I thought because I thought it might be manipulative. She had been through enough. It came and went in a flash—the bravest thing I had ever done. Bravest of all was that I was the only person who knew what I had done.

For once, I understood and respected the decision of whether we tried to make amends again would also be a part of her decision, and I extended that to her. I was able to show that I respected her decision without manipulation. And that, in turn, might've provided a chance.

I had to be genuine enough to say nothing of my intentions. Even speaking with her about that, I felt would be manipulative.

Whenever I was called a hero, it only caused even more of a disparity between what one perceived and what I knew. I felt more alone. If my family loved me unconditionally, I felt undeserving.

* * *

In our next session, Robert suggested expanding my sense of safety, which included verbalizing my thoughts. Joking, he would guess I didn't even sing alone in my car to a favorite song if I felt I might sing off-key. He was right.

His challenge was for me to write a thought, free writing was what he called it, just getting thoughts on a page, followed by reading it out loud when I was in the house. Loudly and confidently. Then, if I didn't like what I wrote, I could shred it. The most important part of the exercise was to verbalize my thoughts aloud.

In fact, Robert was a good advocate for one to enter counseling. One of his few stories was about being able to lift a car, all four tires just on sheer strength alone. A person exhausted themselves trying to no avail.

Then the idea of a pulley was introduced, and suddenly, with a fraction of the effort, one was able to lift the car.

Therefore, he suggested, therapy was the psychological equivalent of mechanical advantage. First, however, one must decide that speaking with some honesty and the level of trust that entailed, was paramount.

Chapter Seven

Imagine That

December 2013

B ETWEEN MY ROUTINE BASED ON mindfulness and my elimination of most maladaptive responses, I began to feel safe in my own body, even becoming aware of things immediately around me.

Sounds in my house announced themselves like a friendly visitor or passed through my awareness politely enough to notify without alarm. If I stayed focused on that, I felt the same way as the first week after Cindy and I bought our house: It was like a summer home.

Robert focused on conditioned deployment associations through assigned activities like gardening, which brought a new association to different shades of newly dug dirt.

I focused on the feeling and smell of my hands in the earth. Eventually, one of my raspberry bushes bore fruit. The turning of the leaves upward, toward the sun, was noticeable over a couple of hours as the middle of the day arrived.

Observing nature was immensely gratifying as if I contributed. I understood how Munawwar, or anyone, loved the idea of nurturing something, and with that, I thought again of our initial meeting. I would've never imagined a sense of fondness for someone who may have killed me if our fates were reversed.

In one therapy session, I said I felt haunted with an ominous feeling whenever I left my house. Shopping was stressful. There was no order, and once I abandoned my cart and moved with my back to the shelves of groceries. I wasn't able to determine how one could be invisible and yet karma's favorite target.

"I think your situational awareness is one of your biggest assets," Robert ventured. "Have you ever had someone say you're a bit of a dreamer?"

I almost laughed out loud. My fourth-grade teacher, Mrs. Artz, dubbed me "Forgetful James," and the name stuck, especially with my older brother Norm, who kept the nickname in use until high school. In a close second was "Walter Mitty," James Thurber's fictional daydreamer who envisioned the mundane activities of his life as heroic and courageous acts.

"How about this, Jim? In some of your stories, you added a lot of detail. You're an observer, I think. When was the last time you looked at clouds in the sky and saw the Alps?"

It had been a long time. For the most part, whatever capacity I had was spent scouring the area for threats or sensing a person behind me in the cereal

aisle. Safety seemed necessary for creativity. I
had begun to write at home and even thought of
taking piano lessons again after almost forty years.

"I don't know what you mean, Robert." I looked
at the counselor whose eyebrows looked like they
may have raised cartoonishly off his forehead
with excitement.

"You don't miss anything, right?" If Robert had
planned it, he did a good job of sounding spontaneous. But the therapist had a plan. I couldn't
do much about a sense of danger being a part of
my new wiring.

By using the mindfulness I'd been practicing, I
could leave my house, just stop and take note of
what I'd see. He asked me to write down or describe every type of flower or tree I saw. There
were always birds on Mamacoke Island. I felt he
wanted me to take stock of the positivity about me.

It was a great idea and easy to oblige, another
breakthrough. A person in a world without enough
safety for imagination and creativity quickly lost
hope. Maybe that was what had happened to me.
My mind filled in any missing piece of a scene
with an imminent threat. It could just as well be a
butterfly farm if that's what I practiced choosing
as a default.

I looked around the room. On the huge mahogany
desk was a Charlie Brown Christmas Tree with a
red ornament pulling the top of the tree endearingly
to the right. There were cards along the windows
just above the clinging and clanging radiators.

In just over a week, I was going to fly to Chicago to see my parents and family. I was happy both Alfonso and Lorenzo were there. Alfonso was happiest he could spend his birthday on the 15th of December in Chicago.

A blizzard was forecast on the day I was scheduled to fly from Providence, Rhode Island to O'Hare.

* * *

I had one final appointment the day before I flew home to see my family. On the way to the appointment, I found myself driving up north from my home. It was a ride Cindy and I used to take at least every weekend. That part of Connecticut was everything Chicago and Miami were not.

Passing the town hall, which was about half the size of my six-flat apartment building, the road weaved through scenic back bays and hills, the smell of pine fresh after precipitation. The hills gave the road the feel of a roller coaster. At the apex of various hills, one could imagine being a bird, soaring high above with its choice of spectacular views and the freedom to raise and lower elevation for the best sunlit effects.

Robert was in a festive mood, ready to head up to his family in Newburyport, Massachusetts, and asked if I'd done my homework, which was to spend a one-hour slot daily doing something creative: writing, drawing, or anything from a book of imagery exercises.

"I'm curious to see which of the activities you chose."

"Well, I went on a date," I spoke soft enough that Robert asked me to repeat it before asking how it had gone.

The truth was I had gone out on an imaginary date, recalling the thrill of meeting a person when everything was new and within the realm of possibility. I admitted I had gone through the day of anticipation like those days long ago, in my flow chart comfort zone, thinking of contingencies that might interfere with making a good impression. Meanwhile, my "date" was nervously anticipating the same thing.

"Tell me about your 'date,'" Robert asked, without the slightest hint of mockery.

I'd imagined her as a person who was intrigued with me and felt an immediate curiosity—that mysterious thing called chemistry. Maybe, I thought, if I told my story the right way it would have a better ending. During the date, I hoped she found a kindred spirit and I felt honored to have earned her trust. I imagined trust as the best possible outcome.

"With women," I felt the need to explain, "trust is more difficult to earn than love."

Robert nodded and wondered what happened next, and I recounted going for that same drive over that hilly, winding road, before heading home and passing the town hall building I'd passed on the way to my appointment.

Just past the town hall was a house that went all out every Christmas. Multi-colored lights practically covered the house, with a sleigh carrying

Santa Claus driving reindeer somehow attached to the roof of his gray wooden A-frame home.

I admitted to Robert my imaginary date had been a recollection of one Christmas season with Cindy.

In previous years, we parked in front of the house, amazed at the artful decorations. After about four or five consecutive Christmas seasons, there were no lights and Cindy remarked they were late decorating that year.

The next night she asked to go to a store just past the house, as if she didn't want to admit to checking up on the decorations, and again the next day. I'd been afraid to even mention it as we drove by, but the lot looked dark and lonely. I was afraid the owner had passed away.

Robert was still engrossed with the story with a kind, appreciative smile.

On December 23rd of that year, after driving by maybe seven nights in a row for various reasons, the house was decorated and seemingly lit up all of Montville, Connecticut. Light snow fell just before we went to the store, yet again.

"The lights! The lights! He decorated! Stop the car!" Cindy screamed, and before the car came to a complete stop, she leapt from the car right there in the snowfall and spontaneously danced some combination of an Irish jig, salsa, and a bunch of other dances which hadn't been invented yet, unable to contain her joy.

I got out and danced with her and Cindy talked me into knocking on the door so she could thank the man for making her Christmas complete. Anyone who knew Cindy knew she would designate eleven-and-a-half months of the year as Christmas season.

The homeowner answered and was overjoyed at the thought we looked forward to his decorations.

All over again, she was the same little girl who was amazed by each quarter she found on the beach with her father, so delighted in life's small joys.

God, I loved her.

* * *

The story came to an abrupt end. I could have fantasized about snorkeling in Bora Bora or hang gliding in Italy's Dolomite Mountains, but foremost on my mind was closer to home.

"It's Christmas, I'm ready to visit my family. Alfonso and Lorenzo will be there, and that time is so precious." Rather than a sense of optimism, I felt desperation.

I was a willing client, earnestly taking suggestions, and avoiding my proclivity for checking my way through some imaginary rubric, but little changed.

Outside of my body and home, I was a stranger to the world and its rhythms. I felt isolated, no closer to reuniting with my family and remaining clueless as to what was missing. A nagging ache in my stomach's pit told me that some people seemed to like me, but sensed that had little to do with me, but rather some resolution to their quandaries. I brought out the polite and tolerant side of humanity.

"Go, Jim. Spend time with your loved ones. You've worked hard. Take a break and just surround yourself in unconditional love."

My yearning to belong to a pack or tribe again was constricted by listening to music or reading books. I ran alongside the author or songwriter, cheering their ability to designate words to wordless feelings, and that met my hope of basking in togetherness without being forced to interact with people. My end goal was no longer belonging. I'd settled for the mere possibility that it was safe and unidirectional without a chance of rejection.

That could not come from anyone but me—no doctor had a prescription for friendship.

Chapter Eight

Miracles

December 2013

C HICAGO'S O'HARE AIRPORT WAS JAM-PACKED
three days before Christmas. I carried a single
carry-on bag. Chaotic and unpredictable movements of airport patrons produced stress. Almost
six years after landing in Atlanta post-deployment, the throng had the same cast of characters with tearful reunions interspersed among
video-gamers, self-empowered women with hair
bouncing like softly coiled springs, and men with
red Marine Corps baseball caps. That time, however, I was anonymous and felt excitement rather
than apprehension.

In an airport full of triggers, I focused my attention and heard the laughter of the children and a
mother and her daughters singing Christmas carols,
instead of thinking of emergency exits and escape
routes for when disaster invariably struck.

It was quite an achievement for a person who had
left a full cart of groceries in the aisle and ran

from the commissary, rather than deal with those dastardly commissary shoppers. Better yet, the transition from the airport to see my sister Julie's family, my parents, and Alfonso was seamless.

On the way to dinner with my family, everyone talking at the same time, I felt a decided heaviness. I acknowledged the laughter of the airport's children made my spirit soar moments before I noticed two elderly women wearing hijabs. I couldn't help but think of Abdul-Hayy's mother, who may have broken into tears at the chatter and uninhibited giggling of children. Somehow, I figured Robert would have approved of my self-permission to think of her.

* * *

I awakened the next morning in the hotel room and opened my computer to search for the latest news about Iraq. Even almost six years after the deployment, I compulsively checked the developments in the Middle East at least a couple of times per day without knowing exactly what I hoped to read outside of a sense that our deployment bore fruit. My computer was extraordinarily slow in pulling up the Internet. Frustrated, I abruptly slammed the computer shut.

"I'm not afraid of you." Startled, I looked to see Alfonso had been standing just inside the corner of the room. There was no way to be sure how long he had been there.

Before I could respond, Alfonso stood there calmly, with barely a blink. "You don't scare me, Dad."

"What did you say?" I stood up slowly and walked toward him.

Alfonso, at eighteen years old, was not much smaller than me. He stood with his hands folded in front of him. Maybe in his mind, he saw the same menacing figure that returned. I felt a squinting of my face as if I hadn't heard him.

As I came within three steps of him, Alfonso didn't move an eyelash, staring into my eyes. His hands remained folded at his belt line in a non-confrontational manner. There was neither fear nor bravery. I found it sadly admirable, sad that he had been terrorized to the point of numbness and admirable that he was reclaiming himself, even if it was finally at my expense.

"I'm not afraid of you," Alfonso said again as I stood right in front of him.

He stood while his weight was balanced between his feet, his posture erect, Alfonso seemed to have no intention of physically confronting me.

"I'm not." He didn't seem controlled by any emotion, what drove him seemed to be his truth. That was something Alfonso had thought about in his detailed autistic mind. If he had considered the consequences, they didn't deter him.

I hesitated. We looked into each other's eyes.

He stood in the corner of the room next to an unlit lamp. The shades were opened, and a bright morning sun lit the room. Alfonso didn't stand in a part of the room with any chance of a contingency plan. There was nowhere to run. But Alfonso stood firmly. I moved forward suddenly and maybe Alfonso didn't know if I was going to strike him for defying me.

About two paces from him, Alfonso's expression was equally resolute, his hands still at his belt.

"Go ahead, hit me if you want to. You still don't scare me, Dad."

I stopped. Alfonso hadn't blinked.

Was that all I had taught him? To calmly face the scariest person in his life? We stood there before we fell into a long, tight hug.

"You're my son, Alfonso, I've never meant to scare you. I love you, but I've frightened you, haven't I?

"You have been like a monster—a big, scary bully."

Temple Grandin, an autistic author who described the realities of her world through the lens of autism, explained slight differences in tone or volume can be deafening, which can bring about a measurable pain.

I was unable to imagine the terror I brought to Alfonso's life or what other physical or emotional cycles I had set in motion.

"I'm sorry for the way I've behaved. I hope you know you can tell me how you felt when I was angry, any time. I promise I will listen and not say a word, okay?"

"I'm angry with you Dad, but I love you."

* * *

There may not be a person in the world who had taught me more about resilience than Alfonso, that beautiful child. In the school districts he attended, he was placed in programs for emotionally or behaviorally disturbed youth. After fights with the district, we were placated by having him in a class with severely physically handicapped students.

Each hard day, he would go to bed saying, "Well, today wasn't too good but tomorrow will be better."

Alfonso's life was a series of minor miracles. He had defied every projection. He would not be empathetic, said one doctor. He will not retain information said another. And each time, Cindy and I counted down the days he would rise above expectations.

One time on the way to Six Flags, Cindy's recent lesson for Alfonso was Eleanor Roosevelt's quote to "do one thing every day that scares you." Lorenzo and I had decided to take a water slide that seemed to be a free fall—a steep decline during which one would feel their seat lifting from the slide for a split second.

Alfonso climbed the stairs behind us. I repeated there were less intimidating slides on the way up and we would meet him at the bottom. Maybe fear could be tackled incrementally. But upward he went with a fear of heights, gripping the handrail.

Lorenzo went down the slide first.

"Face your fears, Dad," said Alfonso as he whipped past me and sat down in one motion.

I was left with a good view of the horizon as he disappeared over the side of the slide. A moment later, I heard a long "Woooooo! Yeah!"

I laughed with joy. By the time I'd gotten to the bottom of the slide, Alfonso was halfway to the top of the stairs to fly down the slide again. Who was the hero?

Then, years later, he fearlessly stared down his monster in the closet. I wasn't the least bit surprised.

* * *

Later that night, Alfonso went to bed early and Lorenzo and I went to the pool for a swim. Because the pool was closed, we took a seat and talked about life. He had never ceased to amaze me with creative stories, much like Robert had been encouraging me to do. He could create a story around any image.

We sat in a quiet area of the lobby. I recounted to him one of my favorite of his stories. It came from build-able toys called Bionicles.

There were two twin monsters named Cahdok and Gahdok who protected a great treasure of huge crystals deep within the earth. The monsters were huge, powerful, and most-assuredly had bad breath. Slowly the army closed in against the seemingly unbeatable enemy. Without thinking about it, I found myself rooting for the army.

Eventually, through bravery and loss, the army conquered all adversity and managed to overcome

Cahdok and Gahdok. Victory, I thought. Lorenzo sat on the floor.

I told him as I remembered it. We looked out at the pool of the hotel. I wondered if that was an eight-year-old's view of my military service.

Then to my shock, Lorenzo revealed a twist to the story.

"What nobody knew," the eight-year-old said without looking up, "was that Cahdok and Gahdok were the guardians of the crystals that sustained life to the entire planet. If they died, the crystals lost their energy, and the planet would die."

Lorenzo continued to play with his Bionicles, and I stood there with my mouth agape.

I recounted that story to a sixteen-year-old Lorenzo, thinking he might not even remember. On so many levels, I was certain it was his perception of my military service.

The tale reminded me of one of Sayyed's responses once to the phrase "history is written by the victors." Without a thought, Sayyed closed the debate by saying "and also, history is written by those who have hung heroes." Silence ensued. The army I was inclined to support had ended life on that planet by not understanding their enemies.

"Did I remember that story correctly?" I asked.

Lorenzo smiled, probably remembering how terrible I was when I would play the Bionicles video game with him. He had corrections and it was simply a part of the history he had learned, but I had internalized it as if it were about me.

I smiled at the thought of Robert appreciating my imagination.

Lorenzo and I shared a good laugh. It didn't matter if I had no natural skills in video games. What mattered was the time we spent together. He reminded me of the entire weekend afternoons we spent making paper airplanes that didn't fly very far. That really wasn't the point, either. I felt such a feeling of satisfaction that I had left a positive imprint somewhere.

It was time to head back up to the room and as we walked back, we had the same idea. We both extended our hands at the same time and held hands through the lobby and back to our room without saying another word.

"We should do this more often, Dad."

"We sure should." I felt such gratitude.

* * *

Over our Christmas vacation in Chicago, I learned a lot of my family's perceptions, those moments onto which I placed so much importance. Lorenzo said he would never forget the image of me, in uniform, reading "Fernando the Bull" to his class just before I deployed. Julie laughed about our attempts to get a picture of Errol Flynn's home during a visit to Los Angeles. My niece, Monica still had a recording my Chaplain in Iraq filmed, meant to be a bedtime story. Dad remembered visiting Maine just after Alfonso was born and seeing me lovingly hold his grandson. Norm recounted the time we ran in a marathon together and, at about the halfway point, when the marathon route turned right, we spontaneously ran straight through the crowd as they booed, and straight into a Chinese buffet.

Mom recounted one time, when I was about eight or so, during a heavy rainstorm. I let her know a dire emergency was right outside our apartment building. Leaves from the curbs were washed down and covered the sewer. Soon, the curb by the drains may have been a foot high because the gutters were slanted downward. I went out in the rain with my yellow raincoat and a big broom and swept the leaves from the sewer cover, allowing the water maybe two houses from the corner to drain. I stood there and as leaves were washed down again, I swept them away.

Within an hour I felt the satisfaction of a job well done. My satisfaction was doubled when Mom told everyone about my project. She was proud that I had seen a problem and did something about it. What I remembered was looking at our first-floor windows to see Mom watching me.

It had been a long time since I'd laughed so hard.

Robert had said that by reconnecting with safety within my own body and mindfulness exercises, that a sense of humor would return, and following the pattern of my relationship with Robert, he had my best interests at heart, and most importantly, he was right.

* * *

The only thing missing was Cindy. But under the cover of the Christmas season, I thought I would call her.

During the Christmas season, she pointed out annually the better moods and sense of community. It was a time of year to count blessings. Not everyone had health and family with which to celebrate.

"Hello?" Cindy answered on the second ring.

We were between Christmas and New Year's, perhaps an ideal time to call. Something in her voice told me she wasn't pressed right then with plans. Maybe later, I thought.

"Merry Christmas from Chicago!"

"Merry Christmas to you," She immediately spoke with the boys and my family.

Our agreement upon separation held—we'd promised not to speak badly of each other. Most of all, we kept Alfonso and Lorenzo out of it. I had the promise of my own not to bring up working things out and instead focused on being a good, uncomplicated friend.

Our separation was mentioned once Mom and I had a quiet moment.

"I just can't understand what happened with you two. You had such a good relationship."

I was happy that both families had reserved judgment and resisted the natural urge to take a side. Time with family gave me a chance to reflect on Iraq's lessons.

Once, I chanced across a meeting at the base entrance with an Iraqi family of a detained man who'd been brutally killed at the hands of fellow detainees. The representative, through an interpreter, could only offer a clinical explanation without the onus of responsibility. Nobody knew what happened and those who did weren't talking.

That did not alleviate the family's grief. They were left to understand what that meant, their imagination likely worse than reality.

Facts were of no use and invariably added to our disconnection of hearts and minds.

I discovered in my own therapy facts were an ineffective way of dealing with emotions. They were of no help to me in counseling. I couldn't help but realize I had brought that disconnect with Cindy by expecting my data to resolve her sense of betrayal or the thought I refused to trust her with my burden.

Once we were back on the phone, we made small talk. Things were going well with her and her family. I ached. I just wanted to scream my litany of regrets. I wanted Cindy to know why I had behaved the way I had.

"Can I tell you something?" Cindy asked after we shared a laugh. "I've had this thought of one time we were arguing, and I told you I wished you would be sent back to Iraq or Afghanistan."

I said I didn't recall, but I did.

"I still feel so bad. You know I would never wish anything like that."

"Oh God, Cindy, please don't feel bad. I've said a hundred things worse than that that I regret." I felt like someone heavy stood on my chest. I was one second from begging her to think of working out our marriage. We hadn't started the divorce paperwork and I felt I was giving it a "pocket veto."

"There is one more thing I have to tell you," she said. I felt our conversation had momentum. "About Iraq, I would never wish what happened, I don't even know what, upon you."

I responded that I knew that.

She had stuck through the worst, and I still had to shatter her in order for her to leave. The ache I felt turned to nausea. Cindy continued.

"This was the first thing in your life that you couldn't compartmentalize and file in its rightful place, before moving ahead as if nothing were wrong."

Sure enough, there were times Cindy accused me of sounding as though I were reading from a book. My coping mechanisms were logical and robotic, she would say.

"I know your heart and I watched how hard you struggled. But those horrible experiences have made you emotionally inaccessible. Even through that, I've seen the person I always knew was in there."

I held the phone away from my mouth in uncontrollable but silent heaves. Cindy asked if I was still there and I collected myself, even practicing saying something as if I were talking to someone in my parents' house.

Cindy continued that if I ever wanted to talk about Iraq that I wouldn't have to go into details of what had happened. I could just talk about how I felt in those moments.

"Cindy," I couldn't contain myself, "how would you feel about trying to work things through?"

I was sorry for bringing it up, but we had been married for twenty-two years. I figured I had at least earned the right, in the middle of the kind of conversation in which I'd fallen in love with her so long ago.

Through our traumas, we'd become witnesses to a brilliant world. As sunlight returned, I felt no longer the color blindness perception of darkness. Although I hadn't thought of it before, I would welcome talking to Cindy about Iraq, and she could tell me about her experiences living with me. I was prepared to be accountable. Pain shared was pain divided

"I think it's a possibility," Cindy said.

"I didn't ask what you thought about it, silly. I asked how you felt. We have work to do, grasshopper."

We both roared with laughter.

Chapter Nine

The Accident

April 2014

RESTLESSNESS OVERCAME MY DESIRE TO sleep and, in my bedroom, I felt too tired to stay awake and too alert to sleep. After midnight on an unseasonably warm night, I decided to grab a couple groceries, providing a chance to reflect. Thinking and driving went together like peanut and jelly or fresh basil and tomato. Wonders I had recently acknowledged brought a stampede of other positive images.

Robert was convinced that each moment of gratitude was a catalyst for healing, and sure enough, the memory of my friend's four-year-old daughter smiling at me and hiding behind her mother's leg made me smile. Then, I pictured a dog, with its tail between its legs, which trusted me enough to cautiously approach when I offered food. They saw something inherently approachable, even trustworthy.

Having those images in my mind seemed like a novel concept. My thoughts shifted to one patient I had on my mobile x-ray job.

"Give me five minutes and I'll tell you the impact of a man's mother in his life," a woman said, as I visited her home for the elderly.

Within a moment of introducing myself, she had been sleeping and in the fog of awakening, she saw her eldest brother who had been killed in World War II. He'd been like a second father to her, she said.

"Anyway, you walked in and I just had a feeling. My brother was considerate and had good manners. That was our mom's influence."

"You're absolutely right, Ms. Davis," I said.

She was the youngest of eight children and awoke when the wheels with my portable x-ray equipment squeaked in the library-like silence. Ms. Davis, at eighty-five years old, insisted her brother walked into the room alongside me. He'd visited her before in glimpses that same way, sometimes as an apparition. Ms. Davis said when she looked across the darkened room into her closet, she saw him there, smiling and watching over her. That a person could look into the shadows and not be terrified, actually finding comfort there, humbled me.

Magic indeed.

* * *

Still thinking of Ms. Davis, I drove past the twenty-four-hour market and looped around in a bowling alley parking lot. I pulled up to a stoplight just on the south side of I-95 from the submarine base. I was suddenly utterly amazed that Robert had seemed to work through a bunch of my maladaptive behaviors without immediately trying to change them. I wondered how tempted he'd been.

At one point though, he said it was more important to distinguish where the true issues were and see differences between cause and effect. Everyone was more than a stranger who introduced himself with conditions.

Thankfully, Robert didn't try to strip my coping mechanisms and even gave them credit for continuing the struggle, until he listened long enough to hear of a better alternative from which I'd relied on in the past. Those threads of resilience had been sewn and had only lived in other people. With gratitude, I felt safe enough to learn in the face of non-judgment. When we went over resilience factors, I was unable to see them or put words to them without a sense of comfort and trust.

Robert quoted Anais Nin and said, *"And then the day came when the risk to remain tight in a bud was more painful than the risk it took to blossom."*

It was an exclamation mark at the end of a session, and I thought he may have waited our entire relationship to say it out loud. The timing was ideal.

The statement sat in the corner of my mind, I had come about self-loathing and worthlessness honestly before that same amount of energy was expended toward healing. Robert supposed I had a lot of energy either way. And yet, much seemed unresolved.

* * *

Like most New England nights in April, the air cooled after dusk. Still, as I sat at the red light, with the windows down and a late-night talk show playing on the radio, I felt an even chillier stillness with the smell of catastrophe. It was as if I had become deaf, there was no sound and dreadful tension spread from my abdomen to my chest. My only sense was that familiar smell, a stink without stench.

I whirled around in my seat. Nobody. No cars behind me at the light. No discernible highway traffic on the overpass, only a single cream-colored SUV going southbound on Route 12. As it passed under the highway, the car slowed slightly as if the driver had lost their bearings or missed a turn. With a median to its left, the best place to turn around was right in front of me at the light.

"He's going to make a U-turn," I deduced.

Looking to the right, I saw a car driving northward, over the speed limit as if hurrying to make the traffic light.

If the car is in the middle of a U-turn, he won't see the oncoming car's lights.

Disaster was imminent and unavoidable, like a movie I'd seen before. I wondered during the deployment if I had a sixth sense and orchestrated the death and destruction which invariably unfolded seconds later. If I could see so clearly, why couldn't I keep it from happening? The SUV, directly in front of me began to make an agonizingly slow U-turn. With the window open, I screamed.

"Hey! Stop!" I yelled.

The SUV seemed to take an hour to complete the turn while the other car didn't slow, and my sense of touch returned. My skin crept with death. A breaking sweat didn't rinse it away.

I swung my door open, which felt weightless, and I ran toward the intersection as the car broadsided the SUV without as much as stepping on the brake, and I jumped over a flying piece of a car grille which landed near my feet.

The SUV balanced on the two driver side wheels as it spun, landing upright clumsily. Glass shattered, metal dented, and tires must have been screeched but I didn't hear them. The other car, upon impact, seemed to rise up only on its front wheels. The entire front end buckled like aluminum foil.

I saw and smelled smoke coming from the SUV. In the other car, two young men and a woman climbed from their vehicle. Right then, I heard the hiss of their leaking radiator, only a single headlight remained lit and turned downward. The windshield was shattered by the buckling hood. My feet crackled on pulverized windshield.

"Everyone okay?" I yelled without slowing my pace.

Two of the three returned my thumbs up, with the third one already dialing a cell phone.

Approaching the SUV, its cab filled with smoke, I saw no movement inside. An arm with an upturned left hand was extended outside the vehicle, palm up. I instantly thought of Munawwar's outstretched left hand. The limp hand sought help.

Just inside, a woman wearing a hijab sat unconscious in an awkward position, her head turned toward her extended hand. Her eyes were glazed and faced without focus toward her extended hand.

She didn't respond to my high-pitched, panicked voice, but she was asking for help. She was. One second later, I almost stopped in mid-step with a clear picture of the woman on the Iraqi roadside begging us to stop. She had asked for help and as we passed, her fate had been sealed. The hand I ran toward wasn't as desperate but was just as doomed if I couldn't extract her in time.

Fortunately, her car had been hit on the passenger side. I pulled on the handle. The door stubbornly creaked open as the engine sputtered before turning off. I caught her outstretched left hand. The gas I smelled and the smoke could be a deadly combination within seconds. The passenger-side wheel had buckled under and the car leaned away from the driver's side.

I managed to urgently undo the seat belt as the woman seemed to stir. I tried to move the steering wheel out of the way to no avail, and swung her legs toward the doorway. Her left hand, which I hadn't let go of, instinctively squeezed mine as I threw her over my shoulder in a Fireman's carry and ran along the median for maybe a hundred and fifty feet.

I gently placed her on her back, praying all the while she didn't have a significant injury. Her right hand had limply struck my back as I ran.

As I placed her on the grass in the median, the woman's headscarf was askew. I pulled her hijab back over her hair, her modesty maintained. As though it had happened before, I began to pray. I felt my incompetence would result in further injury or her death. Sweat soaked through my shirt. I wiped away sweat with my sleeve. It felt so hot that I thought in daylight hours, I would have seen steam dissipating from the ground.

After the physical assessment, it seemed everything was intact. I was speaking out loud before performing each part of a physical exam, regardless of whether she understood me. She stirred.

"Son... my son..." she muttered.

My eyes widened in stunned disbelief as Abdul-Hayy crossed my mind, his graceful hand falling limply. I hadn't noticed anyone else in the vehicle, which hadn't ignited yet.

Not again, I thought, losing track of where I was. If I missed him, it would be me who explained his death to his mother. The woman would feel angry grief toward me, the bungling rescuer.

Sprinting back, I used the driver's door to slingshot myself into the front seat. Nobody. Kneeling in the front seat looking back, I looked through a haze at the back seat, and coughed from the choking smoke, before I waved my hand by the floor behind the front seat, but all I saw was the smoke moving around as my hand passed. Perhaps he had been unconscious and lifelessly slid to the floor.

"Stay with me, do you hear me?" I said.

The child had to have been knocked out. I began to cry until I coughed again from the smoke.

I leapt out and swung the back door open and looked into the storage area behind the back seat. Still nobody. Eyes stinging and almost overcome, I almost fell out of the back seat to the ground, stumbling and coughing.

My hand touched grass that felt damp and again, sensing Connecticut's crisp spring air, I realized the woman who was on the median needed care and I needed to get away from the car.

By then, an ambulance and fire truck had arrived, and two paramedics approached the woman. I reported I hadn't found any injuries besides her level of consciousness.

The sounds of the ambulances and cars passing on the highway overpass returned. Ambulance lights blinded me as the two paramedics lifted the woman onto a stretcher and lifted it. The woman seemed to advance from unconsciousness to a subdued haze. The paramedics had to half-carry, half-roll the gurney over the grassy median.

"I hope she's okay."

"Thank you for your help. We've got it from here." Paramedics in the middle of an accident call aren't overly talkative, I knew.

I lingered near the gurney as it approached the ambulance. One paramedic was talking to the woman and she waved me over.

"Thank you." She had an accent as if Arabic was her first language, maybe she had emigrated to the United States as a young girl. She had a shy smile and my mind flashed. *No, the girl in the detainee's picture in front of her destroyed home would be twelve or thirteen, and Abdul-Hayy's mother about forty.*

"You're in good hands now." Emotions throughout the spectrum passed through me with no resistance. I stood there, suddenly drained as the adrenaline wore off. She reached out and grasped my hand.

The woman looked at me and I saw her lips move. All sound was silenced again, but I wondered if I really had heard her ask, "Who is Abdul-Hayy?"

Had I really shouted those words as I ran to the car?

I walked back to my car, sat down, closed the door—awash in tears. Some were tears of joy. I'd never considered those moments with Munawwar and Abdul-Hayy as stories with a beginning, middle, and end. The story with Abdul-Hayy had a different finale. I was no longer doomed to inevitability.

Outside the rocket attack by the diesel fuel tanks, and those minutes with Munawwar, I'd performed exactly as I had been trained. I was left to choose between family protection, as close to the core of a son, husband, and father as one gets.

On the other side, I thought I could make up for my mistaken belief that I'd seen the first moments of radial violence in America. From that moment, I imagined floating alongside myself—a heavy, drifting sensation.

My narrative over most of the seven months with Robert was the same story, a mishmash of recollections without sequence. Only the ending was predictable. The progress I'd made didn't change the way I felt about myself. In my rational mind, I could reason through the events of the day Munawwar and Abdul-Hayy died and conclude there was nothing I could have done in either case. But I did not feel that way.

The accident gave an alternate view of a flawed character, but one who was profoundly earnest and humane.

I'd had over five years to replay their deaths, over and again, and each time, I had lived through the same ending. That I had hesitated or done nothing was the most consistent part of a seemingly completed narrative, and with each replay, it became etched further into my mind, like adding cement to concrete. Then, almost six years later, that narrative shattered.

Circumstances dictated that the woman and I never spoke again. I felt a familiar rhythm of not being able to continue conversations at the very moment I had something to say.

I began to trust Robert's approach. While we worked on breathing and mindfulness, he introduced part of my deployment bound to bring stress. When I had a reaction, he asked me to monitor my emotions and related physical symptoms. Recognizing those effects seemed important. Once I identified them, he reminded me of the awareness exercises he taught me, and situational awareness of gratitude. Maybe a minute later, he asked again if the symptoms diminished. Just about every time, they had. If they hadn't, we talked about what had crossed my mind. Maybe I had only moved one layer closer to the real issue.

* * *

"Let's say you're back in the moment where you came upon Munawwar. What if you had done with him what you did after the car accident?" Robert asked, right after I explained what had happened in the car accident.

"He would have died. He was really badly injured."

That wasn't Robert's question, so he clarified by having me imagine I was able to perform a miracle, and if so, would I have done so. I could only imagine how torn I was at that moment. I balked and sensing it, Robert asked me what would have happened if I had been there and I had decided to go to Munawwar's aid.

"How would that feel?"

I felt transported to that moment and remembered the looks in our eyes. Still, I was unable to say anything out loud.

"What do you think would have happened if you were able to save him, Jim?"

"I believed we could have negotiated a lasting peace," I said almost inaudibly. Such relief I felt at saying that. I felt a rush of other thoughts.

Another question echoed: "Who is Abdul-Hayy?"

The boy who had such bravery to stand and protect his mother and sisters as pure terror overcame his bodily functions. His love for them, however, remained intact—courage any parents would be proud of.

But what I would share of the lives of Munawwar and Abdul-Hayy was their willingness to forgive. Neither of them, in any of their writings, uttered the word 'hate.'

Chapter Ten

Name That Attune

April 2014

A MONG THE EARLIEST LESSONS I remembered was
touching the burner element on our Frigidaire
Flair. I reacted as most toddlers, not going near
that stove top again. But over time, I learned burn-
ers not in use didn't cause burns. I maintained a
healthy respect around burner elements if they were
a threat to have removed my fingerprints or not.

Iraq had taught me the electric burner was always
energized and was ever dangerous. Every time.

Robert nodded when I explained that to him, as a
person I knew appreciated analogies and suggested
them as an exercise in curiosity and creativity.
If I recounted an experience and connected it to
a present, mindful moment, it was all the better.

* * *

My assignment for the day's appointment was
to think of a time I felt comforted in an awful
moment. I thought of the task as another that

connected me to a sense of gratitude, but Robert had a counselor's ulterior motive.

I told Robert a story of when a bunch of neighborhood families organized a day and reserved a picnic area at a nearby Illinois lake. Maybe I was four or five. Not long after we arrived, we lined the beach as Dad swam out to a set of diving boards protruding from the lake. Always a superior athlete, Dad climbed to the highest of three diving boards and dove off to the applause of the group. *Dad can do anything*, I thought to myself.

The lake also had a swim float with an accompanying metal ladder. My five-year-old brain recognized three girls my age sitting on the raft as an irresistible opportunity. I immediately decided to swim the fifty feet or so.

The lake had a swim area cordoned off by safety ropes with evenly spaced orange and white egg-shaped floating devices in the calm shallow water. Just on the other side of the ropes, the water dropped off, making the water a few forbidding shades darker. The tops of pale green seaweed were visible just under the surface.

My desire to sit on the float with three girls superseded my lack of confidence to swim that far, but I still decided to cut the distance by just swimming outside the lines for a quick second—just across a corner of the roped-off area.

In doing so, I felt the seaweed, like tentacles, wrap around my right ankle. Panicked, I kicked furiously, only to further the seaweed's grip. I screamed for help, feeling the water in my nose and unable to even see which direction I faced.

Within seconds it seemed, Dad flew in and grabbed me with enough strength or adrenaline to lift me almost entirely out of the water. A second later, Dad carried me back toward the collection of picnic tables. Mom waited alongside the lake and walked back with us. Dad assured her I was fine.

As I sat at the picnic bench, Mom came over and spoke softly to me as I stopped crying. Mom reached down stroked my right ankle, exactly where the seaweed had wrapped. Within seconds, I had bounced back and wondered what I was missing with the sounds of activity all around me.

I asked Robert, how could she have reached for that exact spot? Her touch countered the terrible feeling of some mysterious hairy thing leaping from the depths and gripping my ankle.

"The only lasting effect it seemed was an avoidance of kelp no matter what the dietary benefits," I said, noting my tendency to joke or tell a tangential story to avoid emotional intensity.

Robert had deftly danced on the periphery of a topic he recognized as a major issue. But when I displayed a sense of humor or humility, or when I was overcome with sadness, he knew when to probe a little further. In his sense, those exhibited a door. I felt it was likely creativity or reflection or a potential release of emotional weight that he noted. Robert did not miss the signs.

"How does it feel to remember a feeling like that?" Robert had asked a question that brought a flood of memories of the sanctuary in which I was raised.

I felt that illustrated with every narrative adjustment the blessings of resilience and with it, an enormous depth of gratitude. I could have been born anywhere to any parents.

"I felt loved and so lucky."

One-part questions were not a part of the counselor's vernacular. One question folded neatly into the next. I had been reading, writing, and felt reconnected with a sense of creativity, imagination, and playfulness. I had begun to feel I deserved better, and I loved the idea of making my own endings, like dream reconstruction.

"You've spoken about what others have done for you. I would like to hear a time you think you've left another person with that feeling."

I could not think of a single instance until I thought of a story Cindy likely would have given.

* * *

In 1989, my cousin Scott was in Navy Corps School and arranged a double date with two of the girls who were in class with him. We saw the Chicago sites and off-the-beaten track places only a native like me might know. Then, it was on to see a Madonna concert at Soldier Field. Everyone got along very well. At the end of the night, Scott and his girlfriend wanted to check into a motel before continuing their sightseeing the next day.

Over forty miles from Great Lakes, that put the other girl in an awkward position. I could tell she felt obligation's pressure. She avoided eye contact when I glanced in her direction, perhaps feeling betrayed that I had placed a price on an intimate night with her. Any expenditure exchanged for her dignity was too low. Love did not work that way.

"What would like to do, Angie? I could drive you back to the barracks."

Angie's look of fear dissipated into relief and she offered payment for gas. I felt an equal liberation from being the face of her unease.

As we climbed into the car, I apologized for the uncomfortable moment at the motel and asked if we could see each other again before she graduated from Corps School and was given orders. But she had promised her parents she wouldn't get involved while so many transitions occurred in her life. She had gone from Philadelphia to Boot Camp to Corps School to a place yet to be determined. I said I understood it was a lot to ask. I thought maybe I wasn't her type.

We made small talk along the darkened highway with the radio turned to a whisper. When we were silent for a few minutes, I noticed she had fallen asleep. Maybe ten miles down the road as I made a gentle right turn, her body slid, and her head rested on my shoulder. Driving stiffly, I didn't want to awaken her.

With some of the progress I had made since I began seeing Robert, I had an epiphany: I didn't want that moment to end, believing that somewhere within her, she found me trustworthy. I relished the moment, cherishing her trust.

"Right at that moment, you felt as uncomfortable as she did?" Robert asked, putting forward the idea that I had mirrored her mood.

He'd used that situation to ask me what I had really looked for in a relationship. I had no interest in coercing the young woman I had only known for a day. I hoped the day we spent could be parlayed into a second date rather than a shortcut. Robert stopped and exploded the moment and made it a week's worth of discourse.

"Yes," was the short answer.

If she was going to remember me at all, I hoped it would not be because a person she trusted selfishly took advantage of the circumstances. I felt genuine satisfaction. Love did not work that way and on that night, neither did I, even if I were the only person who remembered.

Robert responded he would bet she might recall her fears and my empathetic response—a welcome thought if it were true.

"Is it safe to suggest that you've received, but you've also given? You said this was a story you believe Cindy would tell?"

I thought so. Cindy said I remind her of Jimmy Stewart in *Mr. Smith Goes to Washington*, in which he played an uncompromisingly wholesome legislator in the face of powerful and corrupt government officials. With innocence and a lack of guile, Mr. Smith won out delightfully in the end.

Robert's next question caught me by surprise.

"When you've spoken your goal of reuniting with your family, what do you think this story means?"

I had destroyed Cindy's trust. I knew I had done it deliberately, unilaterally deciding that without dialogue or input. I told Robert, on the way back into her life, I had to untie a marriage with a Gordian Knot of my own doing.

"Tell me about this Gordian Knot."

"I read about it from the times of Alexander the Great. It's a metaphor for an unsolvable problem, a knot that cannot be untied."

Robert smiled, before noting that at least one of many adaptations of the Gordian Knot had Alexander the Great struggling to untie the knot before simply taking his sword, and, with one fell swoop, cut the knot in two.

The perceived parameters of the problem became moot in direct proportion to open and varied possibilities.

* * *

I had at least two great reasons to call Cindy and was thrilled when she answered the phone. She seemed to be in a good mood. I blurted out a story before she could ask how I was.

I had a memory of one afternoon early in the summer of 2008 when we were sitting on the deck, watching the red-tailed hawks circle above against a cloudless, blue sky. Over the following thirty minutes or so, the sky darkened with angry clouds, about to burst with a heavy downpour. By the time we closed the sliding glass door, raindrops hit the deck with loud splats.

I was recounting the story so quickly, Cindy had to tell me to slow down. Until that part of the tale, she didn't recall.

"Then we went inside, and I told you I was in pain, remember?"

Since I'd returned from Iraq, I had a number of aches and pains. I chalked much of it up to the rigors of deploying, not much different than any of my unit's four hundred and twenty-one men and women.

The mention of admitting my pain came one day after Cindy congratulated me on my high pain threshold. So high was my threshold, she said somewhat sarcastically, that I would probably die of some ailment easily detectable and treatable because I would refuse to go to a doctor.

She remembered the day.

"Well, when I said I was in pain, you curled up next to me on the couch and placed your hand on my head, just over my right ear, and said, '*Sana-que, sana, culito de rana, Si no te sanas hoy, te sanas mañana.*' Remember?"

Because she had a clear memory of the day, I had to ask how she knew, of all my aches and pains, that I had a headache in that exact spot?

Cindy said she just knew.

"I want you to know that I appreciate every kindness you've ever extended to me." My voice broke, imagining her placing a gift on the floor, her hands swinging away, like a magician at the end of an intriguing trick. "I'm so sorry for what I've done."

"What have you done?" Cindy asked.

Maybe, I thought, she wanted me to detail what I was sorry for as a way of speaking the unsayable. Perhaps that was the way to accept accountability for my actions.

"Is the list that long that you don't know?" We both broke into laughter and I felt gratitude for the levity.

"Jim—"

"I think of one time just before the deployment," I interrupted.

I had to say I failed to recognize her anxiety of one year without me, instead of screaming at her for worrying about 'small, insignificant details'. She tried to explain, but I screamed louder until eventually she just sat, staring straight ahead, hands obediently folded on her lap but flinching as if an electrical shock passed through her.

The process of dissociation, in order to focus on a family's six-month job at hand, was not unusual. What I had done was abusive. What I mourned was the loneliness and powerlessness she must have felt at my hand. I doubted I had ever cried so hard.

"I don't want you to be sorry, Jim. Please don't be so hard on yourself. I can see how hard you're working. Trying hard was never your problem."

I felt alive during the rocket attack, the echo of the rocket striking the diesel fuel tank. And I felt present in the moments of Munawwar and Abdul-Hayy's death. I was ashamed to admit I also felt alive during arguments. Progress was feeling alive around life and living, even if it meant pain. But then, I'd felt present in my body when feeling gratitude.

One hundred and eighty degrees added to one hundred and eighty degrees had not automatically meant a completed circle. No mathematical equation existed to calculate reconciliation. I thought of the loop closed from the safety of my childhood, at various points in my life, all the way to Cindy touching the precise spot of my headache.

* * *

I described to an Arabic man Munawwar's final words the best I could. He immediately recognized them and repeated them. I was shocked. What did they mean?

We were both saying a prayer of forgiveness to our respective Gods. As the man interpreted that final prayer, my mind wandered toward one of Munawwar's entries, in which he wished his mother could have responded to his letters and given him guidance. That Munawwar slept under the same moon as Ameena, he had reason to persevere.

I had been a fool, blessed with privilege Munawwar and Abdul-Hayy couldn't imagine. I sat 1500 miles, a three-hour flight from Miami. So worried about missing life's landmarks I was, that when they occurred but not in the form I'd imagined, they were overlooked. I didn't know when I saw Lorenzo's joyful skip last or if I would've relished it. Maybe I'd have missed entirely. I pondered if Alfonso continued to await the day which got better.

My mind held an etched image of seven-year-old Lorenzo and I playing a behind-the-back hiding game. When it came to his turn to hide an object because his hands were so small, the object protruded from between his fingers, the object further from the empty hand. He wanted me to succeed.

I was nervous to even say it out loud, but I had one more shocker for Cindy.

"I've been taking dancing lessons." Throughout our marriage, I dreaded those functions at which people were expected to dance. Cindy would joke that she had already signed a waiver if I were to injure her. "Are you there?"

"What has gotten into you?" Cindy asked in disbelief.

"I know, it must be Wacky Wednesday."

During one argument, she had been critical of my judgment and sarcastically suggested that I pretend every day was *Wacky Wednesday*, a Dr. Seuss book I used to read to the boys. In the book, every usual occurrence was reversed with hilarious results.

"Whatever your instincts tell you, just do the opposite," she'd said.

Jim Enderle

I wished for the little things. I looked forward to folding paper airplanes with my sons again. I wanted Cindy to look at me the way she used to. And that walk she had, so light as if to not bend a blade of grass when she thought of me. I held the conviction I could sell one hundred out of one hundred vacuum cleaners in door-to-door sales. I had a plethora of aligned and attuned love in my life and I wished to have it back.

Cindy enjoyed the *Wacky Wednesday* reference. Humor and wit were two qualities Cindy admired. While reading that book to the boys years ago, all four of us laughed at the boys' additions.

The clock on the wall was turned inward and only the wall knew what time it was. It was Wacky Wednesday.

Cindy laughed, and it never sounded or felt so good.

Chapter Eleven

Sting and Relief

June 2014

Growing up, each Sunday our family had a routine that brought a smile. Dad, ever an early riser, went to the early Mass and brought home sweet rolls and coffee cake from Reynold's Bakery. Mom, Norm, Julie, and I went to the 9:15 service before we all met at Grandma's house in time to catch *The Lone Ranger*, *The Cisco Kid*, followed by Charlie Chan. During football season, that brought us right up to the Chicago Bears kickoff.

Once, I arrived early for some reason and found Grandma singing Christmas carols in German, but when she saw me, she stopped. Something registered, but I never really thought much about it,. Embedded in the idyllic scene was an unacknowledged but impactful prospect.

Decades later, I chose Israel as a country for an English thesis paper and decided to interview a local rabbi as a part of my research. As we introduced ourselves, the rabbi was curious about the nationality of my surname and I responded that my mother was Scotch-Irish, Swedish, and Norwegian.

Dumbfounded by my answer, I realized on the way home that for some unknown reason, I felt ashamed by the treatment of Jews at the hands of Germans before and during World War II. It felt like admitting I had thrown that rock at the peaceful demonstration.

Grandma had moved to the United States in 1927. The topic was never broached. I doubted relatives of mine were involved in the Holocaust for obvious reasons—it would have been hard to comprehend with what I knew of my family of German farmers.

But spontaneously, at that moment, I was unable to tell the rabbi my racial identity. The moment was passed down tacitly over generations, and that point became clearer when I read the German language had been outlawed in public in Chicago.

Dad expressed a melancholy pride that Grandma had taken her citizenship so seriously she unselfishly obeyed even discriminatory laws if it were for the betterment of her society, even if that meant Grandma never taught my father the language of his parents beside what he'd picked up at the dinner table. Laws were rules to be honored; that was how citizens made our country great. But to Dad, that also meant a forced denial of his heritage and when he told me that, I sensed his disillusionment.

Years later, I had also denied my heritage with no understanding of the generational connection.

At my next appointment, I wondered aloud what unspoken trauma I had passed to Cindy and my sons, certain the concept of not bringing my Iraq experience home was a fool's errand.

"You mentioned once one of Munawwar's theories, one about a poisonous plant," Robert noted. "Do you remember?"

"It was called sting and relief."

In one essay, Munawwar suggested Ameena search for answers within a physical ailment, like nature's example of a poisonous plant growing within reach of its antidote. He had so often looked to the botany for his answers because nature was close to God even on its worst day.

Fascinated, I researched and found examples like jewel weed and poison ivy, or the Yucatan peninsula's Chechen and Chaka trees which grow right next to each other. I had a fond affection for the symbolism, that a solution to a terrible problem could be within arm's reach.

"How do you think that relates to your grandma and father?"

I felt the basic premise of Munawwar's essays, that difficulties bring our best chance to learn. I had been avoiding so much as a conscious thought of my trials and tribulations when maybe its blessing was right with it, an antidote waiting to be realized.

For months, Cindy and I spoke every night, even if it was only to say goodnight. Once in a while, we talked into the early hours of the morning.

What else in our relationship stemmed from my scars? Stuck in a timeless past, I'd missed all the landmarks I claimed were important to me. I couldn't say when Lorenzo last ran with a skip or if Alfonso were still unshakably optimistic or whether Cindy still looked for quarters in the sand. I'd missed it all.

"I would have to think about how that ties in," I said.

Somehow, my thoughts had found their way into daylight, still a long way from outwardly verbalizing them. I saw a clear obstacle and the idea of it remained stubbornly out of view. In my most secret thoughts, I wondered if I subconsciously wanted or deserved to get better.

Since seeing Robert, a thought crossed my mind that I felt sure would never be spoken aloud. My struggles had defined me, maybe for the first time, and provided leeway. Insecurities left me without the luxury of error. Then, I returned from deployment and my struggles defined me, even made me extraordinary.

Was it true that I stayed at war in my mind because I feared a return to my own unremarkable life, seemingly the only possibility, so part of me willingly clung to an assumption of status in the eyes of others?

If I were serious about reuniting with my family, I had to come to terms with that dilemma—to detach from the limits of diagnoses and the benefits I'd found, which had nothing to do with war. It was possible to enhance social standing as a result of the tragedies and heartbreak I'd witnessed in Iraq. In exchange, I'd stunted my own chances for progress, and was enslaved by my own choices.

* * *

Without any idea of the specifics before I called, I decided to phone Cindy and talk about Iraq as if it had become declassified. When Cindy answered, she said she could feel my smile and wondered what had happened.

I said I'd worked through my experiences, made progress, and would answer whatever questions she had about Iraq. It had never been a matter of trust in her, just my determination to preserve my family. I wanted their endearing naïveté to remain in a world where good always wins. In doing so, I'd ensured disaster. No matter what happened between us in the future, I wanted Cindy to know the separation wasn't her fault.

With newfound permission, Cindy was immediately curious about what happened to the two men I had only mentioned once, before shutting down and refusing to discuss them again.

What transpired was an introduction to Munawwar and Abdul-Hayy without the details of their deaths. I had a plan to talk about how I felt in those moments and what I'd learned of them after their deaths. As I spoke, I was lost in a sense of grief and fell silent.

I felt Cindy's cringe over the phone, and she hesitantly asked if I had killed them. In my own mind, I felt I had been responsible, and I didn't know how to respond. In that long moment, pressure built.

Something about that action moved me past the crime of passion and into premeditation. I knew full well that using my M-9 would be forensically traced, but a piece of rebar picked up with gloves was deniable. Certainly, I was guilty of something. My intent was to kill, and I couldn't comprehend when murder began or ended.

Cindy asked again if I had killed them.

I felt words go from a question of whether I killed Munawwar and Abdul-Hayy to the statement, "You killed them!" It was not the conversation I expected, and I couldn't reel my emotions back in.

"What kind of a question..." I blurted out.

Stunned, it sounded as if Cindy were trying to speak and only bits and pieces of words came out. She said she suddenly wasn't feeling well.

For me, it was a lie to simply say I hadn't been responsible, because I'd been present at life's end of two men, of whom I'd learned enough of their lives to care about and respect, even mourn their loss. Behind every "yes" and "no" was a story five years in the making.

I begged Cindy to stay on the phone, unable to find words. I had never realized it would be so hard to clarify what had happened that day in Iraq just over seven years before.

"What, uh... help me, what don't I know about this?" In the desperate moment, the only words I heard echoing through my mind were Abdul-Hayy's mother's advice on conflict resolution.

Cindy was utterly perplexed. Typically, when my point wasn't clear, I felt the need to speak more. I had thought about the idea of reaching out and listening instead.

"Please, help me understand why your question is so important to you."

Cindy was without words for a long moment. It had been among the first times, in the heat of a conversation that my answer was to elucidate her question. She could only say she tried to understand war and men incapable of killing would be forced to do so. If I'd hurt or killed anyone, she wanted to help me carry that grief, but what my mind heard was Cindy trying to reconcile the man she married with the identity of a murderer.

The idea hadn't occurred to me and I responded without a thought, that my anger was unresolved, manifesting when I didn't have the capacity to hold everything in. It had taken so much energy to maintain numbness, and, as they say in Alcoholics Anonymous, one is only as sick as the secret one keeps.

* * *

So much in life had shifted. In Iraq, people with whom I had interacted had been seen as different, but our lives became intertwined and indistinguishable in humanity. I smiled at the thought that the Dalai Lama, from Tibet, considered his archenemy, the Chinese to be among his greatest teachers.

I didn't apologize in words, but my actions had. Cindy saw that my desire to do better came out in a new way. Still, I felt the need to apologize for acting like an ass. In the normal rhythms of marital conversations, that was usually the time when Cindy said likewise.

"I'm sorry you acted like an ass, too." After a moment's hesitation, we both laughed.

In time, I felt humbled, and two thoughts crossed my mind. I thought about Munawwar's sting and relief and how the antidote to my poison sat nearest to me, if only I had looked, and then, surrounded by people who loved me, I could safely let them in.

Also, in those seconds of humility and vulnerability, I'd received what I'd always wanted. In spite of my perceived averageness, Cindy saw me as taller, darker, more self-confident, twice as smart, and as handsome as Lorenzo Lamas.

I explained what transpired. After a while, Cindy said that through all that, I had been an important testimonial to their lives. Maybe that had been my purpose. Had the events of the day ended any other way, had I not sought Munawwar out, for any reason and not been with him in his final moment, there may be no story remaining of him. With no living relatives, his beautiful letters may have been sent to the burn pit. And had I not seen the reaction of a grieving father and his dying son, the tale of human emotion may have never been told.

From what I believed was poison rose its antidote.

Chapter Twelve

Have Air Conditioner
Repair, Will Travel

July 2014

CONTEMPLATING JUST HOW I WOULD ask Cindy to move to Connecticut was an exercise in frustration. She was happy in Miami and had renewed relationships with relatives and friends. Just like when we met, she had a job she enjoyed that was too far of a drive through Miami traffic. It was a tall order to expect her to leave Miami again when she doubted her sanity of exchanging Miami and Chicago winters the first time. Surely, logistics and snow conspired against me.

Somehow, even though we had been married for twenty-two years, I enjoyed that we finished each other's sentences like two newlyweds in love. Suggesting that Cindy and I look at the moon reminded me of Munawwar's message to Ameena: looking at the moon at the same time shortened the distance between them and closer was always better.

Yet, I felt Cindy had to have held back. I didn't have the nerve to ask about our chances of reuniting—it felt manipulative when it seemed based on a dream more than the reality of almost two years before. We both seemed fearful of the idea.

But a chance presented itself in one phone call.

Cindy said her air conditioning hadn't been working and I pounced. In Miami, in late June. I offered to take a look at it, scratching my head while wondering how exactly one fixes an air conditioning unit. As usual, my strokes of genius were purely accidental and had little to do with expertise.

"Oh my God, could you?" Cindy asked, sounding surprised that over twenty-two years of marriage, she never realized my hidden talent. There we were, flirting as if we just met and were attempting to figure out a way to our first date.

"I should probably come soon. It has to be as hot as Hades there."

Before we hung up, we had set a date for me to fly to Fort Lauderdale.

* * *

But then my emotions took over—an elated feeling as if my feet didn't touch the ground. At the same time, I feared if I'd jumped before we were ready, that chance could have been the last. I suddenly felt less confident. I needed to talk to Robert, who believed I had been making enough progress to set appointments every other week.

I hurriedly placed a call to his office and when I didn't get through, I figured it was only a little out of the way to stop in person.

In his parking lot, I noticed no lights were on in his office. Everyone was due a day off or a vacation.

As I walked through the lobby, the receptionist recognized me and waved me over. It was too urgent to be a friendly wave and my heart sank. I should have checked in at least. Only recently, Robert thought I was doing well enough to try and space out appointments.

"He was transported to the hospital yesterday afternoon. They said Yale."

I imagined Robert, probably in his Harvard sweater with likely a mismatched shirt heading into Yale's emergency room.

Going to the hospital's front desk, I found Robert had been checked in. While walking to the elevators I prayed. "Please Robert, just give me one more day, one more appointment," as he had likely done in my darkest hour when my therapy had begun.

The hospital floor emitted the smell of fresh ammonia, nurses moved purposefully about their rounds. The sun shined as I walked as fast as I could without running, checking room numbers without stopping.

I finally arrived at the room, still praying. I listened for sounds of family but heard none. An ominous feeling set in and I tried to block the thought that the worst might have happened—my post-deployment belief that every bad thought I had, became true. I turned the corner into the room but backed out as it was the wrong room. Checking the room number by the door next to the hand-written room number from the front desk in the lobby, I asked a passing nurse for the correct room.

"Are you a member of his family?" she asked, stepping between me and the sunlight reflecting off the floor.

"A friend," I responded, knowing the shorter my answers were, the sooner my anxiety would abate. She placed her hand on my arm.

"Do you mean the colonel? I'm sorry sir, he passed away a couple of hours ago."

The sunlight off the floor dimmed and the nurse came into view, no longer a silhouette against the sun behind her.

Without answering, I walked back into the empty room. Sheets were stripped from the dark blue plastic mattress and it had been sterilized to make space for the next person.

There was no trace of him as the cleaners moved about without reverence. It wasn't their fault. They didn't know him. Then again, I didn't know him, not even that he had served in Vietnam and made the care of veterans his life's work. I always felt like I was Robert's only patient.

I wasn't sure why, but I placed my hand on the blue mattress. It felt cool to the touch and it sat straight across as if a quarter would bounce. What a special love Robert had for me. He had shown me the loftiness of humility known only by the greatest of mankind—the regality of service to others. Love was only understood by witnesses.

I felt I should cry but did not. I felt both joy and grief and never realized the intimate ballet they danced with each other. Both of them, it turned out, brought me closer to divinity either through elation after a challenge or its balancing sense of meekness hardship and misfortune brought. Both qualities came with their own ironic implied peace, reconciliation, and acceptance I had yearned, only crystallized in that moment.

Robert hadn't specifically said it in words, but I could never have confronted resilience without my imperfect struggle with adversity. Robert taught me of the antidote growing within arm's length of its associated poison like the body rejecting a splinter. My recovery had no guarantees, and around him, I felt protected from the dangers of my worst thoughts.

Robert would never know I had tickets to Florida. He had done his duty as if placed in my life by God Himself. He saved my life and, possibly, my marriage. I felt profound thankfulness.

As I stood there, my hand on the mattress, a nurse entered the room and asked if she could help me. I moved toward the door.

"No, I've already been helped."

Chapter Thirteen

Reflections

July 2014

Vince Lombardi was wrong in the quote "winning isn't everything, winning is the only thing."

Two days after Robert's death, I sat in T. F. Green Airport in Providence, Rhode Island, awaiting a flight to Atlanta on the way to Fort Lauderdale, Florida. Not lost on me was the symbolism of reversing my flight home after my deployment. I stood on the stairs looking down on the kiosk, trying to remember how I had felt. It seemed like another place.

I looked at my watch and saw Robert's funeral service was scheduled to begin in ten minutes in New Haven. He would have been happy I didn't alter my plans on his account. The canned quotes of victories cannot be parlayed into one extra minute of life.

In my friend Jim's final, tormented minutes, where was his victory?

From that day on January 17ᵗʰ, 2008, a large number of people had impacted my life at a time where nothing stood to have been gained by spending a single moment on me. Robert was one of an estimated one hundred and five people dying each minute the world over, all of them tragic in their own way. People like Robert worked their way into communal lives and generations with no names attached.

I felt I understood why Robert requested his surname not be revealed. He only wanted the credit to go to his collective community of Licensed Marriage and Family Therapists (LMFTs). Ideals and ethical principles were only that until some courageous catalyst put them in motion.

Just that I had the words to communicate joy and grief, and know they were different was Robert's last gift. In the whitewashed, disinfected room in which he died, I was instead knee-deep in Euphrates River mud. As Abdul-Hayy had written, I had finally felt worthy of my struggles.

* * *

The flight to Atlanta went quickly and most of the time, I wondered what Cindy was doing at that moment. We were strangers in an odd way again. I felt comforted with the thought we had started almost from scratch. Over the past two years, a courting routine was on full display. I felt I had amends to make and each of the increments folded into our conversations.

At least, in theory, I felt differently. The moment of truth would come if the well-known stranger fell asleep as we drove from one place to another. Would her head rest on my shoulder? I was certain I would drive stiffly so as to not disturb her. Selfishly, I would revel in her trust and swear I would do better. I'd had so many more chances than most. I hoped to tell Cindy my own version of an Irish saying: *She is the place where I stand when my feet are sore.*

Once we landed, I walked through the enormous airport. Almost immediately, I came across the remnants of an Army battalion as they dispersed. I related, as many of them would never hear from others with whom they'd been close and counted upon with their lives. At that point, they looked at their connecting flights and broke off into various directions depending on where their homes were. They were one leg from home, at least I hope that was what each of them found.

As for me, an anonymous civilian, I was also one leg from maybe returning to the arms of my family. I nodded at two soldiers in their crisp uniforms with warfare devices. They walked, staring straight ahead, perhaps uncomfortable with so many people staring. I understood.

Just ahead of me was a young woman in a mid-length black skirt and red-flowered top. She walked with optimistic determination and I smiled wondering if Cindy had walked into her work, her brunette hair bouncing like a gently coiled spring, to tell her co-workers I was flying to see her—her steps so light they wouldn't bend a blade of grass.

I remembered her uninhibited laugh when I said if we were to reunite, I would even let her have the French fries at the bottom of the bag, and I'd never question why her purse should never touch the floor again. I pledged in my mind right then that I'd try to make her laugh like that at least once a day.

I glanced outward at the taxiing aircraft and noticed a man who appeared to be Arabic. He never looked up from his newspaper, oblivious to my presence. In fact, I went entirely unnoticed. I realized the airport loudspeakers blared with various announcements, but I didn't pay attention to them any more than the other travelers. I was just one person in a crowd.

* * *

I sat at the terminal an hour before my flight to Fort Lauderdale and had a daydream.

I stood outside the rail of the George Washington Bridge, only that time I clung to the rail for dear life. My hands sweated so profusely I thought I'd be unable to climb back over the rail toward safety. Passersby ignored my pleas for help before Robert appeared, as if still alive, and explained that in that reverie, I was supposed to let go and trust-fall backward.

That time, as I hung hundreds of feet above the ground, it was meant for me to let go—Let go of all I desperately clutched onto. I could respect and mourn the loss in the eyes of Sayyed, Munawwar, Abdul-Hayy and his family, the blindfolded detainee and his daughter, the young woman left dead on the side of the road. I'd remembered something worthy and lovable in them. In my imagination, people throughout my life came into view, much like my near-death experience during the rocket attack near the diesel fuel tanks.

The black man struck in the temple by a rock in the Chicago demonstration was there, not even scarred. I rejoiced when Munawwar, Abdul-Hayy and his father, and the blindfolded man arrived. In that moment, I no longer felt haunted by freezing in the moment of Munawwar's death. Maybe I'd accidentally afforded him rapid-fire images of every pleasant moment with his loved ones. Even in that vision, he explained the sobering news he still sought his daughter even after all that time. Even daydreams had remnants of heartbreak.

There were my parents, Norm, Julie along with Cindy and her family, Bill, Monica, and Willliam, with Alfonso and Lorenzo. I found myself imperfectly worthy and lovable as well, a person who could behave the exact same with every impactful influence in my family in the room at the same time. For that moment, we were all just human as if their collective hand rested on my shoulder.

Because that moment aligned in my flow-chart brain, I released my hands from the rail and fell backward. For that moment, at least, I was free of that which enslaved me. Through my struggles, I had witnessed an inconceivable brilliance. Not that I was scintillating, mind you, not much more than a bystander basking warmth and light emanated from others' efforts. But something carried me.

I thought back to the single moment I was certain of death in the rocket attack in the field of diesel fuel tanks. The split-second memories of people I had not consciously thought of for most of my life. If they had left my mind, their deeds did not. When I'd thought of death, seemingly so abrupt and random, I'd be yet another human being to fade from view, whose gravestone was worn flat over time, but maybe a deed remained. If I found that community, like Robert, I could know a contribution for goodness' sake. That community would benefit forever. Maybe I could be a selfless catalyst for healing in my own family as Robert had been.

It was the highest goal I could imagine.

* * *

The plane left Atlanta's airport, rising high above the runway and I was thankful for having a window seat. The view was eventually lost as we lifted above clouds, which appeared pillow-soft.

I looked back down at my latest book, Viktor Frankl's *Man's Search for Meaning*. The first words I saw read that architects knew one way to strengthen a decrepit arch was to increase the load which is laid upon it.

Was I prepared for the commitment and determination I would rely on to reunite with my family? I feared I would fail, another scar for them to bear. I was indebted to any of the characters in my life responsible for putting those words before my eyes. It could've been one of them or all of them.

Oh, how I wished Abdul-Hayy's first impression upon seeing an American soldier was that I was there to help. But I might not have had a story to tell. It would have been so easy for me to feel our deployment was validated and go back to my privileged life, never thinking about it again.

The truth about June 9th, 2007, was that I sought to find Munawwar for a single, murderous reason. I spoke of a privileged life—my intentions defined as evil in Iraq, and protective of my family in America.

But had I not been driven to homicide, I would have never stood there, close enough to hear his final prayer or to see his upturned hand or see his eyes—the whole shape of his face softened and human. Had I not seen his eyes, I would have never found out everything I could about him.

Without Sayyed's translations, I would have never had access to Munawwar's words among his loved ones. And without those words, I never would have reunited with my family. Recovery required a series of miracles.

In spite of every failing, I was blessed with a story to tell.

I was at peace with that person who had dug ditches, blocked for or passed to the more skilled athletes and finished 5417 on the Boston Marathon. I felt joy at the thought of a hand on the shoulder of a grieving father, and fearlessness in admitting I became lost and entirely missed Philadelphia.

Nobody just misses Philadelphia.

I'd fancied myself as a world traveler, but the favorite story in my family was the one time I had asked a waitress in Kentucky if I could try one single grit first to see if I liked it. I remained the person who endearingly took the longest route possible.

Some might imagine my unit in Iraq with movie-like heroism, but I remembered us as the unit ordered to kill a stray cat for fear that it had rabies.

The truth was most of us conspired to feed and give the poor animal water until we could give it to an interpreter to bring home to his daughter.

I would never deny any facet of those memories. I knew I could stare over the vast expanse of a desert and see the sparks of love between Sayyed and his wife of forty-one years and the countless hues of the browns against a clear, blue sky.

One didn't have to be a "winner" to see the level of magnificence, but to have seen the splendor in what appeared to be a bleak landscape made me triumphant.

Chapter Fourteen

Miami

July 2014

THE AIRPLANE ROUGHLY LANDED IN Fort Lauderdale, Florida. I habitually placed my hand over my shirt pocket, then went through where I had seen the piece of paper last, before remembering the notebook-sized paper, folded and soaked with sweat or the elements since June 9th, 2007, had disintegrated.

It didn't matter by then, I had memorized a poem Munawwar had written to his love, Manha.

I had mixed emotions about carrying it in my pocket daily since then. On one hand, I hoped I could hand a poem so beautiful to Cindy, while I fought against the idea of bringing even an iota home from Iraq. Over time, I realized that thought process as flawed. From some divine place, it seemed appropriate that it crumble into almost nothing in a similar way that Robert passed away. They had done their good, fulfilled their purpose, found their place in the universe. It was up to me to carry it forward.

The airplane taxied into the terminal and I murmured the lines of the poem, written by Nizar Qabbani:

In the summer I stretch out on the shore
And think of you,
Had I told the Sea what I felt for you,
It would have left its shores, its shells, its fish,
And followed me

I had too many people to thank. I tried to picture each of them: the blindfolded man, the gas station attendant with the kidney stones, Munawwar, Abdul-Hayy and his father, the young woman on the side of the road. I wished we would have stopped for her, consequences be damned.

As I sat in my reserved rental car, I felt mournful. I had learned so much from them and, within hours, my life could change dramatically as a result. How lucky I was, a person no better or deserving than they, just as likely to cry in pain for loved ones in my final agonizing moments or wet my pants before overwhelming force blasting through the door of my home.

I had entered my own home and part of my story included my own family cowering in the corner. Maybe the America Abdul-Hayy imagined did exist. Even with my behavior, I was granted the chance for amends. Perhaps anything was possible in America.

What about those with whom I'd interacted in Iraq? I wondered what I had brought into their lives—the part of me who believed our effort was for the good of their nation. They were only my answers, but I found them in the pleading, desperate cries of the young woman. Munawwar may not have known anything of me besides my swimming in sterilized pools, too good to dip a toe in his beloved Euphrates River.

I looked at fairness and if life were equitable, the blindfolded man would reunite with his daughter and comfort her while he explained war and conflict were over. I would wish that Abdul-Hayy's family could find not just an absence of war, but peace. I could create a wish for those lost besides having tangible evidence that their lives were better, and their sacrifices were honored.

* * *

I looked at the horizon as I drove inland from Fort Lauderdale, the expanse wide and flat with an occasional palm tree and mostly low-lying shrubbery and evenly spaced canals as straight as arrows—a similar landscape to parts of Iraq. I was about an hour from Cindy's apartment.

My thoughts were indeed my own. I felt as if I stood on the confluence of two rivers as they eventually joined into a single current, two disparate tributaries with different identities becoming one with a sole destination. I'd reclaimed myself and resuscitated lost pieces of a soul along the way.

Those who loved me stood on banks on either side, scooped me up in meshed nets and cast me back toward the middle where the flow was strongest. They had left letters, translated them, put the words into motion, and gave them direction. In depending on and trusting those blessings, ironically I was freed.

I had audited an English class at the beginning of 2014 and after one assignment, Professor Collins stated the mechanics of writing could be learned by anyone, but the perspective was not taught. I thought of Munawwar's example of being served a humble meal and elicited gratitude. It certainly did.

* * *

Soon, I had traveled to Miami and recognized landmarks from my many visits there to see Cindy's family. I had a good idea where Cindy's apartment was, and she expected me in the late afternoon. With military punctuality, I would drive up to her apartment almost to the minute. My adrenaline rose and the anticipatory cottonmouth of nervousness struck. I took a deep breath. It seemed hard to do so.

I had no intention of escaping accountability. I hoped Cindy, my sons, and my parents would judge me harshly. I yearned for them to maintain their standards and beliefs. They were not culpable for my actions. That portion of the story would stay with me. I hoped each of their benchmarks would remain in place, and they would not be compromised for me. I had accepted that war's dictates.

* * *

I turned off Route 1 and saw the apartments. I drove slowly over the parking lot speed bumps. I quickly identified the building with Cindy's apartment and stopped just out of view. I straightened my shirt and wondered if I had lost enough weight. I pulled a toothbrush and checked my teeth. I took my glasses off because she never cared for those frames, anyway.

My heart pounded and there I was, like a nervous teenager, only the cause of all that consternation was my wife of almost twenty-three years. I pulled up and parked in front of Cindy's door and couldn't help but notice a sunflower, as tall as I was—its face optimistically turned upward to soak in every ray of the brilliant sun.

I whispered to myself, "I am loved. It raises me above the outgoing tide and brings me home."

Munawwar was correct once again. He had reached me.

The door opened and there she stood. She was always a beauty, the kind that never fades. Good old Cindy, she had always known what to do. Our eyes met.

We smiled.

AFTERWORD

WE'RE BORN A BLANK SLATE. Our experiences come in black and white and our parents are a box of crayons. If you're blessed like my my brother Norm, my sister Julie, and me, you get one of those big boxes with 128 colors and anything you would ever want to draw is possible.

I wrote a letter to Dad after his death, but this story would help those who never met him understand him better.

One time, Norm, Dad, and I were counting down the last seconds of his beloved Notre Dame football team's victory. 3 . . . 2 . . . 1 . . .

"All right, we brought 'em in!" Dad said. He then turned to Norm to his left. "Now Monday, remember you need to stand in the middle of the framed-in part of the sidewalk before the concrete is poured and shovel it toward the back quickly, understand?"

Norm nodded.

He turned to me. "The sidewalk is three feet wide and the slope is three-eighths of an inch away from the foundation. We don't want water sitting on the sidewalk or at the foundation. The temperature will be cold enough that it will take a while longer to cure, so check it periodically to make sure it's not leveling off, got it?

"I got it." I answered. "Hey, what a game. Huh, Dad?"

Dad looked at Norm and me. "The concrete will drop at seven, so be there ready to work at six-thirty."

Dad never allowed the things he liked to get in the way of the things he had to do—the items on his list of responsibilities.

Here's my letter:

Dear Dad,

When I returned from Iraq, you sensed my struggles and pulled me aside. I'd made your list. After you asked a couple of times, I told you about the worst day of our deployment. I'd been back for four years and hadn't spoken a word about it.

When there was silence, you said you wished you could take away the pain—that you could find a way to carry my burden. You spoke as if you believed you could do something about it.

I wondered, *What is available to a man with unshakeable faith?*

That same night I felt it was the most selfish thing I'd ever done—to add something to your list you were powerless to resolve.

Last May you had a stroke. And when things turned for the worst, I left Connecticut and arrived in about eleven hours. 950 miles.

Right now, you're looking down at me doing the math. I'm sorry, I was speeding Dad. I know how you are about rules.

Norm and I stayed up most of the night, talking about you. I thought of a time you sat on my deck and pointed out the hawks circling above. I hadn't noticed them before. But each time I went on the deck after, I'd look up and there they were.

The next morning we visited you, and with all that time to think and all that talking of what I'd like to tell you, I only said one thing. That all of us were going to be okay. I felt certain you were more worried about us than yourself, even as you lay there.

By the time we got to Mom's, the call came. You'd waited, we believed, until we all got there.

Two days later, I left for Connecticut, and somewhere along the way, the sleepless nights caught up with me. I pulled over to take a nap. As I sat in the car, a hawk swooped low over the highway, maybe 150 feet in front of me and rose gracefully up above the treeline.

I suddenly jumped up and fumbled for my phone to check the calendar and realized you left one final gift. You'd completed the last item on your last list and died on the anniversary of my worst day in Iraq. From that moment on, every June 9th I'll think of you instead of Iraq.

You brought 'em in, Dad. I love you.

Jim Enderle

Time for a letter home.

Homecoming Statue 2000 (family at the Navy Home-
coming statue dedication unveiling ceremony on
October 14th, 2000, just after the bombing of the
USS Cole (DDG-67) in Yemen on October 12, 2000)

Kindness to troops (a care package collected and sent to us by a Florida radio station)

Family 2005 (CNIC Atlantic Sailor of the
Year - taken by Cheryl Albanese)

Navy picture (official Navy picture taken in 2010)

About the Author

Jim & Cindy Enderle (Photo credit Tom Bradley)

J IM ENDERLE IS A RETIRED Navy Chief Hospital
Corpsman, and holds a Masters Degree in the
Education of Exceptional Students from North-
central University. He's a longtime DJ at New
London's WCNI Radio. He and his family live in
Quaker Hill, Connecticut.

CPSIA information can be obtained
at www.ICGtesting.com
Printed in the USA
BVHW051949160821
614548BV00018B/553

9 781943 267804